THE
Expositors Bible Commentary

with *The New International Version*

1, 2 PETER • 1, 2, 3 JOHN • JUDE

THE
Expositor's
Bible
Commentary

with *The New International Version*

1, 2 PETER • 1, 2, 3 JOHN • JUDE

Edwin A. Blum &
Glenn W. Barker

ZondervanPublishingHouse

Grand Rapids, Michigan

A Division of HarperCollinsPublishers

General Editor:

FRANK E. GAEBELEIN

Former Headmaster, Stony Brook School
Former Coeditor, *Christianity Today*

Associate Editors:

J. D. DOUGLAS

Editor, *The New International
Dictionary of the Christian Church*

RICHARD P. POLCYN

1, 2 Peter; 1, 2, 3 John; Jude
Copyright © 1996 by Edwin A. Blum, Glenn W. Barker

Requests for information should be addressed to:
Zondervan Publishing House
Grand Rapids, Michigan 49530

Library of Congress Cataloging-in-Publication Data

The expositor's Bible commentary : with the New International Version of the Holy Bible /
Frank E. Gaebelein, general editor of series.
    p. cm.
    Includes bibliographical references and index.
    Contents: v. 1–2. Matthew / D. A. Carson — Mark / Walter W. Wessel — Luke / Walter
L. Liefeld — John / Merrill C. Tenney — Acts / Richard N. Longenecker — Romans /
Everett F. Harrison — 1 and 2 Corinthians / W. Harold Mare and Murray J. Harris —
Galatians and Ephesians / James Montgomery Boice and A. Skevington Wood—Philippians,
Colossians, Philemon / Homer A. Kent Jr., Gurtis Vaughan, and Arthur A. Rupprecht—
1, 2 Thessalonians; 1, 2 Timothy; Titus / Robert L. Thomas, Ralph Earle, and D. Edmond
Hiebert—Hebrews, James / Leon Morris and Donald W. Burdick—1, 2 Peter;
1, 2, 3 John; Jude / Edwin A. Blum and Glenn W. Barker—Revelation / Alan F. Johnson
    ISBN: 0-310-20388-0 (softcover)
    1. Bible N.T.—Commentaries. I. Gaebelein, Frank Ely, 1899–1983.
BS2341.2.E96 1995
220.7-dc 00   94-47450
                                                             CIP

Printed in the United States of America

96 97 98 99 00 01 /❖ DH / 10 9 8 7 6 5 4 3 2 1

CONTENTS

PREFACE

The title of this work defines its purpose. Written primarily by expositors for expositors, it aims to provide preachers, teachers, and students of the Bible with a new and comprehensive commentary on the books of the Old and New Testaments. Its stance is that of a scholarly evangelicalism committed to the divine inspiration, complete trustworthiness, and full authority of the Bible. Its seventy-eight contributors come from the United States, Canada, England, Scotland, Australia, New Zealand, and Switzerland, and from various religious groups, including Anglican, Baptist, Brethren, Free, Independent, Methodist, Nazarene, Presbyterian, and Reformed churches. Most of them teach at colleges, universities, or theological seminaries.

No book has been more closely studied over a longer period of time than the Bible. From the Midrashic commentaries going back to the period of Ezra, through parts of the Dead Sea Scrolls and the Patristic literature, and on to the present, the Scriptures have been expounded. Indeed, there have been times when, as in the Reformation and on occasions since then, exposition has been at the cutting edge of Christian advance. Luther was a powerful exegete, and Calvin is still called "the prince of expositors."

Their successors have been many. And now, when the outburst of new translations and their unparalleled circulation have expanded the readership of the Bible, the need for exposition takes on fresh urgency.

Not that God's Word can ever become captive to its expositors. Among all other books, it stands first in its combination of perspicuity and profundity. Though a child can be made "wise for salvation" by believing its witness to Christ, the greatest mind cannot plumb the depths of its truth (2 Tim. 3:15; Rom. 11:33). As Gregory the Great said, "Holy Scripture is a stream of running water, where alike the elephant may swim, and the lamb walk." So, because of the inexhaustible nature of Scripture, the task of opening up its meaning is still a perennial obligation of biblical scholarship.

How that task is done inevitably reflects the outlook of those engaged in it. Every biblical scholar has presuppositions. To this neither the editors of these volumes nor the contributors to them are exceptions. They share a common commitment to the supernatural Christianity set forth in the inspired Word. Their purpose is not to supplant the many valuable commentaries that have preceded this work and from which both the editors and contributors have learned. It is rather to draw on the resources of contemporary evangelical scholarship in producing a new reference work for understanding the Scriptures.

A commentary that will continue to be useful through the years should handle contemporary trends in biblical studies in such a way as to avoid becoming outdated when critical fashions change. Biblical criticism is not in itself inadmissible, as some have mistakenly thought. When scholars investigate the authorship, date, literary characteristics, and purpose of a biblical document, they are practicing biblical criticism. So also when, in order to ascertain as nearly as possible the original form of the text, they deal with variant readings, scribal errors, emendations, and other phenomena in the manuscripts. To do these things is essential to responsible exegesis and exposition. And always there is the need to distinguish hypothesis from fact, conjecture from truth.

The chief principle of interpretation followed in this commentary is the grammatico-historical one—namely, that the primary aim of the exegete is to make clear the meaning of the text at the time and in the circumstances of its writing. This endeavor to understand what in the first instance the inspired writers actually said must not be confused with an inflexible literalism. Scripture makes lavish use of symbols and figures of speech; great portions of it are poetical. Yet when it speaks in this way, it speaks no less truly than it does in its historical and doctrinal portions. To understand its message requires attention to matters of grammar and syntax, word meanings, idioms, and literary forms—all in relation to the historical and cultural setting of the text.

The contributors to this work necessarily reflect varying convictions. In certain controversial matters the policy is that of clear statement of the contributors' own views followed by fair presentation of other ones. The treatment of eschatology, though it reflects differences of interpretation, is consistent with a general premillennial position. (Not all contributors, however, are premillennial.) But prophecy is more than prediction, and so this commentary gives due recognition to the major lode of godly social concern in the prophetic writings.

THE EXPOSITOR'S BIBLE COMMENTARY is presented as a scholarly work, though not primarily one of technical criticism. In its main portion, the Exposition, and in Volume 1 (General and Special Articles), all Semitic and Greek words are transliterated and the English equivalents given. As for the Notes, here Semitic and Greek characters are used but always with transliterations and English meanings, so that this portion of the commentary will be as accessible as possible to readers unacquainted with the original languages.

It is the conviction of the general editor, shared by his colleagues in the Zondervan editorial department, that in writing about the Bible, lucidity is not incompatible with scholarship. They are therefore endeavoring to make this a clear and understandable work.

The translation used in it is the New International Version (North American Edition). To the International Bible Society thanks are due for permission to use this most recent of the major Bible translations. The editors and publisher have chosen it because of the clarity and beauty of its style and its faithfulness to the original texts.

To the associate editor, Dr. J. D. Douglas, and to the contributing editors—Dr. Walter C. Kaiser, Jr. and Dr. Bruce K. Waltke for the Old Testament, and Dr. James Montgomery Boice and Dr. Merrill C. Tenney for the New Testament—the general editor expresses his gratitude for their unfailing cooperation and their generosity in advising him out of their expert scholarship. And to the many other contributors he is indebted for their invaluable part in this work. Finally, he owes a special debt of gratitude to Dr. Robert K. DeVries, executive vice-president of the Zondervan Publishing House; Rev. Gerard Terpstra, manuscript editor; and Miss Elizabeth Brown, secretary to Dr. DeVries, for their continual assistance and encouragement.

Whatever else it is—the greatest and most beautiful of books, the primary source of law and morality, the fountain of wisdom, and the infallible guide to life—the Bible is above all the inspired witness to Jesus Christ. May this work fulfill its function of expounding the Scriptures with grace and clarity, so that its users may find that both Old and New Testaments do indeed lead to our Lord Jesus Christ, who alone could say, "I have come that they may have life, and have it to the full" (John 10:10).

FRANK E. GAEBELEIN

ABBREVIATIONS

A. General Abbreviations

A	Codex Alexandrinus	MT	Masoretic text
Akkad.	Akkadian	n.	note
ℵ	Codex Sinaiticus	n.d.	no date
Ap. Lit.	Apocalyptic Literature	Nestle	Nestle (ed.) *Novum*
Apoc.	Apocrypha		*Testamentum Graece*
Aq.	Aquila's Greek Translation	no.	number
	of the Old Testament	NT	New Testament
Arab.	Arabic	obs.	obsolete
Aram.	Aramaic	OL	Old Latin
b	Babylonian Gemara	OS	Old Syriac
B	Codex Vaticanus	OT	Old Testament
C	Codex Ephraemi Syri	p., pp.	page, pages
c.	*circa*, about	par.	paragraph
cf.	*confer*, compare	||	parallel passage(s)
ch., chs.	chapter, chapters	Pers.	Persian
cod., codd.	codex, codices	Pesh.	Peshitta
contra	in contrast to	Phoen.	Phoenician
D	Codex Bezae	pl.	plural
DSS	Dead Sea Scrolls (see E.)	Pseudep.	Pseudepigrapha
ed., edd.	edited, edition, editor; editions	Q	Quelle ("Sayings" source
e.g.	*exempli gratia*, for example		in the Gospels)
Egyp.	Egyptian	qt.	quoted by
et al.	*et alii*, and others	q.v.	*quod vide*, which see
EV	English Versions of the Bible	R	Rabbah
fem.	feminine	rev.	revised, reviser, revision
ff.	following (verses, pages, etc.)	Rom.	Roman
fl.	flourished	RVm	Revised Version margin
ft.	foot, feet	Samar.	Samaritan recension
gen.	genitive	SCM	Student Christian Movement Press
Gr.	Greek	Sem.	Semitic
Heb.	Hebrew	sing.	singular
Hitt.	Hittite	SPCK	Society for the Promotion
ibid.	*ibidem*, in the same place		of Christian Knowledge
id.	*idem*, the same	Sumer.	Sumerian
i.e.	*id est*, that is	s.v.	*sub verbo*, under the word
impf.	imperfect	Syr.	Syriac
infra.	below	Symm.	Symmachus
in loc.	*in loco*, in the place cited	T	Talmud
j	Jerusalem or	Targ.	Targum
	Palestinian Gemara	Theod.	Theodotion
Lat.	Latin	TR	Textus Receptus
LL.	Late Latin	tr.	translation, translator,
LXX	Septuagint		translated
M	Mishnah	UBS	The United Bible Societies'
masc.	masculine		Greek Text
mg.	margin	Ugar.	Ugaritic
Mid	Midrash	u.s.	*ut supra*, as above
MS(S)	Manuscript(s)	viz.	*videlicet*, namely

vol.	volume	Vul.	Vulgate
v., vv.	verse, verses	WH	Westcott and Hort, *The*
vs.	versus		*New Testament in Greek*

B. Abbreviations for Modern Translations and Paraphrases

AmT	Smith and Goodspeed, *The Complete Bible, An American Translation*	LB	The Living Bible
		Mof	J. Moffatt, *A New Translation of the Bible*
ASV	American Standard Version, American Revised Version (1901)	NAB	The New American Bible
		NASB	New American Standard Bible
		NEB	The New English Bible
Beck	Beck, *The New Testament in the Language of Today*	NIV	The New International Version
		Ph	J. B. Phillips *The New Testament in Modern English*
BV	Berkeley Version (The Modern Language Bible)		
		RSV	Revised Standard Version
JB	The Jerusalem Bible	RV	Revised Version — 1881–1885
JPS	*Jewish Publication Society Version of the Old Testament*	TCNT	Twentieth Century New Testament
KJV	King James Version	TEV	Today's English Version
Knox	R.G. Knox, *The Holy Bible: A Translation from the Latin Vulgate in the Light of the Hebrew and Greek Original*	Wey	*Weymouth's New Testament in Modern Speech*
		Wms	C. B. Williams, *The New Testament: A Translation in the Language of the People*

C. Abbreviations for Periodicals and Reference Works

AASOR	*Annual of the American Schools of Oriental Research*	BAG	Bauer, Arndt, and Gingrich: *Greek-English Lexicon of the New Testament*
AB	*Anchor Bible*		
AIs	de Vaux: *Ancient Israel*	BC	Foakes-Jackson and Lake: *The Beginnings of Christianity*
AJA	*American Journal of Archaeology*		
		BDB	Brown, Driver, and Briggs: *Hebrew-English Lexicon of the Old Testament*
AJSL	*American Journal of Semitic Languages and Literatures*		
AJT	*American Journal of Theology*	BDF	Blass, Debrunner, and Funk: *A Greek Grammar of the New Testament and Other Early Christian Literature*
Alf	Alford: *Greek Testament Commentary*		
ANEA	*Ancient Near Eastern Archaeology*	BDT	Harrison: *Baker's Dictionary of Theology*
ANET	Pritchard: *Ancient Near Eastern Texts*	Beng.	Bengel's *Gnomon*
		BETS	*Bulletin of the Evangelical Theological Society*
ANF	Roberts and Donaldson: *The Ante-Nicene Fathers*		
ANT	M. R. James: *The Apocryphal New Testament*	BJRL	*Bulletin of the John Rylands Library*
		BS	*Bibliotheca Sacra*
A-S	Abbot-Smith: *Manual Greek Lexicon of the New Testament*	BT	*Babylonian Talmud*
		BTh	*Biblical Theology*
AThR	*Anglican Theological Review*	BW	*Biblical World*
BA	*Biblical Archaeologist*	CAH	*Cambridge Ancient History*
BASOR	*Bulletin of the American Schools of Oriental Research*	CanJTh	*Canadian Journal of Theology*
		CBQ	*Catholic Biblical Quarterly*

CBSC	Cambridge Bible for Schools and Colleges	HUCA	Hebrew Union College Annual
CE	Catholic Encyclopedia	IB	The Interpreter's Bible
CGT	Cambridge Greek Testament	ICC	International Critical Commentary
CHS	Lange: Commentary on the Holy Scriptures	IDB	The Interpreter's Dictionary of the Bible
ChT	Christianity Today	IEJ	Israel Exploration Journal
Crem	Cremer: Biblico-Theological Lexicon of the New Testament Greek	Int	Interpretation
		INT	E. Harrison: Introduction to the New Testament
DDB	Davis' Dictionary of the Bible	IOT	R. K. Harrison: Introduction to the Old Testament
Deiss BS	Deissmann: Bible Studies		
Deiss LAE	Deissmann: Light From the Ancient East	ISBE	The International Standard Bible Encyclopedia
DNTT	Dictionary of New Testament Theology	ITQ	Irish Theological Quarterly
EBC	The Expositor's Bible Commentary	JAAR	Journal of American Academy of Religion
EBi	Encyclopaedia Biblica	JAOS	Journal of American Oriental Society
EBr	Encyclopaedia Britannica		
EDB	Encyclopedic Dictionary of the Bible	JBL	Journal of Biblical Literature
EGT	Nicoll: Expositor's Greek Testament	JE	Jewish Encyclopedia
		JETS	Journal of Evangelical Theological Society
EQ	Evangelical Quarterly		
ET	Evangelische Theologie	JFB	Jamieson, Fausset, and Brown: Commentary on the Old and New Testament
ExB	The Expositor's Bible		
Exp	The Expositor		
ExpT	The Expository Times	JNES	Journal of Near Eastern Studies
FLAP	Finegan: Light From the Ancient Past	Jos. Antiq.	Josephus: The Antiquities of the Jews
GR	Gordon Review	Jos. War	Josephus: The Jewish War
HBD	Harper's Bible Dictionary	JQR	Jewish Quarterly Review
HDAC	Hastings: Dictionary of the Apostolic Church	JR	Journal of Religion
		JSJ	Journal for the Study of Judaism in the Persian, Hellenistic and Roman Periods
HDB	Hastings: Dictionary of the Bible		
HDBrev.	Hastings: Dictionary of the Bible, one-vol. rev. by Grant and Rowley	JSOR	Journal of the Society of Oriental Research
		JSS	Journal of Semitic Studies
HDCG	Hastings: Dictionary of Christ and the Gospels	JT	Jerusalem Talmud
		JTS	Journal of Theological Studies
HERE	Hastings: Encyclopedia of Religion and Ethics	KAHL	Kenyon: Archaeology in the Holy Land
HGEOTP	Heidel: The Gilgamesh Epic and Old Testament Parallels	KB	Koehler-Baumgartner: Lexicon in Veteris Testament Libros
HJP	Schurer: A History of the Jewish People in the Time of Christ	KD	Keil and Delitzsch: Commentary on the Old Testament
		LSJ	Liddell, Scott, Jones: Greek-English Lexicon
HR	Hatch and Redpath: Concordance to the Septuagint	LTJM	Edersheim: The Life and Times of Jesus the Messiah
HTR	Harvard Theological Review		

MM	Moulton and Milligan: *The Vocabulary of the Greek Testament*		*Testament aus Talmud und Midrash*
MNT	Moffatt: *New Testament Commentary*	SHERK	*The New Schaff-Herzog Encyclopedia of Religious Knowledge*
MST	McClintock and Strong: *Cyclopedia of Biblical, Theological, and Ecclesiastical Literature*	SJT	*Scottish Journal of Theology*
		SOT	Girdlestone: *Synonyms of Old Testament*
NBC	Davidson, Kevan, and Stibbs: *The New Bible Commentary*, 1st ed.	SOTI	Archer: *A Survey of Old Testament Introduction*
NBCrev.	Guthrie and Motyer: *The New Bible Commentary*, rev. ed.	ST	*Studia Theologica*
		TCERK	Loetscher: *The Twentieth Century Encyclopedia of Religious Knowledge*
NBD	J. D. Douglas: *The New Bible Dictionary*	TDNT	Kittel: *Theological Dictionary of the New Testament*
NCB	*New Century Bible*		
NCE	*New Catholic Encyclopedia*	TDOT	*Theological Dictionary of the Old Testament*
NIC	*New International Commentary*		
NIDCC	Douglas: *The New International Dictionary of the Christian Church*	Theol	*Theology*
		ThT	*Theology Today*
		TNTC	*Tyndale New Testament Commentaries*
NovTest	*Novum Testamentum*		
NSI	Cooke: *Handbook of North Semitic Inscriptions*	Trench	Trench: *Synonyms of the New Testament*
NTS	*New Testament Studies*	UBD	*Unger's Bible Dictionary*
ODCC	*The Oxford Dictionary of the Christian Church*, rev. ed.	UT	Gordon: *Ugaritic Textbook*
		VB	Allmen: *Vocabulary of the Bible*
Peake	Black and Rowley: *Peake's Commentary on the Bible*	VetTest	*Vetus Testamentum*
PEQ	*Palestine Exploration Quarterly*	Vincent	Vincent: *Word-Pictures in the New Testament*
PNFl	P. Schaff: *The Nicene and Post-Nicene Fathers* (1st series)	WBC	*Wycliffe Bible Commentary*
		WBE	*Wycliffe Bible Encyclopedia*
		WC	*Westminster Commentaries*
PNF2	P. Schaff and H. Wace: *The Nicene and Post-Nicene Fathers* (2nd series)	WesBC	*Wesleyan Bible Commentaries*
		WTJ	*Westminster Theological Journal*
PTR	*Princeton Theological Review*	ZAW	*Zeitschrift für die alttestamentliche Wissenschaft*
RB	*Revue Biblique*		
RHG	Robertson's *Grammar of the Greek New Testament in the Light of Historical Research*	ZNW	*Zeitschrift für die neutestamentliche Wissenschaft*
		ZPBD	*The Zondervan Pictorial Bible Dictionary*
RTWB	Richardson: *A Theological Wordbook of the Bible*	ZPEB	*The Zondervan Pictorial Encyclopedia of the Bible*
SBK	Strack and Billerbeck: *Kommentar zum Neuen*	ZWT	*Zeitschrift für wissenschaftliche Theologie*

D. Abbreviations for Books of the Bible, the Apocrypha, and the Pseudepigrapha

OLD TESTAMENT

Gen	2 Chron	Dan
Exod	Ezra	Hos
Lev	Neh	Joel
Num	Esth	Amos
Deut	Job	Obad
Josh	Ps(Pss)	Jonah
Judg	Prov	Mic
Ruth	Eccl	Nah
1 Sam	S of Songs	Hab
2 Sam	Isa	Zeph
1 Kings	Jer	Hag
2 Kings	Lam	Zech
1 Chron	Ezek	Mal

NEW TESTAMENT

Matt	1 Tim
Mark	2 Tim
Luke	Titus
John	Philem
Acts	Heb
Rom	James
1 Cor	1 Peter
2 Cor	2 Peter
Gal	1 John
Eph	2 John
Phil	3 John
Col	Jude
1 Thess	Rev
2 Thess	

APOCRYPHA

1 Esd	1 Esdras	Ep Jer	Epistle of Jeremy
2 Esd	2 Esdras	S Th Ch	Song of the Three Children (or Young Men)
Tobit	Tobit		
Jud	Judith	Sus	Susanna
Add Esth	Additions to Esther	Bel	Bel and the Dragon
Wisd Sol	Wisdom of Solomon	Pr Man	Prayer of Manasseh
Ecclus	Ecclesiasticus (Wisdom of Jesus the Son of Sirach)	1 Macc	1 Maccabees
		2 Macc	2 Maccabees
Baruch	Baruch		

PSEUDEPIGRAPHA

As Moses	Assumption of Moses	Pirke Aboth	Pirke Aboth
2 Baruch	Syriac Apocalypse of Baruch	Ps 151	Psalm 151
3 Baruch	Greek Apocalypse of Baruch	Pss Sol	Psalms of Solomon
1 Enoch	Ethiopic Book of Enoch	Sib Oracles	Sibylline Oracles
2 Enoch	Slavonic Book of Enoch	Story Ah	Story of Ahikar
3 Enoch	Hebrew Book of Enoch	T Abram	Testament of Abraham
4 Ezra	4 Ezra	T Adam	Testament of Adam
JA	Joseph and Asenath	T Benjamin	Testament of Benjamin
Jub	Book of Jubilees	T Dan	Testament of Dan
L Aristeas	Letter of Aristeas	T Gad	Testament of Gad
Life AE	Life of Adam and Eve	T Job	Testament of Job
Liv Proph	Lives of the Prophets	T Jos	Testament of Joseph
MA Isa	Martyrdom and Ascension of Isaiah	T Levi	Testament of Levi
		T Naph	Testament of Naphtali
3 Macc	3 Maccabees	T 12 Pat	Testaments of the Twelve Patriarchs
4 Macc	4 Maccabees		
Odes Sol	Odes of Solomon	Zad Frag	Zadokite Fragments
P Jer	Paralipomena of Jeremiah		

E. Abbreviations of Names of Dead Sea Scrolls and Related Texts

CD	Cairo (Genizah text of the) Damascus (Document)	1QSa	Appendix A (Rule of the Congregation) to 1QS
DSS	Dead Sea Scrolls	1QSb	Appendix B (Blessings) to 1QS
Hev	Nahal Hever texts	3Q15	Copper Scroll from Qumran Cave 3
Mas	Masada Texts		
Mird	Khirbet mird texts	4QFlor	Florilegium (or Eschatological Midrashim) from Qumran Cave 4
Mur	Wadi Murabba'at texts		
P	Pesher (commentary)		
Q	Qumran	4Qmess ar	Aramaic "Messianic" text from Qumran Cave 4
1Q,2Q,etc.	Numbered caves of Qumran, yielding written material; followed by abbreviation of biblical or apocryphal book.	4QPrNab	Prayer of Nabonidus from Qumran Cave 4
		4QTest	Testimonia text from Qumran Cave 4
QL	Qumran Literature		
1QapGen	Genesis Apocryphon of Qumran Cave 1	4QTLevi	Testament of Levi from Qumran Cave 4
1QH	*Hodayot* (Thanksgiving Hymns) from Qumran Cave 1	4QPhyl	Phylacteries from Qumran Cave 4
1QIsa[a,b]	First or second copy of Isaiah from Qumran Cave 1	11QMelch	Melchizedek text from Qumran Cave 11
1QpHab	Pesher on Habakkuk from Qumran Cave 1	11QtgJob	Targum of Job from Qumran Cave 11
1QM	*Milhamah* (War Scroll)		
1QS	*Serek Hayyahad* (Rule of the Community, Manual of Discipline)		

TRANSLITERATIONS

Hebrew

א = ʼ		ר = d		י = y		ס = s		ר = r	
ב = b		ה = h		כ = k		ע = ʻ		שׂ = $ś$	
ב = b		ו = w		כך = k		פ = p		שׁ = $š$	
ג = g		ז = z		ל = l		פ = p		ת = t	
ג = g		ח = $ḥ$		מ = m		צ = $ṣ$		ת = t	
ד = d		ט = $ṭ$		נ = n		ק = q			

(ה)ָ = $â$ (h)	ֲ = $ă$	ֳ = a	ֲ = a	
ֵי = $ê$	ֵ = $ē$	ֶ = e	ֳ = e	
ִי = $î$		ִ = i	ְ = e (if vocal)	
וֹ = $ô$	ֹ = $ō$	ֹ = o	ֳ = o	
וּ = $û$		ֻ = u		

Aramaic

ʼ $b\ g\ d\ h\ w\ z\ ḥ\ ṭ\ y\ k\ l\ m\ n\ s$ ʻ $p\ ṣ\ q\ r\ ś\ š\ t$

Arabic

ʼ $b\ t\ ṯ\ ǧ\ ḥ\ ḫ\ d\ ḏ\ r\ z\ s\ š\ ṣ\ ḍ\ ṭ\ ẓ$ ʻ $ġ\ f\ q\ k\ l\ m\ n\ h\ w\ y$

Ugaritic

ʼ $b\ g\ d\ ḏ\ h\ w\ z\ ḥ\ ḫ\ ṭ\ ẓ\ y\ k\ l\ m\ n\ s\ ṣ$ ʻ $ġ\ p\ ṣ\ q\ r\ š\ t\ ṯ$

xv

Greek

α	—	a	π	—	p	αι	—	ai
β	—	b	ρ	—	r	αύ	—	au
γ	—	g	σ,ς	—	s	ει	—	ei
δ	—	d	τ	—	t	εύ	—	eu
ε	—	e	υ	—	y	ηύ	—	ēu
ζ	—	z	φ	—	ph	οι	—	oi
η	—	ē	χ	—	ch	ού	—	ou
θ	—	th	ψ	—	ps	υι	—	hui
ι	—	i	ω	—	ō			
κ	—	k				ρ	—	rh
λ	—	l	γγ	—	ng	'	—	h
μ	—	m	γκ	—	nk			
ν	—	n	γξ	—	nx	ᾳ	—	ā
ξ	—	x	γχ	—	nch	ῃ	—	ē
ο	—	o				ῳ	—	ō

1 PETER

Edwin A. Blum

1 PETER

Introduction

1. Simon Peter

According to the four Gospels, Peter was the leader and spokesman for the early disciples (Matt 15:15; 18:21; Mark 1:36–37; 8:29; 9:5–6; Luke 12:41; John 6:68). Peter's original name in Hebrew was "Simeon" (*šimeʿon*). James called Peter by this name at the Jerusalem Council (Acts 15:14; cf. v.7). The only other NT usage of Simeon is in 2 Peter 1:1. The Greek name "Simon" (*Simōn*), however, is applied to Peter forty-nine times in the NT. A third name "Cephas" (*Kēphas*) is a Greek transliteration of the Aramic word *kêpāʾ* ("rock"), which is the same as "Peter" (*Petros*). The NT, therefore, has four names for Peter. The combination "Simon Peter" (Matt 16:16) and the phrase "Simon who was known as Peter" (Acts 10:18) indicate that his new name (Peter) became his common designation.

Simon was one of the first disciples called into the service of Jesus (Mark 1:16–18). He was a fisherman from Bethsaida of Gaulanitis (John 1:44). Gaulanitis was the portion of the Transjordan immediately east of Galilee. Peter had a home in Capernaum (Mark 1:21, 29), which is about five kilometers west of Bethsaida, in Galilee. Peter was married (Matt 8:14; Mark 1:30; Luke 4:38) and took his wife on journeys to churches (1 Cor 9:5). His strong north-country accent marked him as a Galilean (Mark 14:70). Doubtless he was influenced by the preaching of John the Baptist; his brother Andrew was one of the Baptist's disciples (John 1:35–42).

Andrew introduced Peter to Jesus (John 1:42). Peter quickly became the leader of the twelve disciples, and his name always stands first in lists of them in the Synoptics. Of the twelve, Peter was one of the inner three (along with James and John) closest to Jesus (Mark 5:37; 9:2; 14:33). His preaching in the early days of the church (Acts 1–10) shows his great ability. The risen Lord appeared especially to him (1 Cor 15:5) and gave him a special commission (John 21:15–19).

Peter's leadership in the early church is not matched by his literary output. The NT contains only two letters that bear his name. Papias (c.60–c.130) (cited by

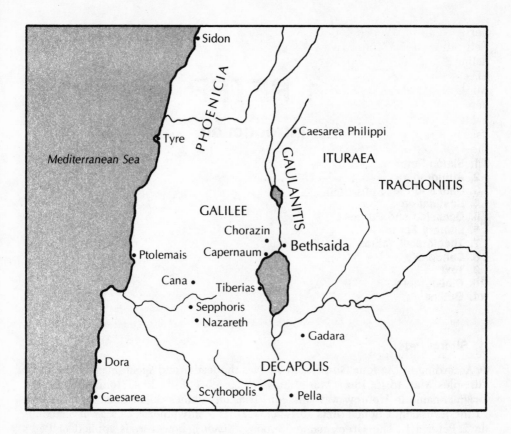

Eusebius *Ecclesiastical History* 3.39.15) and Irenaeus (fl. c.175–c.195) (*Contra Haereses* 3.1.2) state that Mark was the disciple and interpreter of Peter and that he transmitted in writing the things preached by Peter.

2. Authorship

This first letter claims to be from "Peter, an apostle of Jesus Christ" (1:1), who says he was "a witness of Christ's sufferings" (5:1). In addition, it states that he wrote it "with the help of Silas, . . . a faithful brother" (5:12). The reference is undoubtedly to "Silas" of Acts 15:22 and 1 Thessalonians 1:1. Also, the "Mark" mentioned in 1 Peter 5:13 appears to be the same man mentioned in Acts 12:12. Both such references as these together and the strong, early reception of the letter by the church (cf. Bigg, p. 15) led to the almost universal acceptance of it as from Peter, till recent years.

In 1945, F.W. Beare said, "The English reader is here offered for the first time a commentary based upon the thesis, now widely accepted, that First Peter is a pseudonymous work of the post-Apostolic Age" (p. vii). Beare followed the lead of the German commentators Gunkel, Knopf, and Windisch (ibid.). In his third edition (1970), Beare is more dogmatic, claiming that "there can be no possible doubt that 'Peter' is a pseudonym" (p. 44). He bases this claim mainly on his identification of the persecutions mentioned in the book with those of the reign of Trajan (98–117). Since Peter died under Nero's reign (54–68), he could not have written the letter. The dating of the persecutions depends on the commentator's judgment. As Beare says, "The justification of the thesis must depend upon the commentary" (ibid.). In other words, unless there are clear references to dated events in the letter, its dating must depend on (1) evidences of the dependence of 1 Peter on other NT writings, (2) evidences of the use of 1 Peter by later Christian writers, and (3) what sense the letter itself makes when viewed against a specific historical setting. The third factor involves the writing of a whole commentary to determine whether the data fit the supposition. The first two factors are discussed here.

1. E.G. Selwyn finds a variety of materials current in the mid-first-century church: creedal elements, hymns, sermonic forms, catechetical paradigms, and sayings of Jesus—these form a rich traditional deposit behind 1 Peter and other NT books (pp. 365–466). Beare holds that the literary relationship of 1 Peter to the Pauline letters "including the Deutero-Pauline Ephesians" (p. 28) is patent. Bigg (pp. 15–24) prints the parallels with the rest of the NT and concludes his discussion with the remark that "the evidence of style, vocabulary, phraseology does not appear to afford any conclusive evidence of either the absolute or relative date of 1 Peter" (p. 24). The parallels with Ephesians are notable, but what are the correct inferences from them? Beare calls Ephesians "Deutero-Pauline." If this were a fact, and if 1 Peter clearly quotes Ephesians, then a late date would be indicated. But according to Markus Barth, "Rome, about 62, is the best guess for the origin" of Ephesians.[1] It is possible that Peter read Paul's letters. (Second Peter 3:15–16 states that he did.) Did Peter, then, depend on Paul's letters? This is not probable in light of the fact that both Paul and Peter shared the heritage of the oral teaching of the early church. And even if Peter did utilize Paul's wisdom, this is no strong argument against Peter's authorship of 1 Peter. Paul's gifts were well known in the church (Acts 15:1–21; Gal 2:11–24). A good shepherd like Peter would give his sheep the best spiritual food.

2. The evidence for the use of 1 Peter by later writers is helpful but not decisive in fixing its date. The earliest attestation to 1 Peter is 2 Peter 3:1: "This is now my second letter to you." Since 2 Peter is commonly dated late by NT scholars, or since the reference to a "second letter" might not refer back to 1 Peter but to a lost epistle (so Spitta, Zahn), 2 Peter 3:1 does not solve the case. Bigg (pp. 7–9) gives lists of similarities between 1 Peter, the Epistle of Barnabas (c.130), and the writings of Clement of Rome (fl. c.90–100). Once again, the evidence is not clear enough to demonstrate that Barnabas and Clement used 1 Peter. It was not until Polycarp of Smyrna wrote to the Philippians (c.135) that actual citations of 1 Peter demonstrate that it must have been written some time earlier.

Another consideration that led Beare to the dogmatic position that Peter could not have written 1 Peter is that he finds it "scarcely imaginable" that Peter could develop the knowledge of the LXX, the Greek version of the OT (p. 45). In addition, the author of the letter was a master of Greek prose, while Peter, according to Acts 4:13, was "unlearned" (*agrammatos*). Beare (p. 47) argues that this word means "illiterate." But though *agrammatos* means "unable to write," "illiterate," in early Greek, it seems

---

[1]Markus Barth, *Ephesians: Introduction, Translation, and Commentary on Chapters 1–3* (Garden City, N.Y.: Doubleday, 1974), p. 51.

to have a wider meaning in later Greek. Here it can mean "uneducated" and perhaps "lacking in expertise concerning the law" in a Jewish context (cf. BAG, p. 13).

In response to Beare's objections, the following points are offered in support of Peter's authorship of this First Epistle. It is impossible to know to what extent Peter's home was bilingual. It is also very difficult to determine how much fluency in Greek a man like Peter could have achieved. Since use of Greek was widespread in the Middle East, one who was addressing Gentile converts would naturally use the LXX. As to the good literary style of 1 Peter, the book itself states that Peter used Silas as his secretary (5:12), and Silas might have had a part in shaping its style.

The positive case for Peter's authorship rests on these considerations: (1) The self-witness of the book is clear in claiming Petrine authorship. (2) The alternative of a pseudonymous letter is not without serious problems.[2] (3) The church's early and strong reception of the letter as Peter's cannot be overlooked. (4) The letter reveals none of the telltale marks of a late pseudepigraphon. (5) The letter makes good sense when taken at face value as by Peter. Kelley, while noncommittal about the letter's authorship, states that if certain arguments are accepted, "both contents and tone are fully consistent with apostolic times" (p. 31).

3. Date and Place of Origin

First Clement 5:4–7 names Peter and Paul as victims of persecution. The common understanding is that the passage refers to the persecution by Nero at Rome (cf. IDB, 3:755), which began after the disastrous fire in the city of Rome on 19 July 64. First Peter is written from "Babylon" (5:13). This is most likely a code word for Rome (cf. the commentary in loc.; cf. also the similar usage of "Babylon" in Rev 14:8; 17:5) as "the great city that rules over the kings of the earth" (Rev 17:18). If 1 Peter is a genuine letter of Peter, then it was probably written from Rome shortly before Nero's great persecution—that is, in 62–64.

4. Destination

First Peter is addressed to "God's elect, strangers in the world, scattered through-out Pontus, Galatia, Cappadocia, Asia and Bithynia" (1:1)—places in northern Asia Minor or modern Turkey (see map). Peter may have evangelized the northern region of Asia Minor while Paul founded churches in the southern and the western areas of Asia Minor. It is possible that Silas may have ministered in these northern provinces. The churches were no doubt composed of Christians from both Jewish and Gentile backgrounds. But the Christians outnumbered the Jews in these places. Jewish blindness to the gospel was a common phenomenon (cf. Acts 4:17–18; 28:25–28; Rom 10–11; 2 Cor 3:13–15). First Peter 4:3–4 (cf. commentary) supports the thesis that the majority of the Christians had been converted out of paganism rather than out of Judaism.

---

[2]Cf. D. Guthrie, *New Testament Introduction* (Downers Grove, Ill.: InterVarsity, 1970), pp. 786–90, esp. Appendix C: "Epistolary Pseudepigraphy," pp. 671–84.

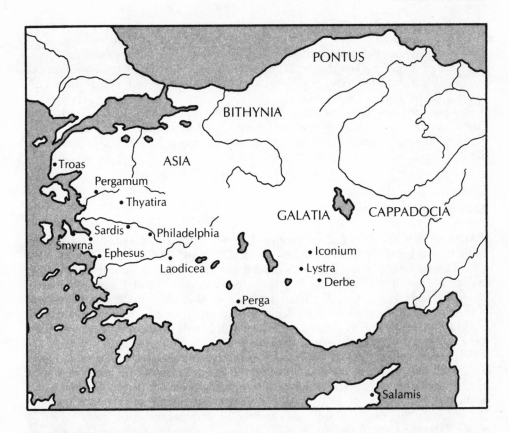

5. Occasion and Purpose

The tone of 1 Peter is a warm pastoral one, full of encouragement. The exhortations are addressed to Christians who are scattered over a wide area. They share a common faith with Christians everywhere and face common problems. Their basic problem is to live for God in the midst of a society ignorant of the true God. Because they are Christians, they are misunderstood and subjected to cruel treatment. Peter's pastoral purpose is to help these early believers see their temporary sufferings in the full light of the coming eternal glory. In the midst of all their discouragements, the sovereign God will keep them and enable them by faith to have joy. Jesus Christ by his patient suffering and glorious future destiny has given them the pattern to follow and also a living hope. Life in a pagan society is difficult and requires humility and submission. The immediate future for the church is an increase in the conflict with the world (*kosmos*) (4:7–18). But God will provide the grace to enable the community of the faithful to grow into maturity. They must help one another and show loving concern lest the members of God's flock be injured (4:8, 10; 5:1–2).

6. Literary Form

First Peter is an epistle, or letter, written in the normal letter form of the NT world. Many scholars have worked to isolate or identify creedal or hymnic fragments in 1 Peter. It has been viewed as a sermon or homily (e.g., a baptismal homily), a paschal liturgy, or even as an early Christian catechesis. (For a survey of these views, cf. Dalton, pp. 62–71.) The rhetorical and didactic nature of the letter may reflect the fact that it was intended to be read aloud to congregations (cf. Col 4:16; 1 Thess 5:27; Rev 1:3 for evidence of the practice).

This commentary takes the view that while Peter may have used material that existed in other forms (possibly material from his past teaching and preaching activity), yet these materials now form a letter the author intends to be intelligible apart from the knowledge of previously existing forms.

7. Theological Values

Although it is not a theological treatise, 1 Peter abounds with valuable theological implications. It presupposes a biblical world view based on God's sovereignty. This is God's world; yet the devil "prowls around like a roaring lion looking for someone to devour" (5:8). People who live in this world are subject to evil desires, ignorance, false gods, and all forms of sinful living (1:14; 4:3–4). God allows people time to repent of their sins, but the time for repentance is limited. He is gracious (5:2, 10), but he is also a righteous and holy Judge who will visit all people, living and dead, with their just deserts (1:17; 2:12, 23; 4:5–6, 17–19).

In common with the rest of the NT, 1 Peter presents a new eschatological perspective. With the coming of Jesus as Messiah, the age-old plan of God is on the way to its consummation (1:20). The writings of the prophets have found fulfillment in the death and resurrection of Jesus (1:11–12). Two major themes of prophetic teaching in 1 Peter are the messianic sufferings and the subsequent messianic glory. The first phase of the messianic times has already occurred! Jesus is the Suffering One who has died and has now been raised. The time is short, and Jesus must soon enter into his full glory. Already God has glorified him in heaven (1:21). All that remains is the final manifestation of the glorious Lord from heaven (1:7, 13; 4:13).

Christians are God's chosen people in an ignorant and rebellious world. In God's grace, the Triune God (1:2) is accomplishing in history a plan of redemption (1:20). The Father's role is extensive (1:1–3, 5, 15, 20–21, et al.) and is neither impersonal nor remote. The Spirit's participation in the salvation of humanity is also shown (1:2, 11–12; 4:14); but as in the other NT writings, the focus in 1 Peter is on the Messiah.

Peter regularly speaks of Jesus as "Jesus Christ" (1:1, 2, 3, 7, 13; 2:5, et al.), indicating his confession and that of the church (cf. Matt 16:16ff.). He also calls Jesus "Lord" (*kyrios*) (1:3; 2:13, 3:15) and recognizes the exaltation of Jesus (cf. Acts 2:36, where Peter, at the conclusion of his sermon on the Day of Pentecost, said, "Therefore let all Israel be assured of this: God has made this Jesus, whom you crucified, both Lord and Christ"). Peter does not develop the idea of the preexistence of Messiah.[3] Yet he declares that the Spirit of Messiah inspired the prophets (1:11) and that the Messiah was "foreknown" before the creation of the world (1:20). Peter implies the deity of Messiah (2:3) by applying Psalm 34:8 to him, where Messiah is called "LORD," which is the Hebrew "Yahweh." The ascription of a doxology to Jesus in 5:11 (if 5:11

---

[3]Cf. R.G. Hamerton-Kelly, *Pre-Existence, Wisdom, and the Son of Man* (Cambridge: Cambridge University Press, 1973), pp. 258–62.

is taken as referring to Jesus rather than to "the God of all grace" [v.10]) reveals his dignity and deity. Jesus is also called "a lamb" (1:19), "the living Stone" (2:4), "the Shepherd and Overseer of your souls" (2:25), and "the Chief Shepherd" (5:4).

In his sufferings, Jesus fulfills the OT Scriptures in types and prophecies. He is the spotless Passover lamb of Exodus (1:16–21), the Suffering Servant of Isaiah 53 (2:24–25), and the scapegoat of Leviticus (2:24a). He carries away the sins of people, takes the punishment on himself, and provides a new life of righteousness. Not only is his death a substitutionary atonement (2:24), but at the same time it provides a pattern for Christian living. Since Jesus was the Suffering Servant, his followers also have a vocation of suffering (2:21).

The key vocabulary in 1 Peter provides insight into one of the letter's distinctive contributions. Peter uses the word *anastrophē* ("way of life," "conduct," "behavior") six times; *paschō* ("suffer"), twelve times; *hypotassō* ("subject," "subordinate"), six times, and *agathopoieō* ("do good"), four times. When we consider these words together, we see that 1 Peter emphasizes the godly life of submission and good deeds in the midst of suffering. By their noble deeds, Christians may glorify God in difficulties (2:12). The sovereign Lord sustains them in adversity and has all power (5:10–11). Thus faith, submission, and trust provide the basis for Christian living.

Commentators have often discerned the close theological unity of 1 Peter with Paul's epistles (cf. Beare, p. 44; Selwyn, p. 363f.)—a unity ought to be expected in view of 2 Peter 3:15–16, which states that Peter knew and respected Paul's letters. Yet the unity between Peter and Paul should not be exaggerated as Beare does (p. 44–45) so as to make Peter dependent on Paul. For 1 Peter has none of the great Pauline emphases on justification by faith and the relation of the Jewish law and circumcision to Gentile Christians. First Peter has a distinctively pastoral tone with a strong emphasis on godly behavior in suffering. It is of great value for Christians today, who are still in a hostile world and many of whom in certain lands are suffering for Christ. A faithful witness for him can be costly, not only under repressive regimes but also in our more open society.

8. Canonicity

Eusebius of Caesarea (c.265–c.339) in his *Ecclesiastical History* (3.25.2) places 1 Peter among the books that were accepted by the church without any doubt (the *homologoumena*) and says that Papias (c.60–c.130) "used witnesses from the first epistle of John and similarly from Peter" (ibid., 3.39.17). There are probably traces of 1 Peter in 1 Clement (c.96) and even more in Ignatius, Hermas, and Barnabas (all in the early second century A.D.).

In his Epistle to the Philippians, Polycarp (c.70–150/166) unmistakably refers to 1 Peter. Though it is not in Marcion's (d.c.160) canon, this is hardly significant since Marcion's mention of letters is limited to the Pauline ones. It is not mentioned (by accident, as some—e.g., Zahn—think) in the Muratorian Fragment (c. late second century), which is in any case an incomplete document. Yet "it is reflected in the *Gospel of Truth,* which seems to use the books regarded as authoritative in Rome c. A.D. 140."[4] After the Polycarp reference, Irenaeus, Clement of Alexandria, Tertullian, and Origen all attest Peter's authorship of the book.

---

[4](A.F. Walls, NBD, p. 974; cf. p. 883).

There is no question of the canonicity of 1 Peter. It was accepted by the church because the church universally recognized its worth and authority. As Bigg (p. 7) states, "There is no book in the New Testament which has earlier, better or stronger attestation, though Irenaeus is the first to quote it by name."

9. Text

F.W. Beare, in the third edition of his commentary on 1 Peter, deals with the text of the epistle (pp. 1–24). It must be remembered that each book of the Bible circulated independently, and therefore each has a different textual history. The text of 1 Peter is reliable and is attested by 3 papyri, 16 uncials, about 550 minuscules, and a fair number of lectionaries. Until some more definitive work on the theory of textual criticism than UBS's eclectic text finds general assent, and until progress is made in the utilization of the mass of material, the commentator on 1 Peter can do little more than use the third edition of the UBS Greek text and its companion work by Metzger.[5] The earlier work of Tischendorf and von Soden should be supplemented by the materials in Beare's Introduction (pp. 1–24). Most notable is Beare's claim that there is no evidence for a "Western" text type in 1 Peter (p. 24).

10. Bibliography

For extensive bibliography, see Dalton, xv–xxiv, Goppelt, 11–26, Reicke, *Disobedient Spirits*, pp. 249–69, or Schelkle, pp. 249–55.

Balz, Horst, and Schrage, Wolfgang. *Die "Katholischen" Briefe*. DNTD. Göttingen: Vandenhoeck & Ruprecht, 1973.
Barnett, Albert E. *The Second Epistle of Peter*. Vol. 12. IB. New York: Abingdon, 1957.
———. *The Epistle of Jude*. Vol. 12. IB. New York: Abingdon, 1957.
Beare, Francis W. *The First Epistle of Peter*. 3d ed. Oxford: Basil Blackwell, 1970.
Best, Ernest. *I Peter*. NCB. London: Oliphants, 1971.
Bigg, C. *The Epistles of St. Peter and St. Jude*. ICC. Edinburgh: T. & T. Clark, 1901.
Blenkin, G.W. *The First Epistle General of Peter*. CGT. Cambridge: Cambridge University Press, 1914.
Calvin, John. *Calvin's Commentaries: The Epistle of Paul The Apostle to the Hebrews and The First and Second Epistles of St. Peter*. Translated by W.B. Johnston. Edited by D.W. and T.F. Torrance. Grand Rapids: Eerdmans, 1963.
———. *Calvin's Commentaries: A Harmony of the Gospels Matthew, Mark and Luke and The Epistles of James and Jude*. Translated by A.W. Morrison. Edited by D.W. and T.F. Torrance. Grand Rapids: Eerdmans, 1972.
Chaine, Joseph. *Les Épitres Catholiques*. 2d ed. Etudes Bibliques. Paris: J. Gabalda, 1939.
Clark, Gordon H. *Peter Speaks Today*. Philadelphia: Presbyterian and Reformed, 1967.
———. *II Peter: A Short Commentary*. Nutley, N.J.: Presbyterian and Reformed, 1972.
Cranfield, C.E.B. *I & II Peter and Jude*. TBC. London: SCM, 1960.
———. *The First Epistle of Peter*. London: SCM, 1950.
Cross, F.L. *I Peter: A Paschal Liturgy*. London: Mowbray, 1954.

---

[5](Bruce M. Metzger, *A Textual Commentary on the Greek New Testament*, corrected ed. [New York: UBS, 1975]).

Dalton, William J. *Christ's Proclamation to the Spirits*. Rome: Pontifical Biblical Institute, 1965.

Goppelt, Leonhard. *Der Erste Petrusbrief*. 8th ed. Edited by Ferdinand Hahn. KEK. Göttingen: Vandenhoeck & Ruprecht, 1978.

Green, E.M.B. *2nd Peter Reconsidered*. London: Tyndale, 1961.

_____. *The Second Epistle General of Peter and the General Epistle of Jude*. TNTC. London: Tyndale, 1968.

Hort, F.J.A. *The First Epistle of St. Peter*. I.1–II.17. London: Macmillan, 1898.

Hunter, A.M. *The First Epistle of Peter*. Vol. 12. IB. New York: Abingdon, 1957.

James, Montague R. *The Second Epistle General of Peter and the General Epistle of Jude*. CGT. Cambridge: Cambridge University Press, 1912.

Kelly, J.N.D. *A Commentary on the Epistles of Peter and of Jude*. HNTC. New York: Harper and Row, 1969.

Lawlor, George L. *The Epistle of Jude*. Nutley, N.J.: Presbyterian and Reformed, 1972.

Leaney, A.R.C. *The Letters of Peter and Jude*. Cambridge: Cambridge University Press, 1967.

Mayor, Joseph B. *The Epistle of St. Jude and the Second Epistle of St. Peter*. 1907. Reprint. Grand Rapids: Baker, 1965.

Moffatt, James. *The General Epistles. James, Peter, and Judas*. MNTC. London: Hodder and Stoughton, 1928.

Reicke, Bo. *The Disobedient Spirits and Christian Baptism*. Copenhagen: Ejnar Munksgaard, 1946.

_____. *The Epistles of James, Peter, and Jude*. AB. Garden City, N.Y.: Doubleday, 1964.

Schelkle, Karl H. *Die Petrusbriefe der Judasbriefe*. 4th ed. HTK. Freiburg: Herder, 1976.

Schlatter, Adolf. *Petrus und Paulus nach dem ersten Petrusbrief*. Stuttgart: Calwer, 1937.

Schneider, Johannes. *Die Briefe des Jakobus, Petrus, Judas und Johannes*. NTD. Göttingen: Vandenhoeck & Ruprecht, 1967.

Selwyn, Edward G. *The First Epistle of St. Peter*. 2d ed. London: Macmillan, 1947.

Sidebottom, E.M. *James, Jude and 2 Peter*. CB. London: Nelson, 1967.

Stibbs, Alan M. *The First Epistle General of Peter*. TNTC. Grand Rapids: Eerdmans, 1959.

Wand, J.W.C. *The General Epistles of St. Peter and St. Jude*. WC. London: Methuen & Co., 1934.

Windisch, Hans. *Die Katholischenbriefe*. HzNT. 3d ed. Revised by H. Preisker. Tübingen: J.C.B. Mohr, 1951.

11. Outline

    I. Salutation (1:1–2)

   II. The Privileges and Responsibilities of Salvation (1:3–2:10)
     A. God's Plan of Salvation (1:3–12)
      1. The praise of God for salvation (1:3–9)
      2. The prophecy of salvation (1:10–12)
     B. The Lifestyle of Salvation (1:13–25)
      1. A life of hope and holiness (1:13–16)
      2. A life of reverence before God (1:17–21)
      3. A life of love (1:22–25)
     C. Growth in Salvation (2:1–10)
      1. Growth through the pure milk (2:1–3)
      2. Participation in the temple and priesthood (2:4–10)
       a. Christ the Rock and the Christian living stones (2:4–8)
       b. The nation of priests (2:9–10)

  III. Christian's Submission and God's Honor (2:11–3:12)
     A. The Noble Life and God's Glory (2:11–12)
     B. The Duty of Christian Submission (2:13–3:7)
      1. The submission to civil authority (2:13–17)
      2. The submission of slave to master (2:18–25)
       a. The submission of household slaves (2:18–20)
       b. The example of Christ's submission (2:21–25)
      3. The submission of Christian wives (3:1–6)
      4. The obligation of Christian husbands (3:7)
     C. The Call to Righteous Living (3:8–12)

  IV. The Suffering and Persecution of Christians (3:13–5:11)
     A. The Blessing of Suffering for Righteousness (3:13–17)
     B. The Pattern of Christ's Suffering and Exhaltation (3:18–22)
     C. Death to the Old Life (4:1–6)
     D. The Life for God's Glory (4:7–11)
     E. Consolations in Suffering (4:12–19)
     F. The Shepherd's Suffering Flock (5:1–4)
     G. Humility and Watchfulness in Suffering (5:5–9)
     H. The Sustaining Grace of God (5:10–11)

   V. Final Words (5:12–14)
     A. Silas's Role Writing the Letter (5:12)
     B. The Greeting From Rome (5:13)
     C. A Final Exhortation and a Prayerful Wish (5:14)

Text and Exposition

I. Salutation

1:1–2

> ¹Peter, an apostle of Jesus Christ,
> To God's elect, strangers in the world, scattered throughout Pontus, Galatia, Cappadocia, Asia and Bithynia, ²who have been chosen according to the fore-knowledge of God the Father, through the sanctifying work of the Spirit, for obedience to Jesus Christ and sprinkling by his blood:
>
> Grace and peace be yours in abundance.

1 Peter begins by using his name in its most common NT form. His name in Hebrew was probably "Simeon" (Acts 15:14; 2 Peter 1:1 [Gk.]), the Greek equivalent of which was "Simon." He also had the Aramaic nickname of "Cephas" (John 1:42; Gal 2:11 [Gk.]). "Peter" is the Greek translation of "Cephas" or "rock." Cullmann suggests that to bring out the power of the nickname and to follow the common NT practice ("Simon Peter"), Peter should be called "Simon Rock" (TDNT, 6:101). "An apostle of Jesus Christ" indicates the dignity and authority as one selected by Jesus and given unique responsibilities of ministry in the establishment of the Christian church (Matt 16:18–19; Mark 1:16f.; 3:16; John 1:42; John 21:15–19).

As is common in Greek letters of the NT era, the writer first identifies himself, then identifies the recipient, and finally gives a word of greeting. Peter begins by designating those he is writing to as "God's elect." In biblical teaching, election is a central theme and the foundation of spiritual blessing (cf. Deut 4:37; 7:6; 14:2; Ps 105:6, 43; Isa 45:4; Eph 1:4–5). No believer should ever feel threatened by the doctrine of election, because it is always presented in Scripture as the ground of comfort. So here the designation of "elect" reminds the scattered Christians in danger of persecution that God's purposes for them are certain and gracious. "Strangers in the world" (*parepidēmoi*) points to the fact that Christians are "pilgrims" who do not reside permanently on earth. They belong to the heavenly realm (cf. Eph 2:19; Phil 3:20; Heb 11:13–16). The destination of the letter is "Pontus, Galatia, Cappadocia, Asia and Bithynia." These were the Roman provinces north of the Taurus Mountains in what is today Turkey.

2 Peter next announces some basic themes of his letter ("foreknowledge of God the Father," "sanctifying work of the Spirit," and "obedience to Jesus Christ and sprinkling by his blood") that will later be expanded and developed. Here he reminds his readers of their Triune faith and of the Triune work of God. While Peter does not go into the developed theological form of the Trinitarian faith, the triadic pattern of the Christian faith is already evident in his words. The "foreknowledge of God" is more than God's simply knowing what will take place in the future, for it includes God's special relations with mankind even before creation (cf. 1:20; Amos 3:2; Acts 2:23; Rom 8:29–30; 11:2). The "special relations" include God's election and his special plans for his people (cf. TDNT, 1:714). The "sanctifying" of the Spirit is his operation of applying the work of redemption to the Christian, purifying him and setting him to tasks of service. The goal of election and redemption is obedience that grows out of faith (cf. Paul's reference to "the obedience that comes from faith" in Rom 1:5). The salutation closes with the wish for the multiplication of God's grace and peace to the believers.

II. The Privileges and Responsibilities of Salvation (1:3–2:10)

A. *God's Plan of Salvation* (1.3–12)

1. *The praise of God for salvation*

1:3–9

> ³Praise be to the God and Father of our Lord Jesus Christ! In his great mercy he has given us new birth into a living hope through the resurrection of Jesus Christ from the dead, ⁴and into an inheritance that can never perish, spoil or fade—kept in heaven for you, ⁵who through faith are shielded by God's power until the coming of the salvation that is ready to be revealed in the last time. ⁶In this you greatly rejoice, though now for a little while you may have had to suffer grief in all kinds of trials. ⁷These have come so that your faith—of greater worth than gold, which perishes even though refined by fire—may be proved genuine and may result in praise, glory and honor when Jesus Christ is revealed. ⁸Though you have not seen him, you love him; and even though you do not see him now, you believe in him and are filled with an inexpressible and glorious joy, ⁹for you are receiving the goal of your faith, the salvation of your souls.

The first major section of Peter's letter concerns salvation (*sōtēria*), the key term of this unit that occurs at 1:5, 9–10 and 2:2 but nowhere else in the book. Its basic meaning is "deliverance," "preservation," or "salvation" (BAG, p. 808–9). In 1:9 Peter defines his use of it as "the salvation of your souls" (cf. below). The section closes with an OT quotation, as the next major division also does (cf. 3:10–12).

3–4 The nature of this salvation as a new birth according to the mercy of God evokes praise to God the Father, who is the source of salvation. The new birth is the work of the Holy Spirit, as Jesus taught in John 3:3–8. The Christian has a "living hope" because Jesus has been raised by the Father (cf. Titus 2:13). This hope is further described in v.4 as an inheritance "that can never perish, spoil or fade." The concept of inheritance is one of the major Bible themes and stresses family connection and gift. As Paul wrote to the Galatians, "God in his grace gave it [the inheritance] to Abraham through a promise" (3:18; cf. 1 Peter 3:9; Matt 5:5; 19:29; 25:34; see also DNTT, 2:295–303). The inheritance is kept (*tetērēmenēn*, perfect tense) or reserved by God for his people in "heaven."

5 God's people are described as "the ones being guarded" (*tous phrouroumenous*, present passive; NIV, "who are shielded"). This stresses the continued activity of God in their lives, while the phrase "through faith" stresses the believers' activity. The divine protection and the final salvation are only for believers. The salvation "ready to be revealed in the last time" looks at the final aspects or realization of what Christians already have and enjoy.

6 "In this" (*en hō*) probably refers to anticipation of the future deliverance. As the Christian longs for his inheritance, he can "rejoice" (*agalliasthe*, which is best taken as a present indicative). Bultmann says, "God's help is always the theme of [*agalliaē*] which is a jubilant and thankful exultation" (TDNT, 1:20). The participle *lypēthentes* (grieve) is concessive, as the translation "though now for a little while you may have had to suffer grief" shows. The Greek emphasizes that the suffering is brief, for the present time (*arti*), and necessary (*ei deon*). The aorist participle also plays down the duration of the grief of the believer. That Peter uses *peirasmoi* ("trials") instead of *diōgmoi* ("persecutions") or *thlipseis* ("tribulations") is significant. While they are not technical terms (cf. BAG, s.v.), *diōgmoi* or *thlipseis* are not found in Peter's epistles. Peter is thinking in terms of the broadest category of the pagans' attitude toward Christians rather than of specific actions, and this may be an evidence of the early dating of the book.

7 Gold is one of man's most prized objects. When it is refined, its impurities are removed by a fiery process. Though extremely durable, gold belongs to the perishing world-order. Faith, which is more valuable than gold because it lasts longer and reaches beyond this temporal order, is purified in the tests of life. Gold, not faith, is presently valued by men. But God will set his stamp of approval on faith that has been tested and show this when Christ is revealed. Then the believer will openly share in the praise, glory, and honor of God.

8 Faith is directed toward Jesus Christ and produces love and joy in Christians. Without seeing Jesus (either because they were second-generation believers or because they were geographically removed), Peter's readers have come to love Jesus because they believe he has loved them enough to die for them. Christians do not rejoice because of sufferings but because of the glorious expectation of their future with Christ. "This is a mystery of faith contradicting everyday experience, and so the *joy* is *inexpressible*" (italics his) (Kelly, p. 57).

9 "For you are receiving" (*komizomenoi*, a present causal participle) gives the reason for the paradoxical joy while stressing that the anticipated salvation is even now in the process of realization. The "goal" (*telos*) or consummation of faith is "the salvation of your souls." No soul-and-body dichotomy of Greek thought is implied. The "soul" is used in the Semitic biblical sense of "self" or "person." Therefore the thought of this section closes with the believers' enjoyment of the future salvation in this present age.

Notes

3–13 A.B. du Toit has an instructive article on the argument here (cf. "The Significance of Discourse Analysis for New Testament Interpretation and Translation: Introductory Remarks with Special Reference to 1 Peter 1:3–13," *Neotestamentica* 8 [1974], 54–79).
6,8 Ἀγαλλιᾶσθε (*agalliasthe*, "you rejoice") may be taken as a command or as a future present. The indicative seems to fit the argument best.

2. *The prophecy of salvation*

1:10–12

> ¹⁰Concerning this salvation, the prophets, who spoke of the grace that was to come to you, searched intently and with the greatest care, ¹¹trying to find out the time and circumstances to which the Spirit of Christ in them was pointing when he predicted the sufferings of Christ and the glories that would follow. ¹²It was revealed to them that they were not serving themselves but you, when they spoke of the things that have now been told you by those who have preached the gospel to you by the Holy Spirit sent from heaven. Even angels long to look into these things.

10–11 This salvation was the subject of the OT prophecies of the messianic sufferings and glories. The prophets not only spoke to the situation of their contemporaries, but they also spoke of the longed-for messianic times. In predicting the future, they did not always understand their utterances. The clearest example is Daniel and his visions (8:27; 12:8) and his study of other prophets (9:2ff.). The prophets longed to see the messianic time and so searched into what they could know of it (cf. Luke 10:24). The motivating force in prophecy is not the human will (cf. 2 Sam 23:2: "The Spirit of the Lord spoke through me; his word was on my tongue"; cf. also 2 Peter 1:21); it is the Holy Spirit. The content of the prophecies embraced both the "sufferings" and the "glories" of Christ (cf. Luke 24:26). Both words are plural. The gospels list various aspects of the predicted sufferings of Christ—e.g., hatred by his people, betrayal by his friend, being forsaken by his flock, his scourging and crucifixion, etc. His glories include his transfiguration (2 Peter 1:17), his resurrection (1:21), his glorious return, and his reign.

12 Through revelation the prophets learned that some of their utterances related to future generations. The writings of the prophets contain both "near" and "far" aspects. Yet the prophets were unable to understand the time significance of their prophecies or to understand fully the relation of the sufferings of the Messiah to his glory. Denial or ignorance of these things has led to denial of supernatural predictive prophecy. The word translated "serving" (*diēkonoun*) is significant, for it points to the fact that the writings of the OT are of service to the new community—the church. The unity of the OT and NT writings centers in Christ and his salvation. This message of salvation has come to humanity through men under the power of the Holy Spirit, who has come from heaven.

The last statement of v. 12 is especially significant—"even angels long to look into these things." The Scriptures reveal that the angels have intense interest in human salvation. They rejoice at the conversion of a sinner (Luke 15:10); they observed Jesus in his early life (1 Tim 3:16); they will rejoice in songs of praise at the completion of redemption (Rev 5:11–14).

The verb *parakyptō* (NIV, "long to look") means "to stoop over to look." It implies willingness to exert or inconvenience oneself to obtain a better perspective. Here the present tense gives it a continuous aspect. The verb is also used in Luke 24:12; John 20:5, 11; and James 1:25. It means continuous regard rather than a quick look.

The Bible says nothing about salvation for angels. On the contrary, they learn about it from the church (Eph 3:10); and they serve the church (Heb 1:14).

B. The Lifestyle of Salvation (1:13–25)

1. A life of hope and holiness

1:13–16

> [13]Therefore, prepare your minds for action; be self-controlled; set your hope fully on the grace to be given you when Jesus Christ is revealed. [14]As obedient children, do not conform to the evil desires you had when you lived in ignorance. [15]But just as he who called you is holy, so be holy in all you do; [16]for it is written: "Be holy, because I am holy."

13 "Therefore" (*dio*) relates this section to the former one, which is the basis of the commands in these verses. The general meaning is that the reception of salvation must issue in a life of holiness, reverence, and love. Moreover, since the prophets and the angels take great interest in this salvation, how much more should Christians pay careful attention to its results. The Greek syntax is significant. Peter used the indicative mood in stating the nature of the Christian faith in vv.3–12. In this section (1:13–2:5) he changes to the imperative. Most of these commands are in the aorist tense, and NIV correctly reflects their significance—e.g., "Set your hope" (1:13). The alternation of the indicative and imperative moods throughout Peter's writing differs from Paul's style. Paul tends to group his indicatives first and follow them with imperatives in the last portions of his letters (cf. Rom 12:1ff.; Eph 4:1ff.).

"Prepare your minds for action" (NIV) replaces KJV's literal translation "Gird up the loins of your mind." The figure is of a man gathering the folds of his long garment and tucking it into his belt so that he can move freely and quickly (cf. 1 Kings 18:46; Jer 1:17; Luke 17:8). Related uses of the figure occur in Luke 12:35 and Ephesians 6:14. Selwyn (p. 140) offers "Pull yourselves together" as a comparable English idiom. "Be self-controlled" renders the Greek present participle *nēphontes* and implies another figure. The original meaning of *nēphō* related to abstaining from excessive use of wine. In the NT its sense broadens to "live soberly"—a meaning that embraces sound judgment in all areas of life (TDNT, 4:936–38).

The main emphasis of v.13 is on putting one's hope wholly in the eschatological consummation of the grace of God in Jesus Christ. At the present time, we enjoy only a beginning of that grace. Now we are God's children, John wrote, but when Christ returns, we will be like him (1 John 3:2–3). This longing for the Parousia permeates the NT writings (cf. Acts 1:11; Rom 11:26; 1 Cor 15:51; 1 Thess 4:13ff.; Heb 9:28; James 5:8; 2 Peter 3:12–13; Rev 1:7; 19:11ff.; 22:7–20). For Christians, the consummation of this grace occurs at the unveiling of Jesus the Messiah at the second coming (1 Thess 4:13ff.).

14 The Christians' lifestyle is not to conform to the base desires that formerly dominated them and kept them from God. The imperatival participle *syschēmatizomenoi* ("do not conform") is passive (BAG, p. 803) and is found only here and in Romans 12:2 in the NT. (Ph's tr. of Rom 12:2 is a happy one: "Don't let the world around you squeeze you into its own mold, but let God remold your minds from within.") Peter exhorts Christians to control their desires rather than to be controlled by them. Formerly Christians were in ignorance; now they have come to know God and his will. They are to be "children of obedience"—a Semitic expression describing not only their quality but also their nature.

15–16 God is first described as the one who "called." Here the Greek verb *kaleō* ("call") implies the divine calling or what theologians term "efficacious grace" (cf. DNTT, 1:275). God is described as "holy." Holiness embraces purity and moral integrity. Those called to be God's children are to be like him. Peter reinforces this command by citing Leviticus (cf. 11:44–45; 19:2; 20:7). The basic idea of holiness in the Bible is that of separation from all that is profane. The developed sense of holiness includes various meanings translated into English as "purify," "sanctify," "separate from," "dedicate," etc. The simplest understanding of holiness is that of loving conformity to God's commands and to his Son (cf. 1 John 2:4–6).

2. A life of reverence before God

1:17–21

> [17]Since you call on a Father who judges each man's work impartially, live your lives as strangers here in reverent fear. [18]For you know that it was not with perishable things such as silver or gold that you were redeemed from the empty way of life handed down to you from your forefathers, [19]but with the precious blood of Christ, a lamb without blemish or defect. [20]He was chosen before the creation of the world, but was revealed in these last times for your sake. [21]Through him you believe in God, who raised him from the dead and glorified him, and so your faith and hope are in God.

17 In the Greek, this verse begins with *kai* ("and"), which links it with vv. 13–16 and carries on the call to a lifestyle that is different from that of non-Christians. Peter reminds Christians that they invoke God as "Father" and that as his children (v.14) they should indeed call on him constantly in prayer. But God is Judge as well as Father, and those who call on his name must remember that he is impartial in judgment. Simply because some people call themselves Christians does not mean that all will be well for them in the Judgment. Justified persons are persons changed by grace and they must walk in good works as the evidence of grace (Eph 2:10).

As for sinners, they "will not stand in the judgment" (Ps 1:5–6). This means that at the Last Judgment the unregenerate will be doomed. The regenerate will have their lives evaluated by God also (Rom 14:10–12; 1 Cor 3:13–17; 2 Cor 5:10) and will receive according to what they have done. Justified persons, however, cannot be condemned (Rom 8:1, 34). But only the Lord who knows the hearts knows who the justified are.

Since judgment is certain, Christians are to live in reverential awe of God—yet not in terror, for peace is one of their prerogatives (1 Peter 1:2). The Christian life is a temporary stay on this earth (cf. comments on 1:1). So the brief time granted us should be used carefully (cf. TDNT, 5:848–53).

18–19 "For you know" translates the Greek participle *eidotes* and is grammatically subordinate to the command "Live your lives" (*anastraphēte*) of v.17. The logic is "Live . . . because you know!" That is, the Christian life is lived out of knowledge of the redemption that Christ has accomplished. What do Christians know? Peter reminds his readers of the cost of redemption. The value of redemption is the value of the Person of the righteous Messiah himself.

The Greek word *lytroō* ("redeem") goes back to the institution of slavery in ancient Rome. Any representative first-century church would have three kinds of members:

slaves, freemen, and freed men. People became slaves in various ways—through war, bankruptcy, sale by themselves, sale by parents, or by birth. Slaves normally could look forward to freedom after a certain period of service and often after the payment of a price. Money to buy his freedom could be earned by the slave in his spare time or by doing more than his owner required. Often the price could be provided by someone else. By the payment of a price (*lytron, antilytron*), a person could be set free from his bondage or servitude. A freed man was a person who formerly had been a slave but was now redeemed. (See A.A. Rupprecht, "The Cultural and Political Setting of the New Testament," EBC, 1:483ff.) Jesus described his ministry in Mark 10:45: "The Son of Man . . . [came] to serve, and to give his life as a ransom [*lytron*] for [*anti*, 'in the place of'] many."

The redemption of Christians is from the "empty" (*mataios*) lifestyle of their ancestors. This implies a pagan lifestyle rather than a Jewish one because the NT stresses the emptiness of paganism (cf. Rom 1:21; Eph 4:17; TDNT, 4:521–24).

Verse 19 stresses the value of the purchase price of redemption and at the same time identifies the blood as that of a spotless lamb—the Messiah. When Israel was in bondage in Egypt, the Passover lamb was killed and the blood provided release from bondage and judgment. Because Jesus is without sin, he is unique and his life is of infinite value as the Sacrificial Lamb of the Passover (cf. Exod 12:46; John 19:36; 1 Cor 5:7).

20 "He was chosen before the creation of the world." The Greek word for "chosen" is *proegnōsmenou*, often translated "know before." The meaning, however, must be more than "foresight." For why would Peter at this point make the obvious statement that God knew before about Jesus and his death? The word connotes purpose (cf. Rom 11:2). Kelly (p. 75) translates this clause as "predestined before the foundation of the world." The redemption was in the plan of God before Creation occurred. And now this redemption has been "revealed" in Jesus of Nazareth "in these last times." With the coming of Jesus, the last age has come (cf., e.g., Acts 2:17; Heb 1:2; 9:26). The salvation in Christ purposed from eternity is now made plain, Peter tells his readers, "for your sake." He personalizes it so as to spur them to a life of response to God.

21 The paragraph (vv. 17–21) closes with a statement about the believers' faith in God. Their faith in (*eis*) God comes through the work of Jesus because he is the one who reveals the Father (John 1:18) and because he is the means of reconciliation (2 Cor 5:19; cf. Kelly, p. 77). Peter identifies the Father (v. 17) as the God who raised Jesus and glorified him with the result that believers have faith and hope in God. Jesus' resurrection is the foundation of our faith, and his glorification is the pledge of the hope of our new future (cf. Rom 8:17–30; 1 Cor 15:1–11; Heb 2:10).

Notes

18 On redemption, cf. the following for the various words used in the NT: Acts 20:28; Gal 3:13; 4:4; 1 Cor 6:19–20; Eph 1:7,14; 1 Tim 2:6; Titus 2:14; Heb 9:12. See also, B.B. Warfield, "The New Testament Terminology of Redemption," PTR, 15 (1917), 201–49; Leon Morris, *The Apostolic Preaching of the Cross* (Grand Rapids: Eerdmans, 1955), pp. 9–59; and TDNT, 4:328–56.

For valuable background on slavery, cf. J. Scott Bartchy, ΜΑΛΛΟΝ ΧΡΗΣΑΙ " *First-Century Slavery and the Interpretation of 1 Corinthians 7:21* (Missoula, Mont.: Society of Biblical Literature, 1973).

---

3. *A life of love*

1:22–25

22Now that you have purified yourselves by obeying the truth so that you have sincere love for your brothers, love one another deeply, from the heart. 23For you have been born again, not of perishable seed, but of imperishable, through the living and enduring word of God. 24For,

"All men are like grass,
    and all their glory is like the flowers of the field;
the grass withers and the flowers fall,
25 but the word of the Lord stands forever."

And this is the word that was preached to you.

22 In the third subdivision of this section on the Christian way of life, Peter adds to the command to be holy and to reverence God the command to love. This command is supported by two participles—one before and one after—that explain the reasons for Christians to love one another. The first participle (*hēgnikotes*, "now that you have purified yourselves") is in the perfect tense, stressing the state that results from regeneration. The word itself is not common in the NT nor in the LXX, but its sense is clear. It denotes the moral purity that comes to Christians through the gospel.

The means of this purification is "by obeying the truth," or obeying the gospel (cf. Acts 15:9: "He purified their hearts by faith"; Rom 10:16; 2 Thess 1:8). The Good News carries with it a command to repent and believe. In the early church, this was commonly tied to baptism. Not that the church believed that baptism itself saved; rather, it was the focal point of decision (cf. Acts 2:38). Being purified from sin enables Christians to show genuine family love for God's children. Yet this love is not entirely a foregone conclusion, because it can be and is commanded. Here the command is in the aorist tense, which often expresses "the coming about of conduct which contrasts with prior conduct; in this case it is ingressive" (BDF, par. 337).

This love is to be "from a pure heart" (NIV mg.). So Peter exhorts Christians—because they are purified—to love fellow Christians purely and fervently. Love for non-Christians is not in view here, but of course it is also part of Christians' obligations (cf. Matt 5:44; Luke 6:27, 35). The NT teaches that there are different kinds of love and different emotions of love. Yet Christians are enabled to love all people with agape love—viz., a self-sacrificing desire to meet the needs of others that finds expression in concrete acts (cf. 1 John 3:14–18).

23 The second reason for Christians to love others is expressed by the second participle (*anagegennēmenoi*, "for you have been born again"). This participle is also in the perfect tense and stresses the state into which Christians come at conversion. What is the "seed" that gives the new birth? Schulz claims that it is "the living and abiding divine word of baptism by which Christians are born again" (TDNT, 7:546). Others connect it with "the word" (cf. Luke 8:11: "The seed is the word of God") or with the "seed" of the divine life (1 John 3:9). Perhaps it is best explained as the life-giving message about Jesus' death and resurrection. Peter explains that the new birth comes through the living and abiding word of God. By the "word" (*logos*), he probably means "God's self-revelation," which would include both his spoken message and his written one. God's word is living because it imparts life (cf. Ps 33:9; Isa 55:10–11; Heb 4:12). His word endures because the God who speaks it is the eternal, faithful, powerful one who keeps his promises.

24 The quotation from Isaiah 40:6–8 supports the assertion of the character of God, with its stress on the abiding faithfulness of the Lord's statements. The quotation comes from the "Book of Comfort" in Isaiah as the prophetic message of God to an exiled and oppressed people. How fitting the application is to pilgrim Christians (cf. 1 Peter 1:1) in the light of their oppression by the pagan world! (And what Christian is not in some sense a pilgrim?) The theme of Isaiah's prophecy is the perishable nature of all flesh and the imperishable nature of the Word of God. To the exiles in Babylon, the message was that "human help is weak and perishable, but God's promise of restoration can never fail" (Blenkin, p. 41).

25 Here Peter gives us the application of Isaiah's words. In the Hebrew and in the Greek of the LXX, it is the "word of *God*" that is spoken of. Peter says it is the utterance (*rhēma*, not *logos*) of the Lord (*kyrios*) that endures. So he stresses the specifically Christian application, for Jesus is *kyrios*. The message about Jesus was proclaimed to Peter's readers, and it is utterly reliable. This message gives life and transforms life so that Christians are able to love.

Notes

22 After τῆς ἀληθείας (*tēs alētheias*, "the truth") most minuscules add διὰ πνεύματος (*dia pneumatos*, "through the Spirit"). If this reading is accepted, the idea of how a person is purified would be expanded to state the Spirit's divine working in regeneration-conversion. But most textual critics regard the reading as a later theological expansion introduced by a copyist (cf. Bruce M. Metzger, *A Textual Commentary on the Greek New Testament*, corrected ed. [New York: UBS, 1975], p. 688).

C. Growth in Salvation (2:1–10)

1. Growth through the pure milk

2:1–3

> ¹Therefore, rid yourselves of all malice and all deceit, hypocrisy, envy, and slander of every kind. ²Like newborn babies, crave pure spiritual milk, so that by it you may grow up in your salvation, ³now that you have tasted that the Lord is good.

This section (2:1–10) flows logically ("therefore," *oun*) out of the previous section. Peter uses a variety of images to describe the Christian life. He begins by speaking of "stripping off" habits like garments and then compares Christians to babies. Next he likens them to stones in the temple and finally to a chosen, priestly people.

1 "Therefore" points directly to the conversion of Peter's Christian readers, when they obeyed the truth of the gospel and were purified (1:21). "Rid yourselves" represents the aorist participle *apothemenoi,* not an imperative. This translation may be misleading because it implies that Peter is assuming that the Christians he is addressing have made a real break with pagan vices. But he is probably reminding them of their baptism, which was the focal point of their commitment to Christ, when they stripped off the old life and made a new beginning in repentance and faith. Vice lists such as this were common in the ancient world and also in the NT (cf. Mark 7:21–22; Rom 1:29–31; 13:13; 1 Cor 5:10; Gal 5:19–20; 2 Peter 2:10–14; and the appendix to Eric H. Wahlstrom's *New Life in Christ* [Philadelphia: Muhlenberg, 1950], pp. 281–87).

2 The young Asian Christians whom Peter addresses were, in the main, new converts, i.e., "new born" (*artigennēta*). A major characteristic of a healthy new baby is its instinctive yearning for its mother's milk. Christians are to crave what is "pure" (*adolos*) in contrast to the "deceit" (*dolos,* v.1) of the old life. The "spiritual milk" (*logikos gala*) is probably a reference to the Word of God (*logos*). Therefore the translation might be expanded to "crave the unadulterated spiritual milk of the word." The continuous nourishment from the "milk" causes the newborn to "grow up in [their] salvation." Salvation is the present possession of Christians as well as their future goal (cf. 1 Peter 1:5, 9). After conversion, their lives should be marked by continuous growth (cf. 1 Cor 3:1–4; Heb 5:11–14). This growth comes from the teaching about Christ and God the Father that is at the core of the Word, or the Bible.

3 "Now that you have tasted" has the Greek *ei* or *eiper* (lit., "if") introducing a first-class conditional sentence, which implies that they have tasted the goodness of the Lord. The image of "tasting" the Lord goes back to Psalm 34:8: "Taste and see that the Lord is good." In the psalm, the Lord is Yahweh. In his writings, Peter applies *kyrios* ("Lord") to Jesus, who is the exalted Lord. Once a person has come to taste the graciousness or goodness of the Lord, he should have a continuing appetite for spiritual food.

2. Participation in the temple and priesthood (2:4-10)

a. Christ the Rock and the Christian living stones

2:4-8

⁴As you come to him, the living Stone—rejected by men but chosen by God and precious to him— ⁵you also, like living stones, are being built into a spiritual house to be a holy priesthood, offering spiritual sacrifices acceptable to God through Jesus Christ. ⁶For in Scripture it says:

"See, I lay a stone in Zion,
a chosen and precious cornerstone,
and the one who trusts in him
will never be put to shame."

7Now to you who believe, this stone is precious. But to those who do not believe,

> "The stone the builders rejected
> has become the capstone,"

8and,

> "A stone that causes men to stumble
> and a rock that makes them fall."

They stumble because they disobey the message—which is also what they were destined for.

4 This section (2:4–8) is connected to the previous one by the relative clause *pros hon proserchomenoi* ("to whom coming"; NIV, "As you come to him"), by the continued use of Psalm 34, and by the concept of Christians' finding in Christ great value. So the figure changes. Now Peter presents Christ not as food but as a rock or a stone. The "rock-stone" imagery is common in Scripture. As Hillyer says, "There is, for example, the stumbling stone of Isaiah 8:14, the foundation-stone of Isaiah 28:16, the parental rock of Isaiah 51:1f., the rejected but vindicated building-stone of Psalm 118:22, the supernatural stone of Daniel 2:34, and the burdensome stone of Zechariah 12:3" (Norman Hillyer, " 'Rock-Stone' Imagery in 1 Peter," *The Tyndale Bulletin*, 22 [1971], 58). There is fair evidence that "Rock/Stone" was a messianic title among the Jews as well as among Christians (cf. Selwyn, p. 158–59; TDNT, 4:274–77).

"As you come to him" (*pros hon proserchomenoi*) probably reflects Psalm 34:5 (LXX 33:6, *proselthate pros auton*, "come to him"). Christians "come" to Christ in salvation, but their continual "coming" may also be included in the present tense. Jesus Christ is identified as the "living Stone," which refers to his stability as the risen Lord. God's raising of Jesus from the dead shows Jesus' value and God's choice of him. The "rejection" of Christ is, first, the valuation of Jesus by the nation (Matt 26:14–15; Acts 2:22–24; 3:13–15; 4:10–11) and, second, the current rejection of him by the disobedient in every land.

5 Jesus' great prophecy to Peter (Matt 16:18f.) concerned Jesus' building of his church. Peter sees, in the coming of individuals to Jesus the Rock, the building of a new spiritual edifice. Solomon was amazed at the thought of God's gracious condescension in dwelling among his people and in a house (temple) that Solomon built (1 Kings 8:27). Now the localized manifestation of God's presence on earth is replaced by his indwelling of all believers (1 Cor 3:17; 6:19).

"Are being built" (*oikodomeisthe*) is best taken as an indicative (NIV) rather than an imperative: "Be yourselves built" (RSV). The verb is to be understood as customary or timeless. Thus the thought is that when anyone comes to Christ, a new stone is added to the "spiritual" house. The use of the word "spiritual" does not mean that what Peter is speaking of is less "real" than a material house or material sacrifices. Rather, the material sacrifices and temples that were shadows of the reality to come are now superseded. The OT spoke of the offerings of prayer, thanksgiving, praise, and repentance (Pss 50:14; 51:19; 107:22; 141:2) in addition to the material sacrifices and offerings. The NT speaks of the offering of "faith" (Phil 2:17), gifts as "a fragrant offering" (Phil 4:18), "your bodies as living sacrifices" (Rom 12:1), "a sacrifice of praise"

(Heb 13:15), the conversion of the Gentiles as "an offering acceptable to God" (Rom 15:16), and Paul's coming death as "a drink offering" (2 Tim 4:6; cf. Schelkle, pp. 58–59).

The great new truth Peter states here is the revelation that "through Jesus Christ," i.e., through his work on the Cross, every Christian is part of a new priestly order. This truth of the "priesthood of all believers" was rediscovered and restressed during the Reformation. It means that every Christian has immediate access to God, that he serves God personally, that he ministers to others, and that he has something to give. It does not mean that each Christian has public gifts of preaching or teaching. In this verse Peter is stressing the reassuring fact that through Christ the believer is able to worship and serve God in a manner pleasing to him.

6 Next Peter cites Scripture to support his teaching. The quotation of Isaiah 28:16 refers to God's foundation stone, carefully chosen and very costly, placed in position in Zion. The picture is from the building of a temple. At great cost and care the corner foundation stone was obtained, moved, and laid. Hillyer mentions one stone in a quarry that was sixty-nine feet by twelve feet by thirteen feet ("'Rock-Stone' Imagery," p. 66, n.34). There are similar large foundation stones in many sites in the Middle East—e.g., Baalbek. Once this large foundation corner stone was in place, the rest of the building was determined. Isaiah uses this figure to encourage his people to build on the Lord himself, the one who is immovable and unchangeable, rather than on lies and falsehood. The applications of Peter's use of the figure are self-evident. God has set Jesus forth in Jerusalem as the foundation of the new temple. Whoever builds on this foundation will be established and will never be ashamed (cf. 1 Cor 3:10; Eph 2:20).

7 "Now to you who believe, this stone is precious." Here the Greek literally reads, "For you, therefore, who believe [is] the honor" (*timē*, cf. BAG, p. 825, 2b). The honor for Christians is linked to their union with Christ. Since Christ is honored by God, so will all who participate in Christ. But for unbelievers two other "stone" citations from the OT are strong warnings. The first is from Psalm 118:22, where the builders rejected a building block that later turned out to be the final stone in the building (cf. Mark 12:10–12; TDNT, 1:792; 4:278). In the same way, Jesus, who was rejected by men, has been exalted by God.

8 The second warning quotation is from Isaiah 8:14, where the disobedient are portrayed as stumbling over the stone. So Peter warns that those who refuse to believe in Jesus as Messiah stumble—"which is also what they were destined for." What is "destined"? The unbelief of men or the stumbling that is the result of the unbelief? It is common to argue that only the result or stumbling was ordained (so Beare, p. 126; Bigg, p. 133). Peter probably means to say that the appointment of God embraces both the setting forth of Christ and his work and the rejection by men. Peter's preaching in Acts 2:14–40 makes the same emphasis (cf. esp. v.23). Scripture in other places teaches that human disobedience is within the plan of God (cf. Rom 11:8, 11, 30–32). Yet it must be recognized that though human disobedience is within God's plan, it does not become less blameworthy (cf. Acts 2:23). It is important to recognize also that human disobedience is not necessarily final or irretrievable (cf. Hort, p. 123; Selwyn, p. 164–65). Paul says, "God has bound all men over to disobedience so that he may have mercy on them all" (Rom 11:32).

b. *The nation of priests*

2:9–10

> ⁹But you are a chosen people, a royal priesthood, a holy nation, a people belonging to God, that you may declare the praises of him who called you out of darkness into his wonderful light. ¹⁰Once you were not a people, but now you are the people of God; once you had not received mercy, but now you have received mercy.

9 "But you" marks the contrast with the disobedient who were mentioned in vv. 7–8. Peter applies to the church various terms originally spoken concerning Israel (cf. Exod 19:5–6; Deut 4:20; 7:6; Isa 43:20–1). But this does not mean that the church is Israel or even that the church replaces Israel in the plan of God. Romans 11 should help us to guard against that misinterpretation. Why then does Peter apply OT terminology to the church? He does so chiefly because of the conviction of the church that the OT writings are for it (2 Tim 3:16) and that these writings speak of Jesus and his times. The functions that Israel was called into existence to perform in its day of grace the church now performs in a similar way. In the future, according to Paul, God will once again use Israel to bless the world (cf. Rom 11:13–16, 23–24).

The title "chosen people" stresses God's loving initiative in bringing the church to himself. "Royal priesthood" may be understood as "a royal house," "a body of priests" (see Notes). Both titles stress the dignity of the church because of its union with Christ. Jesus is King, and all in his "house" belong to a royal house. Calling the church "a body of priests" emphasizes its corporate role in worship, intercession, and ministry. "Holy nation" shows that God has "set apart" the church for his use. The title "a people belonging to God" stresses ownership (cf. Titus 2:14: "A people that are his very own"). "That you may declare the praises" gives the purpose of grace to men. "The praises" (*aretai*) often mean his "self-declarations" or his manifestations to men (cf. TDNT, 1:457–61). So then the church is to "advertise" (Selwyn, p. 167) the noble acts of God in history and thus make him known. Specifically, the Father ("him who called" [cf. 1:15]) is revealed by Jesus in his death and resurrection. Light–darkness is a common dualism in the Bible to describe God–evil, good–bad, revelation–ignorance, new age–old age (e.g., Isa 8:21–9:2; John 1:4, 8–9; Eph 5:8; 1 John 1:5–2:2). Christians are once again reminded of God's action in bringing them out of darkness into his marvelous light (cf. Ps 34:5: "Those who look to him are radiant").

10 Peter closes this section with another free use of the OT. This time the words of Hosea (1:6, 9–10; 2:23) are put together. In their original context they describe God's rejection of disobedient Israel followed by future restoration to grace. Here Peter applies them to the salvation that has come to the Asian Christians. Once they were not a people (*laos* is used for Israel; the nations were *ethnē*), now they are "God's people" (lit. Gr.).

Notes

2:1–10 is extremely rich theologically, and a great amount of literature has been devoted to it in recent years. The most important is J.H. Elliott, *The Elect and the Holy* (Supplements to N.T. XII) (Leiden: Brill, 1966). See also Norman Hillyer's " 'Rock-Stone' Imagery," pp. 58–81. Ernest Best, "1 Pet. II:4–10—A Reconsideration," NovTest, 11 [1969], 270–93.

III. Christian's Submission and God's Honor (2:11–3:12)

A. *The Noble Life and God's Glory*

2:11–12

> [11]Dear friends, I urge you, as aliens and strangers in the world, to abstain from sinful desires, which war against your soul. [12]Live such good lives among the pagans that, though they accuse you of doing wrong, they may see your good deeds and glorify God on the day he visits us.

11 This division of the letter deals with some practical implications of what it means to be God's people in a hostile world. Peter begins by reminding them of their position. He calls them "Dear friends" (*agapētoi*, "beloved") because they are bound together by Christ's love. Next he exhorts them as "foreigners and strangers." These titles are rich in content, going back to Abraham (cf. Gen 23:4; cf. also Ps 39:12; Heb 13:14; 1 Peter 1:1, 17). Christians are only in the world, not of it, for their true destiny is the renewed and redeemed earth in which righteousness will dwell. Therefore, they are not to derive their values from what is transitory. So Peter warns of the "passions" (*sarkikōn epithymiōn*) or "sinful desires."

The body's desires are not wrong or sinful in themselves, but sin perverts these desires; and the Christian is tempted to satisfy the bodily desires in ways contrary to God's will. "Which war against your soul" speaks of the warfare that is a mortal threat against the self (cf. TDNT, 7:712; 9:639). Schweizer calls this use of *psychē* in 2:11 "the most strongly Hellenized *psychē* passage in the NT" (TDNT, 9:653). The issue is whether we are to understand Peter as teaching that the sinful desires war against a part of a person (his soul) or against the whole person. Peter's usage of *psychē* elsewhere favors the understanding "against the person" in this location (contra Schweizer) (cf. 1:9 and comments). Peter's exhortation means that the Christian is not to participate in pagan immorality.

12 Instead, Christians are to have a "noble lifestyle" (*kalē anastrophē*) among the pagans. The purposes of the godly life of Christians are twofold. First, as the pagans take careful notice of our good works, they will not slander us. Second, in the future they will glorify God. What kind of charges did non-Christians make in Peter's time? Some of the more common were disloyalty to the state or Caesar (John 19:12), upsetting trade or divination (Acts 16:16ff.; 19:23ff.), teaching that slaves are "free" (cf. 1 Cor 13:13; Gal 3:20), not participating in festivals because of "hatred of mankind" (cf. Col 2:16), holding "antisocial" values, and being "atheists" because they had no idols (cf. Acts 15:29).

The meaning of "on the day he visits us" (*en hēmera episkopēs*) is problematic. Does Peter mean "on the return of the Lord" or "on God's gracious visitation of salvation that may come to the non-Christian?" In favor of the latter is the word "see" (*epopteuontes*), which suggests that the pagans will continuously observe the good works and perhaps God will grant them repentance unto life.

B. *The Duty of Christian Submission* (2:13–3:7)

1. *The submission to civil authority*

2:13–17

> [13]Submit yourselves for the Lord's sake to every authority instituted among men: whether to the king, as the supreme authority, [14]or to governors, who are sent by him to punish those who do wrong and to commend those who do right. [15]For it is God's will that by doing good you should silence the ignorant talk of foolish men. [16]Live as free men, but do not use your freedom as a cover-up for evil; live as servants of God. [17]Show proper respect to everyone: Love the brotherhood of believers, fear God, honor the king.

13–14 Submission (*hypotassō*; cf. 2:13, 18; 3:1) is the key theme of this section of the letter. The word in general means to "subject oneself." In this location, it is the acquiescence in the divinely willed order of society. NIV translates *anthrōpinē ktisei* as "every authority instituted among men." There seems, however, to be better reasons for understanding the phrase as "every human creature" (cf. TDNT, 1:366; 3:1034; Kelly, p. 130; Goppelt, p. 182). The noun *ktisis* in the NT always means "creature" or "creation." The thought is that of a Christian who does not seek his own interests but rather assumes a "voluntary ordination of [himself] to others" (Kelly, p. 109).

The reason for this submission is expressed in the phrase "because of the Lord" (*dia ton kyrion*). Is "the Lord" the Creator or Christ? The question does not seem to be correctly put, since the NT sets Christ forth as the Creator (John 1:1–4; Col 1:16; Heb 1:2). But if we ask whether the reference is to Christ in his creative activity or in his humiliation or exaltation, then the answer would appear to be that Christ in his lordship order as manifest in his creative activity is in mind.

Peter then mentions the rulers of the time. The "king" (*basileus*) is the title used in the East for the emperor who had the "supreme authority" among people. The governors (*hēgemones*) are the legates, procurators, or proconsuls charged with carrying out the imperial will of punishing the disobedient and rewarding the good.

15 Peter is speaking of ordinary situations and not of persecutions (cf., e.g., Acts 4:18ff.; 5:18ff.) when he speaks of governors as commending the good. Later in this epistle, Peter deals with the more difficult situation of governmental persecution of those who do good (3:14, 17; 4:1, 12–19). No government that consistently rewards evil and punishes good can long survive, because evil is ultimately self-destructive. It is God's will for Christians by their submission to the state authorities to "silence" (*phimoun*) the "ignorance" (*agnōsia*)—a kind description—of "foolish" men. The word *aphronōn* ("foolish") is a common biblical adjective for an obstinate sinner. Three different Hebrew words are commonly translated in the LXX by this Greek word (cf. Derek Kidner, *The Proverbs: An Introduction and Commentary* [London: Tyndale, 1964], pp. 39–42).

16 Christians are free because the service of God is freedom (cf. John 8:32; Rom 6:15; Gal 5:13). It is freedom from bondage to sin, Satan, and selfish desires. Christians are not to misuse their freedom in Christ and invoke "freedom" as a covering for wickedness. Christ himself said, "I tell you the truth, everyone who sins is a slave to sin"

(John 8:34). In Plato's *Gorgias* (491), the question is asked, "How can a man be happy who is the servant of anything?" The Christian response is that the service of God, who is the source of joy, is indeed perfect freedom, because Christ frees us from the bondage of sin.

17 Peter next sums up the social obligations of Christians in four succinct commands: (1) "Honor all men" ("Show proper respect to everyone," NIV). Here *timēsate* ("honor") is a constative aorist and is not to be taken as a general heading to be completed by the present tenses that follow (BDF, par. 336[2]). The honor is the recognition of the value of each man in his place as the creature of God. (2) "Love the brotherhood." Special love is due to others within the family of believers because they are brothers and sisters. (3) "Fear God." (4) "Honor the king" (*basileus*). God is to be feared, but the emperor was only to be honored. Christ taught, "Do not be afraid of those who kill the body but cannot kill the soul. Rather, be afraid of the one [i.e., God] who can destroy both soul and body in hell" (Matt 10:28). Normally duties to God and Caesar do not conflict, and Christians can obey both (Matt 22:15–21); but in special cases their higher loyalty is clear: "We must obey God rather than men!" (Acts 5:29).

2. The submission of slave to master (2:18–25)

a. The submission of household slaves

2:18–20

> [18]Slaves, submit yourselves to your masters with all respect, not only to those who are good and considerate, but also to those who are harsh. [19]For it is commendable if a man bears up under the pain of unjust suffering because he is conscious of God. [20]But how is it to your credit if you receive a beating for doing wrong and endure it? But if you suffer for doing good and you endure it, this is commendable before God.

18 (On slavery, see the literature cited at notes, 1:18.) It is difficult for twentieth-century Christians to understand the slavery of the ancient world. During the time of the NT writings, slavery was not as bad as that practiced in America before the Civil War. Ancient slaves had fairly normal marital lives. Often people sold themselves into slavery (for a period of time) as a way to get ahead in the world. Nevertheless the lot of a slave could be very hard if the master was unkind. Here "slaves" (*oiketai*) means "house-servants"—i.e., domestic slaves. Their Christian duty was submission and loyalty to their master, even if he was harsh (*skolios*, "perverse").

19 Peter now motivates this. "For it," he writes, "is commendable"—i.e., a grace (*charis*). It is an attractive quality in the sight of God when because of conscience (or perhaps "consciousness" of God) a Christian slave puts up with pain as he suffers unjustly. (On the conscience, cf. DNTT, 1:348–53.)

20 To endure a well-deserved beating is nothing extraordinary. The word "beating" (*kolaphizomenoi*, "strike with the fist") is used in Mark 14:65 of Christ's treatment at his trial. However, it is "commendable" (*charis*) in the sight of God to do good and to endure suffering. The "commendable" thing is not the suffering but being so committed to God's will (the "good") that devotion to him overrides personal comfort.

b. *The example of Christ's submission*

2:21–25

> 21To this you were called, because Christ suffered for you, leaving you an example, that you should follow in his steps.
>
> 22"He committed no sin,
>   and no deceit was found in his mouth."
>
> 23When they hurled their insults at him, he did not retaliate; when he suffered, he made no threats. Instead, he entrusted himself to him who judges justly. 24He himself bore our sins in his body on the tree, so that we might die to sins and live for righteousness; by his wounds you have been healed. 25For you were like sheep going astray, but now you have returned to the Shepherd and Overseer of your souls.

21 Peter's exhortation for Christians to be submissive now receives a christological foundation. The "calling" (*kaleō*) is God's grace that brings them to salvation (cf. comments on 1:15) and includes the divine ordination in all aspects of their life (Rom 8:28–30), "because [*hoti*] Christ also [*kai*] suffered for you." The sufferings of Christ referred to here are exemplary as well as expiatory on behalf of Christians. "Leaving you an example" (*hypogrammon*, lit., "model, pattern to be copied in writing or drawing," BAG, p. 851) shows that Christ is the pattern for believers to copy in their lives. Just as in his life Christ suffered unjustly for doing God's will, so Christian slaves may have this calling. Servants are to follow their Master's tracks (cf. Matt 10:38; Mark 8:34; John 13:15).

22–23 The preeminent OT passage on the suffering of the Messiah is Isaiah's fourth Servant Song (Isa 52:13–53:12). Peter quotes Isaiah 53:9 to stress the submission of the innocent Sufferer. Other echoes of Isaiah 53 sound in the next verses—viz., 53:12 in v.24a; 53:5 in v.24b; 53:6 in v.25.

Throughout his earthly ministry, Jesus was reviled (cf. Matt 11:19; 26:67; 27:30, 39–44; Mark 3:22). In all these situations, he was ever the patient sufferer who was able to control his tongue. He committed his case to the heavenly Judge whom he trusted to give a just judgment. "Entrusted" (*paredidou*) is an imperfect tense in Greek, describing continual activity in the past.

24–25 Peter explores the sufferings of the Messiah more deeply. Peter has stated that Christ was patient and innocent. Moreover, his sufferings for us are indeed expiatory and substitutionary. He did no sin (v.22) and he "bore *our sins*"(v.24; cf. John 1:29). The exact figure is not clear. Some commentators see a reference to the scapegoat (Lev 16) and others to Levitical sacrifices (cf. Lev 14:20 LXX; Isa 53:12). Peter is probably looking at the basic ideas involved in the sacrificial system. The location of the expiatory offering was "in his body on the tree" (*xylon*, lit., "wood"; cf. Deut 21:23; Gal 3:13; Col 1:22). The purpose of the death of Christ is to produce new life in the believer. By means of Christ's death on the cross, whoever comes to him ends his old life and begins a new one devoted to righteousness (cf. Rom 6:1–14, 18–19; 2 Cor 5:14–15; Gal 2:20; 6:14).

"By his wounds you have been healed" is Peter's application of this precious truth from Isaiah to Christian slaves who had received lashes unjustly. Formerly they were straying sheep (Isa 53:6; Luke 15:3–7) but now they "have returned." The aorist (*epestraphēte*) looks at the decisive action in contrast to their former habitual wandering (*planōmenoi*, present participle; NIV, "going astray"). Jesus is now described as the "Shepherd and Overseer of your souls." (For Jesus as shepherd, cf. TDNT, 6:486–98.)

3. *The submission of Christian wives*

3:1–6

> ¹Wives, in the same way be submissive to your husbands so that, if any of them do not believe the word, they may be won over without talk by the behavior of their wives, ²when they see the purity and reverence of your lives. ³Your beauty should not come from outward adornment, such as braided hair and the wearing of gold jewelry and fine clothes. ⁴Instead, it should be that of your inner self, the unfading beauty of a gentle and quiet spirit, which is of great worth in God's sight. ⁵For this is the way the holy women of the past who put their hope in God used to make themselves beautiful. They were submissive to their own husbands, ⁶like Sarah, who obeyed Abraham and called him her master. You are her daughters if you do what is right and do not give way to fear.

1 "In the same way" (*homoiōs*) in both v.1 and v.7 points back to 2:13. Christian wives are not to be in subjection like slaves but rather the principle of Christian subjection to God's will relates to every class and every situation. Rules for wives occur in other locations in the NT (Eph 5:22; Col 3:18; 1 Tim 2:9–15; Titus 2:4–5). The order for family life in NT times was still clearly patriarchal. Yet in religious matters women are coheirs with men (v.7) when both come to faith.

The phrase translated "so that" (*hina kai*) introduces the purpose of the command. Literally the translation is "in order that *also*." Here the evangelistic motivation is added to the general necessity of the divine order. As the gospel was proclaimed, it was always possible for a wife to be converted before the husband. In such a situation where the man is disobedient to the gospel message (*tō logō*, lit., "the word"; cf. 1:23–25), he may be "won over" (*kerdainō*, "a missionary term," TDNT, 3:672–3) for the faith "without talk" (lit., "without a word") by the way his wife lives.

2 The husband will then observe purity of life (on purity, see TDNT, 1:122–24) lived in the "fear" (NIV, "reverence") of God. Kelly (p. 128) aptly cites Augustine's account of how his mother influenced his father. "She served her husband as her master, and did all she could to win him for you, speaking to him of you by her conduct, by which you made her beautiful. . . . Finally, when her husband was at the end of his earthly span, she gained him for you" (*Confessions* 9.19–22).

3–4 The divinely intended manner of life for wives is inward, not outward. Mankind constantly makes superficial value judgments: "Man looks at the outward appearance, but the LORD looks at the heart" (1 Sam 16:7). Many have taken Peter's words to be an absolute prohibition of any outward adornment. The early fathers Tertullian and

Cyprian did this, and many rigorists have followed them. But Peter's emphasis is not on prohibition but on a proper sense of values.

The "inner self" is literally the "hidden person [man] of the heart," or the character of a person. In biblical psychology the "heart" is the central psychological term and refers to the faculty where man relates to God and makes his basic decisions (cf. Prov 3:5; 4:23; 21:1; DNTT, 2:180–84). The Christian woman is to cultivate an inner disposition (*pneuma,* "spirit") of a submissive (*praeōs,* "meekness," as of Christ; cf. Matt 11:29) and quiet sort that is imperishable or "unfading"—an attitude God highly values. Today, when the world's values governed by materialism, self-assertion, and sex obsession are seeping into the church, Peter's words need to be taken seriously (cf. Isa 3:16–24).

5–6 Next Peter turns to the OT in support of his exhortation—first broadly and then from the example of Sarah. The major characterization of these women who were "holy" because they were set apart to God was their hope in God. They trusted the promises of God and longed for the messianic salvation (cf. 1:3, 13; 3:15; Heb 11:13). In so doing, they were habitually adorning themselves with an inner beauty.

The great model of womanly submission is Sarah, whose respect and obedience to Abraham extended to her speech—she "called him her master." Such terminology was not uncommon in the ancient world (cf. Gen 18:12). Peter does not hesitate to apply Sarah's example to his readers: "You are her daughters if you do what is right." The norm for wifely conduct should be submission to God and devotion to the development of Christian character. Moreover, wives are "not [to] give way to fear"; their submissive trust in the living God will keep them from undue apprehension.

4. *The obligation of Christian husbands*

3:7

> 7Husbands, in the same way be considerate as you live with your wives, and treat them with respect as the weaker partner and as heirs with you of the gracious gift of life, so that nothing will hinder your prayers.

7 Peter's instructions for the Christian husband are brief, probably because the family normally followed the husband's religious choice. Yet the husband needs instruction concerning the care of his wife for several reasons. The phrase "in the same way" does not refer to subjection to the wife but rather that the husband "likewise" in the relationship of marriage is to do everything possible to foster the spiritual life of the home. A harsh or unthinking Christian husband could cause a hindrance to the family's spiritual growth. The woman is called the "weaker partner" (*skeuos,* lit., "vessel"); but this is not to be taken morally, spiritually, or intellectually. It simply means that the woman has less physical strength. The husband must recognize this difference and take it into account. "As you live with" probably refers to sexual intercourse in addition to the broader aspects of living together. The husband is to show his wife "respect" (*timēn,* "honor") and not despise her physical weakness.

Men are also to remember that women are coheirs of "the gracious gift of life." The sexual function and sexual distinctions are only for this age. Women will have an equal share in the new age; and even now in the life of the new age, they experience the grace of God equally with men (cf. Gal 3:28). Men must also remember that selfishness and egotism in the marriage relationship will mar their relationship with God.

Notes

7 The exact metaphorical meaning of σκεύει (*skeuei*, "vessel") is disputed. In Gr. usage, it is a common term for the body as the container of the soul. In the rabbinic background, a Heb. equivalent of this word was used for "wife" or "sexual partner." The dispute regarding it extends to the exegesis of 1 Thess 4:4 as well as 1 Peter 3:7. For an extended discussion, cf. TDNT, 7:358–67.

C. *The Call to Righteous Living*

3:8–12

> [8]Finally, all of you, live in harmony with one another; be sympathetic, love as brothers, be compassionate and humble. [9]Do not repay evil with evil or insult with insult, but with blessing, because to this you were called so that you may inherit a blessing. [10]For,
>
> > "Whoever would love life
> > and see good days
> > must keep his tongue from evil
> > and his lips from deceitful speech.
> > [11]He must turn from evil and do good;
> > he must seek peace and pursue it.
> > [12]For the eyes of the Lord are on the righteous
> > and his ears are attentive to their prayer,
> > but the face of the Lord is against those who do evil."

8 Peter brings his treatment of the duties of Christians, considered in various groupings, to a close with general practical advice for the whole community. His use of "Finally" (*to telos*) and his citation of Psalm 34:12–16 show the concluding character of this passage. In v.8 he gives several imperatives for Christians' getting along together; in v.9 he gives them a basic imperative for dealing with those who are hostile to them. The five virtues in v.8 have many illustrations in the life of Jesus and parallels in the other epistles. They are normative qualities every person united to Christ should manifest. (On "harmony," see Rom 12:16; Phil 1:27; 2:2; on "be sympathetic," Rom 12:15; 1 Cor 12:26; on "love as brothers," 1 Thess 4:9–10; for "be compassionate," see Christ's example in Matt 11:29; and concerning "humble," see Christ's example as set forth in Phil 2:6ff.)

9 Here Peter turns to Christ as the pattern for relating to a hostile pagan society. The natural response to hostility is retaliation. But Jesus in his teaching (Matt 5:44) and in his practice responded to hostility with grace (Luke 23:34; 1 Peter 2:21–22). What does it mean to "bless" our enemies? "Bless" translates *eulogountes*, which literally means "to speak well [of someone]." The word occurs over four hundred times in the LXX, often in opposition to cursing. H.G. Link suggests that "blessing here [1 Peter 3:9] means simply a friendly disposition towards enemies" (DNTT, 1:215). But the instruction and practice of Jesus and the apostles goes beyond a "friendly disposition" to active prayer and intercession (cf. Acts 7:60; 1 Cor 4:12). The great desire of Christians must not be revenge but for God to grant the gift of repentance to those who do not know him. The phrase "because to this" is not immediately clear. Does

Peter mean that intercession will bring rewards to Christians? Or that the calling of Christians to grace should make them gracious to others? The second seems best in this context.

10–12 "For" (*gar*) introduces an explanatory quotation that reinforces the teaching of non-retaliation. The source is Psalm 34:12–16, which Peter has already alluded to in 2:3. In the psalm, the "life" and the "good days" refer to earthly life and joys. Peter's use of these terms is not limited to this life but goes beyond it to eschatological salvation. Yet it is still true in this age that being gracious to others may lead to longer life and better days. On the contrary, a life of evil and strife may be shortened and marred. "The way of transgressors is hard" (Prov 13:15 KJV).

Christians should desire life in its goodness. Therefore, they must guard their ways and their tongues. Most importantly, they are to overcome evil with the good (cf. Rom 12:21). Since peace between people is elusive and hard to achieve, Christians must actively seek and pursue it. The fear (reverential awe) of the Lord provides a rationale for godly living and a warning to the wicked. Our "eyes," our "ears," and our "face" speak of our personal relation to God. The "eye" of the Lord over the righteous reminds us of his providential care for his people (cf. Exod 2:25), and his "ear" is open to our cries for help in prayer (cf. Exod 3:7). The "face" of the Lord is a Hebrew expression for "God's countenance, i.e., the side he turns to man" (TDNT, 6:772). Here it relates to his anger against evil doers.

IV. The Suffering and Persecution of Christians (3:13–5:11)

A. *The Blessing of Suffering for Righteousness*

3:13–17

> [13]Who is going to harm you if you are eager to do good? [14]But even if you should suffer for what is right, you are blessed. "Do not fear what they fear; do not be frightened." [15]But in your hearts set apart Christ as Lord. Always be prepared to give an answer to everyone who asks you to give the reason for the hope that you have. But do this with gentleness and respect, [16]keeping a clear conscience, so that those who speak maliciously against your good behavior in Christ may be ashamed of their slander. [17]It is better, if it is God's will, to suffer for doing good than for doing evil.

Peter's major emphasis in this letter is on Christian conduct under persecution (cf. Introduction: Occasion and Purpose). Especially from now on (3:13–5:11), this is Peter's chief concern. Dalton divides his treatment of 3:13–5:11 into two main sections (each with three subdivisions)—"Persecution viewed in calm detachment," 3:13–4:11; "Persecution faced realistically," 4:12–5:11 (pp. 72–86). These two headings capture the essence of the rest of the letter.

13 While suffering and unjust treatment have been in the background (1:6–7; 2:12, 15, 19ff.; 3:9), now they come to the fore. In the Greek, v.13 begins with "and" (*kai*), which shows the connection with the preceding section. If Christians have the zeal for good that Psalm 34 speaks of, who will do them harm? The "harm" Peter alludes to must be understood in the light of Paul's rhetorical question "If God is for us, who can be against us?" (Rom 8:31) and his reference to Christians as being like "sheep to be slaughtered" and yet being "more than conquerors" (Rom 8:36–37). Kelly (p. 140) cites an interesting parallel from Plato (*Apology* 41d) concerning Socrates before his judges: "No harm can befall a good man, either when he is alive or when he is dead, and the gods do not neglect his cause."

14 "But even if you should suffer" (*all' ei kai paschoite*) is a conditional clause in the Greek (fourth class) that has a "future less probable" sense. The use of this construction (optative) points to the fact that suffering is not the expected outcome of zeal for good. The suffering Peter is considering is that which results from righteousness—i.e., from the kind of life that conforms to God's standard. If this should happen to his readers, they are "blessed" (*makarioi*). This blessedness or happiness is the certainty that comes from belonging to God and his kingdom with the promises of future vindication (cf. Matt 5:3–10; "blessing" in DNTT, 1:215–17). The last part of v.14 and the beginning of v.15 are built on the words of Isaiah 8:12b–13:

> Do not fear what they fear,
>   do not dread it.
> The LORD Almighty is the one you are to
>   regard as holy.

In the Isaiah passage, the prophet admonishes the godly in Israel not to fear the impending invasion as the unbelievers in the nation do. Instead, godly reverence is to be their concern (cf. Matt 10:28).

15–16 So Peter admonishes his readers not to be afraid of men but acknowledge "Christ as Lord." This passage is important for Peter's Christology. The "Lord" as applied to Christ refers to "Yahweh of armies" in Isaiah 8:13. The literal Hebrew of "Yahweh of armies" is "LORD Almighty" in NIV. (See Preface to NIV [p. ix] for an explanation of the principle involved in its translation of "Yahweh of armies.") The Christians Peter is writing to are to acknowledge in their hearts Christ as the Holy One. In biblical revelation, the heart is the religious center of man (cf. DNTT, 2:180–84). When the center of one's life is rightly related to God, he is able to respond properly to the vicissitudes of life.

One of the distinguishing marks of Christians is their possession of hope (*elpidos*, cf. 1:3, 21; Rom 4:18; Eph 2:12; Titus 2:13; DNTT, 2:238–44). Christian hope is so real and distinctive that non-Christians are puzzled about it and ask for a "reason" (*logos*, "account"). The type of questioning could be either official interrogations by the governmental authorities—the word for "answer" (*apologia*) can relate to a formal inquiry (cf. Acts 25:16; 26:2; 2 Tim 4:16)—or informal questioning.

Christians should respond with care. "Gentleness" (or "meekness") is the quality that trusts God to do the work of changing attitudes (cf. 2 Tim 2:24–25; cf. also Prov 15:1: "A gentle answer turns away wrath, but a harsh word stirs up anger"). The "respect" (*phobos*, "fear") is reverential awe of God (cf. 1:17; 2:17; 3:2). The "clear conscience" relates to the liberty and boldness that come from living before God in purity (cf. Acts 24:16; 1 Tim 1:19). So in the case in which non-Christians slander believers the statement of the truth may shame them into silence (cf. Luke 13:17). "Speak maliciously" (*epēreazontes*) is a word classical writers used of false accusations; in the NT papyri it is used of "treating wrongfully" (MM, p. 232).

17 Peter next states that it is better to suffer for doing good than for doing evil. Suffering is a just recompense for doing evil. But if one does good and still suffers, there is no disgrace—if his conscience is clear before God—for he can have confidence that his suffering was not caused by his sin. There must be a providential reason for it—perhaps to prick the conscience of some and bring them to salvation. Or suffering may be a necessary prelude to glorification.

B. The Pattern of Christ's Suffering and Exaltation

3:18–22

> [18]For Christ died for sins once for all, the righteous for the unrighteous, to bring you to God. He was put to death in the body but made alive by the Spirit, [19]through whom also he went and preached to the spirits in prison [20]who disobeyed long ago when God waited patiently in the days of Noah while the ark was being built. In it only a few people, eight in all, were saved through water, [21]and this water symbolizes baptism that now saves you also—not the removal of dirt from the body but the pledge of a good conscience toward God. It saves you by the resurrection of Jesus Christ, [22]who has gone into heaven and is at God's right hand—with angels, authorities and powers in submission to him.

18 This section contains some of the most difficult exegetical problems in the NT. (For more extensive treatment, see the literature cited in the Notes.) Before giving the exposition of the passage, a brief view of the major types of interpretations is in order. The three main groups of interpretation may be easily differentiated if the following questions are kept in mind: (1) Who are the "spirits" to whom Christ made a proclamation? (2) When was this proclamation made? (3) What was its content?

1. In the first group of interpretations, Christ during the interval between his crucifixion and resurrection went down to the realm of the dead and preached to Noah's contemporaries. This group is subdivided by various opinions on the nature of the proclamation. (1) Christ's soul ministers an offer of salvation to the spirits. (2) He announces condemnation to the unbelievers of Noah's time. (3) He announces good tidings to those who had already been saved.

2. In the second interpretation group, the pre-existent Christ is viewed as preaching in the time of Noah to Noah's sinful generation.

3. In the third interpretation group, Christ proclaimed to the disobedient spirits (fallen angels) his victory on the cross. This proclamation took place either (1) during the three days in a descent into hell or (2) during his ascension. The writer takes the position that after Christ's death, he made a victorious proclamation to the fallen angels during his ascension. The exposition of 3:18–4:6 develops and defends this position.

The main purpose of the first subsection (3:18–22) is fairly clear. "For Christ died" (v.18) translates *hoti kai Christos . . . epathen* (UBS 3d ed., see Notes) (lit., "because Messiah also . . . suffered"). Dalton says, "The development beginning with 3:18 has for its purpose the doctrinal justification of the main topic of the preceding section (3:13–17), which is Christian confidence in the face of persecution" (p. 84). Thus the example of Christ's experience through suffering into victory gives assurance that those joined to him will share the same destiny. "For Christ died for sins once for all" stresses the definitive and final work of Jesus in salvation (cf. Rom 6:10). "For sins" is a phrase describing the reason for his death (cf. Rom 4:25; 1 Cor 15:3; Gal 1:4; Heb 10:12). "The righteous for the unrighteous" points to Jesus as the Righteous Servant of Isaiah 53 (cf. Acts 3:13f.), who suffers in the place of the sinners (cf. Isa 53:5–6, 11–12) and thus dies a substitutionary death. The purpose of his death is "to bring you [other MSS read 'us'] to God." For the verb "bring" (*prosagagē*), see Luke 9:41; Acts 16:20. The noun form (*prosagōgē*) is used by Paul of Christ's work of opening the way to God (Rom 5:2). BAG (p. 718) cites a parallel from Xenophon "of admission to an audience with the Great King" (cf. also TDNT, 1:131–34).

"He was put to death in the body but made alive by the Spirit." Behind the NIV translation stand a number of problems. The antithesis is between "flesh" and "spirit." "Flesh" and "spirit" do not refer to two "parts" of Christ, i.e., his body and his soul; nor does the "spirit" refer to the Holy Spirit or Christ's human spirit. Rather, "flesh" refers to Christ in his human sphere of life and "spirit" refers to Christ in his resurrected sphere of life (cf. Dalton, pp. 124–34; TDNT, 6:417, 447; 7:143). (For similar "two sphere thinking," cf. Rom 1:3–4; 1 Tim 3:16.) If this view is adopted, the exegesis makes good sense. The Greek is literally "put to death in flesh, made alive in spirit." To translate one member of the antithesis as a dative of sphere or reference and the other as a dative of cause or instrument is inconsistent. It is best to take both as datives of reference (or "adverbial" or even "of sphere") and to translate both "in the sphere of" (cf. Dalton, p. 134).

19 "Through whom" translates *en hō* ("in which"). But the way v. 18b is interpreted is determinative. "Once we take πνεύματι [*pneumati*] as 'in the sphere of the spirit,' then we should take ἐν ᾧ [*en hō*] as 'in this sphere,' 'under this influence,' or even 'as one now made alive in the spirit.' In other words, the person who does the preaching in 3:19 is the risen Lord" (Dalton, p. 140). So the NIV translation might be corrected to read, "in which state [of resurrection] he went and preached."

To whom did he preach? What did he preach? The "spirits" have been understood as the souls of men, fallen angels, or both. The best explanation is that the "spirits" (*pneumata*) are fallen angels (BAG, p. 682; Dalton, p. 150; Kelly, p. 153; Reicke, *Disobedient Spirits*, pp. 90–91 [with possible addition of offspring of fallen angels]; idem. AB, p. 109; Selwyn, p. 353). Jesus, then, in his resurrection "goes" to the place of angelic confinement. Since this is in another realm, we cannot locate it spatially. However, there does not seem to be good evidence for seeing here a "descent into hell." The same word *poreutheis* ("went") is used in v. 22 of his ascension.

The content of the proclamation is not stated. The verb *kēryssō* means "to proclaim" or "to announce." The choice of this verb rather than *euangelizō* ("to proclaim good news"), which is used in 4:6, appears to be significant. Christ does not announce the gospel or Good News to the fallen angels. The thought of salvation for angels is foreign to the NT (Heb 2:16) and also to Peter (cf. comments on 1:12). The announcement is of his victory and of their doom that has come through his death on the cross and his resurrection.

To sum up, the thought of vv. 18–19 may be paraphrased as follows: "He was put to death in the human sphere of existence but was made alive in the resurrection sphere of existence, in which state of existence he made a proclamation of his victory to the fallen angels." As for the pastoral significance of these verses, it is one of comfort because through suffering Christians go to victory. Those who oppose Christians will be defeated (Col 2:15; 2 Thess 1:6–8).

20 The fallen angels (spirits) are identified as those who were disobedient at the time of Noah. This connects with the rebellion of Genesis 6:1–4, which is referred to in Jude 6 and 2 Peter 2:4. Verse 20 makes a connection between the disobedience of the spirits and the Flood-judgment. The Flood-judgment is a warning to humanity of God's coming eschatological judgment on the disobedient world (cf. Matt 24:37–41; 2 Peter 3:3–7). The ark that saved a few through water portrays the salvation now available in Christ.

21 Although the parallel between the OT deliverance of Noah's family and NT salvation through Christ is not precise in every detail, Peter says that the water of the Flood-judgment portrays the water of baptism: "And this water symbolizes baptism." Baptism is an antitype (Gr. *antitypos*) or counterpart of the type (*typos*, cf. TDNT, 8:246–59). Baptism is the "copy," the "representation," or even the "fulfilment" (BAG, p. 75) of the OT deliverance from judgment. How does baptism "save"? Peter says it does not concern an external washing from filth but relates to the conscience. In the proclamation of the gospel, salvation from sin and its punishment is announced through Jesus' death and resurrection. The announcement of the penalty for sin stirs the conscience and the Spirit brings conviction (John 16:8–11; Acts 2:37f.; 13:37–41).

"The pledge of a good conscience toward God" renders a difficult expression in Greek. The thought appears to be as follows: The conviction of sin by the Spirit in the mind calls for a response of faith or commitment to Christ and his work. This is concretely and 'contractually" done in the act of baptism. Saving faith ("saving" because of its object—Christ) is expressed in baptism (cf. Acts 2:38–39). Salvation comes to men because Christ has risen from the dead.

22 Not only has Christ been raised from the dead, but in his victory he "has gone" (*poreutheis*, the same verb tr. "went" in v. 19) into heaven to the place of power and authority (cf. Ps 110:1; Rom 8:34). "With angels, authorities and powers" now under him, he is the supreme Lord. Therefore, the oppressed Christians in Asia Minor to whom Peter is writing need not fear anyone. Psalm 110:1 speaks of Messiah sitting at God's right hand "until I [God] make your enemies a footstool for your feet." So now even the fallen angels are subject to Jesus the Messiah (cf. Rom 8:38–39; 1 Cor 15:24ff.).

Notes

18ff. The literature on the problem passages from 3:18–4:6 is extensive, perhaps because of the article in the Apostle's Creed that states, "He descended into hell." Roman Catholic scholars have done excellent work in this area. Dalton's work is outstanding. For later literature, cf. A. Grillmeier, "Der Gottessohn im Totenreich," in *Mit ihm und in ihm: Christologische Forschungen und Perspektiven* (Freiburg: Herder, 1975) pp. 76–174.

18 Ἔπαθεν (*epathen*, "suffered"; NIV, "died") is the reading of the UBS 3d ed. text, which lists nine variants in the apparatus. The translation and meaning, however, are not seriously affected. Πάσχω (*paschō*, "I suffer") is commonly used for death when applied to Christ (TDNT, 5:913, 917).

C. Death to the Old Life

4:1-6

> [1]Therefore, since Christ suffered in his body, arm yourselves also with the same attitude, because he who has suffered in his body is done with sin. [2]As a result, he does not live the rest of his earthly life for evil human desires, but rather for the will of God. [3]For you have spent enough time in the past doing what pagans choose to do—living in debauchery, lust, drunkenness, orgies, carousing and detestable idolatry. [4]They think it strange that you do not plunge with them into the same flood of dissipation, and they heap abuse on you. [5]But they will have to give account to him who is ready to judge the living and the dead. [6]For this is the reason the gospel was preached even to those who are now dead, so that they might be judged according to men in regard to the body, but live according to God in regard to the spirit.

1 NIV renders *pathōn sarki* ("suffered in his body") in both clauses in v.1 (cf. BV, NEB, and others). But it may be better to be more literal and follow KJV, RSV, and NASB with "suffered in the flesh." *Sarki* ("flesh," "body") is the same as in 3:18 (cf. comments there). The suffering of Christ was "unto death" as in 3:18. The thought appears to be this: Since Christ suffered to the extent of death in the realm of fleshly existence, Christians are to arm themselves with the same attitude that guided Christ.

"He who has suffered in his body is done with sin" (*ho pathōn sarki pepautai hamartias*) is often taken as a proverbial expression (Beare, p. 179) and linked in thought to Romans 6:7. It is also possible to refer this statement to Christ and the finality of his work against sin (Kelly, p. 166). Many commentators see the purging effects of suffering in the sanctification process (Selwyn, p. 209). But the expression "is done with sin" (*pepautai hamartias*) is a perfect tense and looks to a definite past act. So this difficult statement is probably best understood in the Pauline sense of Romans 6. By union with Christ, the Christian is to understand that his conversion is a death to sin. Thus he is "done with sin" (BAG, p. 643; cf. Gal 5:24; 6:14).

2 Peter gives a twofold purpose for Christians' arming themselves with Christ's attitude. (For the "arming" metaphor, cf. Rom 13:12; 2 Cor 10:4; Eph 6:11–17; 1 Thess 5:8.) First, "he does not live the rest of his earthly life for evil human desires." "His earthly life" is *en sarki;* the word *sarki* ("flesh") is found twice in v.1 and once in 3:18. The rest of life after conversion is not to be lived according to human passions (flesh), but the ruling principle is the will of God. Christ is the doer of God's will (John 8:29: "I always do what pleases him"; cf. John 4:34; 5:30; 6:38–40; 7:16–17); and he taught his disciples to pray, "Your will be done" (Matt 6:10; cf. TDNT, 3:55–62).

3 The counsel of the pagans (*boulēma tōn ethnōn*) is now contrasted with the will of God. (For comments on the catalogs of pagan vices, cf. comments on 2:1.) This verse clearly supports the position that the recipients of the letter had, before their conversion, been pagans. The "detestable idolatry," or "illicit idolatries," distinguished the Jews from their pagan neighbors. The other items listed are the common excesses of drink, sex, and wild parties found among the non-Christians then and also now.

4–5 The Christian lifestyle of sober, godly living is a condemnation of the values of pagan society. The pagan response will be one of astonishment when Christians refuse to plunge into the "flood of dissipation" (*tēs asōtias anachysis;* cf. the prodigal son's "wild living" [asōtōs] in Luke 15:13). Christians are expected by pagans to "run with them" (syntrechontōn; NIV, "plunge with them") into the pleasures of the satisfaction of the flesh. But Peter's denial is at once a warning and a judgment on the life lived in such a fashion. The pagan amazement will often turn to hatred and evil speaking (cf. John 3:19–21, esp. v.20: "Everyone who does evil hates the light").

The Christian is supported in his stand against the ungodly life by the basic truth of the coming judgment. In the OT and the NT, God is the Judge (cf. DNTT, 2:362–67). Yet the NT also shows that the Father has given judgment into Jesus' hands (John 5:22–23). This judgment is near (4:7); and it will be universal, for it will embrace all the living and all the dead. In it unbelievers will have to give an account of their lives and will not be able to withstand the divine scrutiny (cf. Ps 1:5–6).

6 The interpretation of this verse is often linked to 3:19, but the vocabulary of the text and its context differ. (See the Notes for other views.) This verse makes good sense in its own setting. "For this is the reason" (eis touto gar) is not retrospective but prospective. The coming judgment not only will bring sinners into account (v.5) but will also reverse the judgments of men (v.6). The Good News was proclaimed (euēngelisthē) to those (Christians) who are now dead (nekrois, same word as in v.5). Even though pagans might condemn Christians and put them to death in the realm of the flesh (sarki), yet in God's judgment there will be a reversal. Christians will live (zōsi) in a new realm—namely, in the spiritual realm.

Notes

6 Dalton (p. 42) outlines the history of the interpretation of this passage and finds four main solutions:

1. Christ, while in his three-day death, went and preached salvation to all the dead, offering salvation to those who lived in pre-Christian times.

2. Christ, while in his three-day death, went and preached salvation to the just of OT times.

3. The theme is the preaching of the gospel by the apostles and others on this earth to those who were spiritually dead.

4. The dead are Christians, who had the gospel preached to them and who then died (or were put to death). In the judgment of God, the opinions of men will be reversed and they will live in the new resurrection realm. I have adopted view 4, which is held by Dalton, Kelly, Moffatt, and Selwyn. The main advantages are (1) it takes "dead" in vv.5–6 in the same physical sense. (2) The terms σαρκί (sarki, "flesh") and πνεύματι (pneumati, "spirit") are taken in the same sense as in 3:18. (3) It solves the problem of a "second chance" (or opportunity after death) for conversion, which seems quite contrary to NT theology. (4) The μὲν (men, "on the one hand") and the δὲ (de, "on the other") are given full weight as contrasting man's view with God's judgment.

D. *The Life for God's Glory*

4:7–11

⁷The end of all things is near. Therefore be clear minded and self-controlled so that you can pray. ⁸Above all, love each other deeply, because love covers over

a multitude of sins. ⁹Offer hospitality to one another without grumbling. ¹⁰Each one should use whatever gift he has received to serve others, faithfully administering God's grace in its various forms. ¹¹If anyone speaks, he should do it as one speaking the very words of God. If anyone serves, he should do it with the strength God provides, so that in all things God may be praised through Jesus Christ. To him be the glory and the power for ever and ever. Amen.

7 As is common in the NT, the end or final salvation is set before Christians to stimulate their faith and to encourage them in difficulty. Most translations (including NIV) miss the connective *de* that joins this unit to the previous one, with its statement of God's readiness to judge. It should be translated as "now" or "but." "Is near" is in the Greek a perfect tense, which has the sense "has drawn near." All is in readiness. "Therefore" (*oun*) introduces the ethical implications of eschatology. Jesus taught responsible living in the light of his return (cf. Luke 12:35–43; 17:26–27). Christians are not to give way to "eschatological frenzy" but to practice self-control and be active in prayer. (Peter had set a negative example in his failure to watch and pray in the Garden [Matt 26:40–41].)

8 "Above all" (*pro pantōn*) reminds us of the primacy of agape love among fellow Christians. This love is to be "eager," "earnest" (*ektenē*, lit., "strained," BAG, p. 245; NIV, "deeply"). Agape love is capable of being commanded because it is not primarily an emotion but a decision of the will leading to action. (On the necessity of Christians' loving one another, see Mark 12:30–33; John 13:34f.; 15:12–17.) The reason for us to show love is that "love covers over a multitude of sins." This quotation from Proverbs 10:12 does not mean that our love covers or atones for our sins. In the proverb the meaning is that love does not "stir up" sins or broadcast them. So the major idea is that love suffers in silence and bears all things (1 Cor 13:5–7). Christians forgive faults in others because they know the forgiving grace of God in their own lives.

9 Hospitality between Christians was an important, concrete expression of love in a world without our modern inns and hotels. This virtue was required of the bishops and widows (1 Tim 3:2; 5:10; Titus 1:8) and is commanded for us all (Matt 25:35ff.; Rom 12:13; 3 John 5–8; cf. TDNT, 5:20–36). Hospitality is to be "without grumbling" —a phase that connotes the difficulty of carrying out this command. In certain cultures that are strongly family-orientated, the bringing of strangers into a house may be somewhat shocking. Yet Christians overcome these conventions because God's love has made them into a single great family.

10–11 Hospitality is not a one-way virtue; every Christian is in some way capable of ministering to others. Every Christian has a gift (Rom 12:6–8; 1 Cor 12:12–31) that he has received from God—whether at birth, rebirth, or sometime after is not stated. Since every Christian has a gift, his being equipped with it apparently takes place with the indwelling of the Holy Spirit at regeneration. That the Holy Spirit can take "natural" talents and abilities and redirect them for Christ was most dramatically shown in Paul's ministry. The believer is not only to view himself as gifted but also as a steward (*oikonomos*, "a responsible slave"; cf. TDNT, 5:149–51) and a minister (*diakonountes*). One of the longstanding misconceptions in church practice is the idea that only one person is to "minister" in the local church. The biblical principle is that all can and should minister in one way or another.

The grace of God is "variegated" (*poikilēs*), or "manifests itself in various ways" (BAG, p. 690).

Peter puts these manifestations of grace in two broad categories: "speaking" and "serving" (v. 11). Speaking (*lalein*) covers all forms of oral service—teaching, preaching, prophecy, perhaps even tongues. "The very words of God" translates *logia* or "oracles," which are utterances from God's mouth. So what one says is to be as God says it (cf. 2 Cor 5:20; 1 Thess 2:13). As for service it is to be empowered "with the strength God provides," which means by dependence on God's help by the Spirit (cf. Eph 3:16). The verb translated "provides" (*chorēgei*) originally meant to "supply a chorus" and later was used of lavish provision (cf. MM, pp. 689–90).

The purpose of mutual Christian service is that through Jesus Christ God will be glorified. Serving fellow Christians does glorify God because people will praise him for his grace that comes to them through Jesus and through his followers.

Peter adds a doxology—something that is not uncommon in Christian letters at various places besides the end (cf. Rom 11:33–36; Eph 3:20–21). In "To him be the glory and the power," "be" is supplied; the sentence is elliptical (i.e., without a verb). Perhaps "is" would be better, since God possesses the glory (cf. Isa 6:1ff.) and the power (cf. Isa 46:9–10). The "Amen" signifies assent—"So it is!"

E. *Consolations in Suffering*

4:12–19

> [12]Dear friends, do not be surprised at the painful trial you are suffering, as though something strange were happening to you. [13]But rejoice that you participate in the sufferings of Christ, so that you may be overjoyed when his glory is revealed. [14]If you are insulted because of the name of Christ, you are blessed, for the Spirit of glory and of God rests on you. [15]If you suffer, it should not be as a murderer or thief or any other kind of criminal, or even as a meddler. [16]However, if you suffer as a Christian, do not be ashamed, but praise God that you bear that name. [17]For it is time for judgment to begin with the family of God; and if it begins with us, what will the outcome be for those who do not obey the gospel of God? [18]And,
>
> > "If it is hard for the righteous to be saved,
> >   what will become of the ungodly and the sinner?"
>
> [19]So then, those who suffer according to God's will should commit themselves to their faithful Creator and continue to do good.

12 "Dear friends" (*agapētoi*, "beloved," as at 2:11; cf. its use in 2 Peter 3:1, 8, 14–15, 17) marks the beginning of a new section. Some scholars have argued that since the situation revealed in 4:12–5:14 is so different ("distress and terror occasioned by an actual persecution," so Beare, p. 188) from the general tenor of the letter, 4:12–5:14 is the real letter. The preceding section (1:3–4:11) was, they assume, only hypothetical and was perhaps general baptismal instruction. But the letter makes good sense as a whole, and 4:12–5:14 makes a fitting climax to its argument. There are also a number of unifying items that reveal connections between this section and the previous one. See, for example, the use of *xenizein* ("be surprised") in 4:4 and 4:12. This verb is uncommon in the NT and only occurs in Acts (seven times) and in Hebrews (once). The idea of the glory of God occurs in 4:11 and 4:14, 16. Eschatology and the judgment of evildoers are also common to both units (cf. Kelly, pp. 183–84).

Suffering is not to be regarded as something foreign to Christian experience but

41

rather as a refining test. Peter has already mentioned the necessity of faith being refined through suffering and testing (1:6–7). Here the idea of refining is found in the word "painful" (*pyrōsis*, lit., "burning"), which occurs in the Greek OT (LXX) in the metaphor of the refining of metals (TDNT, 6:951). Jesus said, "If the world hates you, keep in mind that it hated me first" (John 15:18); and John writes, "Do not be surprised, my brothers, if the world hates you" (1 John 3:13). In the light of Jesus' experience and teaching, his followers should expect troubles, but troubles should only encourage them (cf. John 16:33).

13 In contrast to the usual response of sorrow and shock to suffering and persecution, the Christian is to rejoice because he is participating in Christ's sufferings. (For the idea of suffering with Christ in other NT writings, cf. Rom 8:17; 2 Cor 1:5–7; Phil 3:10.)

For illustrations of Christians' rejoicing because they had been counted worthy of suffering disgrace for the name of Christ, see Acts 5:41 (of all the apostles) and Acts 16:22–25 (of Paul and Silas). Christian rejoicing rests on the fact that as Christians share in Christ's suffering, so they will share in his glory with great joy. The prospect of Christ's full manifestation in all his glory fills the believer with joy and comfort.

14 Jesus said, "Blessed are you when people insult you, persecute you and falsely say all kinds of evil against you because of me. Rejoice and be glad" (Matt 5:11–12). Here in 1 Peter we have a fulfillment of the Lord's own promises to his disciples. In Matthew the cause for happiness is the reward in heaven. Here it is the possession of the messianic Spirit: "For the Spirit of glory and of God rests on you." (Many ancient MSS add "and of power" after "glory.") Verse 14 is based on Isaiah 11:2 (and perhaps Ps 89:50–51). One of God's great characteristics is his glory (Acts 7:2; Eph 1:17), and in Jesus his glory is revealed (John 1:14, 18).

The Spirit of the Father and of the Son now rest on and in every believer. The martyrdom of Stephen illustrates this. He is described as "a man full of faith and of the Holy Spirit" (Acts 6:5, cf. v.8). In his defense his face was like that of an angel (Acts 6:15), and he saw the "glory of God" (7:55; cf. DNTT 2:44–51).

15 The promise of the blessing of the Spirit resting on believers is not universal. Not all who suffer are sharing in Christ's sufferings. Much suffering is the punishment or consequence of sin. Christians must have really broken with sin (4:1–3; cf. Rom 6:1ff.; 1 Cor 6: 9–11). If they suffer, it should be because of their union with Jesus, not with evil. The sins mentioned here characterize a pagan, not a Christian, lifestyle. Yet it is possible for Christians to fall in times of weakness. The NIV choice of "meddler" to translate *allotriepiskopos* (a rare word that may have been coined by Peter) is a happy one. Other scholars have taken *allotriepiskopos* to mean "spy," "informer," "false guardian," or "revolutionist" (cf. discussions in BAG, p. 39; TDNT, 2:620–22).

16 But to suffer as a "Christian" is no shame. The title *Christianos*, which is now so common, was just coming into use when Peter wrote. At first Christians were known as "Jews," "disciples," "believers," "the Lord's disciples," and those "who belonged to the Way" (cf. Acts 1:15; 2:44; 6:1; 9:1–2). It was not till the church took root in Antioch that the use of "Christians" for believers began (Acts 11:26). "Christian" is a Latinism of pagan origin (cf. IDB, 571–72). Goppelt (p. 309) lists its NT, patristic, and classical usage: Acts 11:26; 26:28; 1 Peter 4:16; *Didache* 12.4; Ignatius *Ephesians*

11.2; idem, *Romans* 3.2f.; idem, *Polycarp* 7.3; Tacitus *Annales* 15.44; Suetonius *Vita Nero* 16.2; Pliny *Epistolae* 10.96.1–3; Lucian *Alexander* 25.38.

"Do not be ashamed"—i.e., to suffer as a Christian—recalls Peter's own shame at his betrayal of Jesus (Mark 14:66–72). "That you bear that name" (lit., "in this name") could refer to (1) Christ (v.14), (2) the name "Christian," or (3) in "this category" or "under the heading of" (Kelly, pp. 190–91). Most commentators take the second view.

17–18 Paul said, "We must go through many hardships to enter the kingdom of God" (Acts 14:22). Before the full unfolding of the messianic kingdom, there are to be judgments. In the Prophets, mention is made of judgment coming first upon the people of God (Ezek 9:6; Zech 13:7–9; Mal 3:1–5) before coming upon the nations. Here in 1 Peter the idea seems to be that the coming of the Lord in his eschatological judgment has, as a harbinger, a beginning of "birth pains" that will purify believers (cf. 1:7). (This judgment is not, of course, a punishment for the believers' sins, which were laid on Jesus.) Now if the preliminary judgment (Christian suffering) is already taking place, the final doom on the disobedient is certain to follow shortly. Peter cites Proverbs 11:31 (LXX) to reinforce this thought. The righteous are *just* saved. The rest come far short, and only a great disaster awaits them.

19 The conclusion to this section is that the Christians who are suffering according to the divine will (1:6; 3:17) are to "commit [*paratithesthōsan*] themselves" to God. In his seventh word from the Cross, Jesus used *paratithemai* in committing his Spirit to God (Luke 23:46, which probably reflects a Jewish evening prayer in Ps 31:5; so TDNT, 8:163). Peter described God as the "faithful Creator"—an unusual designation because only here in the NT is God called *ktistēs* ("Creator," cf. TDNT, 3:1000–1035). The combination of "faithful" and "Creator" reminds the believer of God's love and power in the midst of trials so that they will not doubt his interest or ability. The continuation in good works or action is a concrete sign of the faith that is the essence of being a Christian (cf. 2:15, 20; 3:6, 17).

F. *The Shepherd's Suffering Flock*

5:1–4

> [1]To the elders among you, I appeal as a fellow elder, a witness of Christ's sufferings and one who also will share in the glory to be revealed: [2]Be shepherds of God's flock that is under your care, serving as overseers—not because you must, but because you are willing, as God wants you to be; not greedy for money, but eager to serve; [3]not lording it over those entrusted to you, but being examples to the flock. [4]And when the Chief Shepherd appears, you will receive the crown of glory that will never fade away.

1 The "elders" are the leaders of the local congregations. The institution of a group of older and wiser men providing direction and rule goes back to the early days of Israel as a people. This was done both nationally and locally. Thus there were "elders" of the Sanhedrin in Jerusalem as well as "elders" of local synagogues (cf. TDNT, 6:651–83; DNTT, 1:188–201). The institution of eldership was adopted by the Jerusalem church (Acts 11:30; 21:18), and Paul and Barnabas applied it to the local congregations they founded on their missionary journeys (Acts 14:23; 1 Tim 3:1–7; Titus 1:5ff.). Peter, therefore, addresses the elders because of their vital role in the life of the congregation. NIV does not translate the *oun* ("therefore") in v.1 that links this section and the preceding one. Because of suffering and persecution, the need of pastoral leadership was important for the local churches. According to Titus 1:5, 7, the words *presbyteros* ("elder") and *episkopos* ("bishop," or "overseer," cf. v.2 here) are interchangeable. The early church utilized more people than the church today does (see comments on 4:10; cf. Eph 4:12) and so put the spiritual leadership in the hands of a plurality.

The basis of Peter's exhortation to the elders (*presbyteroi*) is threefold: (1) He is their fellow elder. In John 21:15–19, Jesus charged Peter with the care of his sheep. (2) He is a witness (a giver of testimony) of Christ's sufferings. (3) He is a sharer of the coming glory. It is notable that he does not command as an apostle (much less as a "pope") but views himself as an elder, as does John also (2 John 1, 3 John 1). As a "witness" (*martys*), it is possible Peter is referring to the sufferings of Jesus that he had seen. But the stress is on the testimony he gives (cf. Luke 24:45–48; Acts 1:8).

2–3 Peter's command is to "shepherd" (*poimanate*) God's "flock" (*poimnion*). The comparison of God's people to a flock of sheep and the Lord to a shepherd is prominent in Scripture. (See, for example, Jacob's words: "The God who has been my Shepherd all my life" [Gen 48:15]; David's Shepherd Psalm [Ps 23]; Ps 100:3: "We are his people, the sheep of his pasture"; Isa 53:6–7; Luke 15:3–7, the parable of the lost sheep; and John 10:1–16.)

The verb *poimainō* ("shepherd") occurs in Christ's command to Peter (John 21:16) and Paul's charge to the Ephesian elders (Acts 20:28). Its meaning embraces protecting, leading, guiding, feeding, etc. (cf. BAG, p. 690). Peter reminds the elders that the flock is God's and that they are responsible for its loving care. "Serving as overseers" (*episkopountes*) reveals the interchangeability of the terms "overseer" and "bishop." Elder (*presbyteros*) denotes the dignity of the office; "bishop" (*episkopos*) denotes its function—"to oversee."

Peter's exhortation to the elders "Be shepherds of God's flock" is followed by three contrasting statements that tell how this responsibility is not to be carried out and how it should be carried out: "Serving as overseers . . . because you are willing . . . eager to serve." These words remind us of what Paul wrote to Timothy: "If anyone sets his heart on being an overseer, he desires a noble task" (1 Tim 3:1).

Since the responsibilities of the office of elder are great and since elders will be required to give account of their work (Heb 13:17), no one should be forced into this position ("not because you must," v.2). God will work in men's lives and make them willing to do his will. The motivation of elders will be divine, not human. It is not to be financial, though elders were evidently paid in the early church and handled the finances of the congregations (cf. 1 Cor 9:7–11; 1 Tim 5:17). Not money but enthusiasm and zeal for God and his work will motivate elders. They are not to be "lords" over "those entrusted to" (*kleroi*, "allotted to") them. Probably in each congregation, individual elders had portions of the congregation for which they were particularly responsible. Elders should endeavor to be patterns for Christ's sheep.

4 For faithfulness, elders will receive a "crown of glory that does not fade away." The "crown" could be a "garland" or "wreath" made of leaves or of gold. (In Christ's suffering it was ironically made of thorns [Matt 27:29].) The unfading "crown of glory" makes a striking contrast to the "use of *withered* parsley for the crown at the Isthmian games" (DNTT, 1:406). The glorification will take place at the manifestation of the True Shepherd or Chief Shepherd (cf. Rom 8:17ff.; 1 John 3:2).

G. *Humility and Watchfulness in Suffering*

5:5–9

[5]Young men, in the same way be submissive to those who are older. Clothe yourselves with humility toward one another, because,

"God opposes the proud
but gives grace to the humble."

[6]Humble yourselves, therefore, under God's mighty hand, that he may lift you up in due time. [7]Cast all your anxiety on him because he cares for you. [8]Be self-controlled and alert. Your enemy the devil prowls around like a roaring lion looking for someone to devour. [9]Resist him, standing firm in the faith, because you know that your brothers throughout the world are undergoing the same kind of sufferings.

5 "Young men," or "younger members," may refer only to young men in general, to an office of younger men (cf. Acts 5:6, 10), or to all the younger people (spiritually) in the congregation. The first is the most likely interpretation. The women are not mentioned because their activity in the churches was very limited in Peter's time. "In the same way" (*homoiōs*) indicates a new unit of instruction (cf. 3:1, 7). The exhortation to submission is not limited to a few, but all (*pantes*) Christians are to manifest this quality.

"Clothe yourselves" (*egkombōsasthe*) is a rare word that refers to a slave putting on an apron before serving. So Christians are to imitate their Lord, who girded himself and served (John 13:4–17). The reason for humility is based on a text from Proverbs (3:34; cf. James 4:6) that states God's provision of grace to the submissive and God's opposition to the proud. The verbs are present tenses, with something of the timeless character of a proverb, and stress that these actions are God's constant activity.

6 Christians should, therefore, submit themselves to God's "mighty hand." In the OT, God's hand symbolizes discipline (Exod 3:19; 6:1; Job 30:21; Ps 32:4) and deliverance (Deut 9:26; Ezek 20:34). Both meanings are appropriate in view of the sufferings of the Asian Christians. Once more Peter ties his exhortation to humility to eschatology. The "due time" (*en kairō*) is the time God sets for Christ's appearing. Thus the whole destiny of Christians—whether suffering or glory—is God-ordained.

7 "Cast all your anxiety on him." Here the verb *epiripsantes* is aorist and means "to throw upon," indicating a decisive act on our part. Peter does not say what the anxiety is; perhaps he had persecution in mind. The application of his exhortation embraces all the difficulty a believer who wants to live godly in a fallen world must face. The "casting" entails an act of the will and would be done prayerfully and in obedience to Jesus' teaching about anxiety (Matt 6:25–34). "He cares for you" means that God is not indifferent to our sufferings. This conception of God's concern for human affliction is one of the peculiar treasures of the Judeo-Christian faith; though Greek philosophy at its highest could formulate a doctrine of God's perfect goodness, it could not even imagine his active concern for mankind (cf. Beare, p. 204). The Incarnation reveals a caring God, and Christ's teaching about his heavenly Father stresses his intimate concern for his children (Matt 10:29–31).

8–9 Belief in the sovereignty of God and in his fatherly concern for us (vv.6–7) does not permit us to sit back and do nothing. We are to "work out [our] salvation" because "it is God who works in [us]" (Phil 2:12–13). So here Peter warns his flock of the danger of making the fact of God's sovereign care an excuse for inactivity. "Be sober, be watchful" perhaps reflects Peter's own experience in which Satan had "sifted" him (Luke 22:31) and he had failed to "watch" (Matt 26:38; Mark 14:34). God's sovereignty does not preclude peril to the Christian life. Peter calls Satan "your enemy the devil" and likens him to a lion in search of prey. The word "enemy" (*antidikos*, "adversary") meant an opponent in a lawsuit (BAG, p. 73; cf. Job 1:6ff.; Zech 3:1; Rev 12:10). "Devil" (*diabolos*) is the Greek translation of the Hebrew "Satan" (1 Chron 21:1; Job 2:1), which means "slanderer" (cf. TDNT, 2:71–81; 7:151–65). According to Scripture, he has great power on earth, "being the prince of this world" (John 14:30) and "the ruler of the kingdom of the air" (Eph 2:2). But God has limited his activity. Through his captive subjects (Eph 2:2; 2 Tim 2:25–26), the devil attempted to destroy the infant church by persecution.

The Christian response to satanic opposition is not panic or flight but firm resistance in faith (v.9). "Resist" (*antistēte*) is the same word as that found in Ephesians 6:11–13 and James 4:7 in contexts of struggle against hostile spiritual forces. This implies a common "resist-the-devil" formula in the early church (cf. Selwyn, p. 238). Stibbs illustrates the idea of resistance "in the faith" from Revelation 12:10–11 (where Satan is overcome): "They overcame him by the blood of the lamb and by the word of their testimony; they did not love their lives so much as to shrink from death." "In the faith" (*tē pistei*) is not so much then "the Christian faith" or "your faithfulness" but rather "your positive faith and trust in God" (Kelly, p. 210).

Support in the struggle also comes from the realization that the sufferings of the Asian Christians were not unique (cf. 1 Cor 10:13). The same kinds of sufferings (unusual in Gr.; cf. Selwyn) are afflicting "your brothers." The word *adelphotēs* ("brothers") stresses the solidarity of the Christian body. All who are in union with Christ may expect suffering (John 15:18–20; 16:33), and the whole body is joined together in suffering (1 Cor 12:26). The "world" (*kosmos*) is that orderly system under Satan that is opposed to God and his Messiah (cf. Ps 2:1–12). Verse 9, then, relates to the common lot of believers in Christ (cf. John 16:33).

H. *The Sustaining Grace of God*

5:10–11

> [10]And the God of all grace, who called you to his eternal glory in Christ, after you have suffered a little while, will himself restore you and make you strong, firm and steadfast. [11]To him be the power for ever and ever. Amen.

10–11 "And" (*de*) might well be translated "but" to show the contrast between satanic opposition and God's purpose and enablement. For Christians God has as his gracious purpose bringing his children himself to share in his glory (cf. Ps 73:23–24; John 17:22, 24; Rom 8:30—"called . . . glorified"). "Called" (*kaleō*) in the Pauline and Petrine writings stresses God's sovereign working (DNTT, 1:275–76). The eternal glory contrasts with the temporal trials Christians suffer. "Restore you and make you strong, firm and steadfast" translates four future indicative verbs in the best-attested reading. (Some MSS have these verbs in the optative.) The four verbs emphatically promise divine aid. "Restore" (*katartisei*) means "make complete" or "put in order." "Make you strong" (*stērixei*) means "strengthen one so he can stand fast in persecution." "Strengthen" (*sthenōsei;* NIV, "make you . . . firm") is found only once in the NT but more often in the papyri. (The exact difference between *stērixei* and *sthenōsei* is difficult to determine.) "Settle" (*themeliōsei;* NIV, "make you . . . steadfast") is to put on a firm foundation.

With this brief doxology, Peter closes the main part of his letter. Since the verb is not expressed, it may be either "is" (NIV) or "be" (RSV and others).

V. Final Words (5:12–14)

A. *Silas's Role Writing the Letter*

(5:12)

> 12With the help of Silas, whom I regard as a faithful brother, I have written to you briefly, encouraging you and testifying that this is the true grace of God. Stand fast in it.

12 Silas (or "Silvanus," here Gr. text has *dia Silouanou* ["with the help of Silvanus"]) is undoubtedly the same person as the one mentioned in Acts 15:22–33; 15:40–18:5; 1 Thessalonians 1:1; 2 Thessalonians 1:1 (on *Silas, Silouanos,* see BAG, p. 758). As Selwyn says, "There is no reason for disputing the identity" (p. 10). If this is correct, Silas was one of the leading men in the early church. What help he gave Peter in writing this letter is uncertain. If he was the amanuensis, it would have been normal for him to have a significant part in writing. Sometimes the amanuensis took shorthand and at other times he used his own words to convey his employer's message.

Peter says this letter is brief (*di' oligōn*), and he characterizes it as exhortation and testimony ("encouraging you and testifying"). The reference to exhortation (*parabaleō*) reminds us of the commands for ethical living he has given his readers while the reference to testimony stresses the reliability of what he has borne witness to. His final exhortation "Stand fast in it" relates to the "grace of God," which no Christian earns or merits but which all Christians are obligated to abide in.

B. *The Greeting From Rome*

5:13

> 13She who is in Babylon, chosen together with you, sends you her greetings, and so does my son Mark.

13 Who is "she" whom Peter calls "chosen together [*syneklektē,* 'coelect'] with you"? Who is the Mark referred to? What and where is Babylon? "She" could be Peter's wife (Mark 1:30; 1 Cor 9:5), and "Mark" his own son. Most, however, think "she" refers to the church (which is feminine in Gr.) and "Mark" to John Mark (cf. Acts 12:12, 25; 15:36–39; 2 John 1, 13). Strong early tradition links John Mark with Peter and his Gospel. "Babylon" could be (1) in Mesopotamia, (2) a town in Egypt, or (3) a cryptic reference to Rome. The last view is best because (1) according to early church tradition Peter was in Rome; (2) there is no evidence for Peter's having been in Egypt or Mesopotamia; and (3) the reference may be cryptic because of persecution, or it may be an allusion to the "exile" of God's people on the pattern of the exile of ancient Israel in Babylon.

C. *A Final Exhortation and a Prayerful Wish*

5:14

14Greet one another with a kiss of love. Peace to all of you who are in Christ.

14 The formal kiss was common among early Christians as an expression of agape love in the church. From the third century A.D., the sexes were separated (TDNT, 9:143) in the practice of the "kiss of love." But we do not know how old the practice of the formal kiss was. Peter ends his letter with a wish that all his readers who are believers—i.e., who are "in Christ"—may have God's peace. Such a wish is also a prayer. "Peace" reflects the common Hebrew blessing "Shalom." Peter's first letter begins (1:2) and ends with peace.

2 PETER

Edwin A. Blum

2 PETER

Introduction

1. Authorship and Canonicity

Among all the books of the NT, none has been more disputed as to canonicity and authorship than 2 Peter. There is no assured reference to it in the early Christian writings till Origen (c.185–c.254), who first attributed it to Peter. Doubt about it persisted into the fourth century. It may, however, be reflected in Clement of Rome, the Epistle of Barnabas, and in noncanonical Petrine writings, though this is only a possibility (cf. INT, pp. 387–89). The Gospel of Truth and the Apocryphon of John probably quote or allude to 2 Peter, and this might imply acceptance of it in the second century.[1] Also, "the very early (third-century) Bodmer papyrus designated P72 shows acceptance of 2 Peter as canonical, for in that manuscript 2 Peter shares with 1 Peter and Jude a blessing on the readers of these sacred books and receives even more elaborate support than the other two epistles."[2]

Yet while early support of 2 Peter may not be entirely lacking, it is less well attested than the other NT writings. However, it was admitted to the canon[3] and, despite widespread questioning of its Petrine authorship, it still speaks with the authority of Scripture.

Canonicity and authorship, though not synonymous, are often related. In the early church, one of the main reasons for acceptance of a book as authoritative was its apostolic authorship or authorization. The canonicity of 2 Peter was questioned primarily because of doubts about its Petrine authorship. These doubts about the authorship, and therefore the authority, of 2 Peter reappeared at the time of the Reformation. Today they are widespread among contemporary scholars, many of whom deny that the apostle Peter wrote the letter. Kelly, for example, rejects the Petrine authorship (p. 235) but still accepts the letter as revealing "remarkable spiritual insight and power" (p. 225). His attitude is not unusual, for rarely does one

---

[1]Cf. R.H. Gundry, A Survey of the New Testament (Grand Rapids: Zondervan, 1970), p. 353.
[2]Ibid.
[3]EBC, 1:631–43.

51

hear a call to excise 2 Peter from the NT canon. Yet rejection of the Petrine authorship of the letter is very common.

There are approximately eleven arguments against Petrine authorship. Eusebius[4] and Jerome[5] give us the first two: (1) No long line of tradition for 2 Peter could be traced to their day. (2) Its style is different from that of 1 Peter, which was strongly accepted by the church as Petrine.

Two other arguments also stem from the time of the ancient church: (3) Peter's name was used in connection with some Gnostic literature. (4) Knowledge of 2 Peter was geographically limited.

In addition, modern scholars have added these arguments: (5) Petrine authorship is forbidden by its literary dependence on Jude. (6) The conceptual and rhetorical language is too Hellenistic for a Galilean fisherman. (7) The problem of the delay of the Parousia is a second-century one. (8) The collection of Pauline Letters referred to in 2 Peter 3:15–16 was made in the second century. (9) Second Peter is not mentioned by Christian writers in the second century. (10) The letter sounds like "early Catholicism" rather than first generation Christianity. (11) If Peter wrote it, why is there all the doubt about it and reluctance to accept it? In the light of these arguments, the majority of NT scholars today reject 2 Peter as authentic.

Yet there is more to be said. As the following discussion seeks to show, there is another side to the case against 2 Peter; and no single argument is conclusive enough to finally rule out its apostolic authorship.

1. Because of the letter's brevity, governmental persecutions of the early churches, and communication problems in the ancient world, the lack of a long tradition for 2 Peter is hardly surprising. If the letter had been sent to an area not in the main travel routes or one that suffered sudden persecutions, normal circulation patterns may have been hindered.

2. The style does differ from that of 1 Peter, but this may be explained by the use of a different amanuensis (cf. 1 Peter 5:12). If 1 Peter was written by Peter with the assistance of Silvanus, 2 Peter could either be in Peter's own style or in his style with the assistance of a different amanuensis. Moreover, stylistic arguments are hard to evaluate because the criteria for the identity and distinctiveness of writers are not settled. Bruce discusses the interplay of personality, subject, and the freedom of the scribe as a possible solution to stylistic problems within the Pauline corpus.[6]

The work of the Spirit in inspiration may well extend to the amanuensis who in certain cases may even be termed a coauthor. For example, Timothy is associated with Paul's name in the salutations of 1 and 2 Thessalonians, Philippians, Colossians, and Philemon. The stylistic differences in the Pastoral Epistles have long been recognized. In 2 Timothy 4:11, Paul says, "Only Luke is with me." Perhaps Luke served as Paul's amanuensis. So the Pastorals would have a different style from other of Paul's letters. Yet their authority would not be inferior because the superintendence of the Spirit would be over the amanuensis as well as over Paul. The same factors may apply to Peter's letters. Strangely, Morton has argued on the basis of various data, including cumulative sum analysis on a computer, that 1 and 2 Peter are "linguistically

---

[4]*Ecclesiastical History* 3.3.1–4; 25.3–4.

[5]*Scriptorium Ecclesiasticorum* 1, *Letter to Hedibia* (*Epist.* 120.11).

[6]F.F. Bruce, *The Letters of Paul: An Expanded Paraphrase* (Grand Rapids: Eerdmans, 1965), pp. 10–11.

indistinguishable."[7] Such a conclusion, which can only cause most NT Greek scholars to shake their heads in wonder, should at least call for scholarly caution in making dogmatic statements based on stylistic considerations.

3. The argument that the appearance of Peter's name on certain Gnostic writings led to some hesitation in the acceptance of 2 Peter by the early church has a factual basis. But that the early church accepted 2 Peter in spite of the circulation of spurious works bearing the apostle's name shows that it recognized a difference in character between the two epistles and the other works bearing his name.

4. As for the contention that knowledge of 2 Peter was geographically limited, it could be that persecution, the brevity of 2 Peter, or its remote destination resulted in its not being widely circulated in the first hundred years of the church.

5. The literary dependence of 2 Peter on Jude is not conclusively settled (see below, Special Problem). But even if Peter quoted or utilized a substantial part of Jude's letter, this would neither preclude Peter's authorship of the second letter nor its inspiration. For scholars to accept Mark's priority and Matthew's use of Mark is not incompatible with a high view of biblical inspiration and authority.

6. In answer to the claim that the language of the letter is too Hellenistic for a man of Peter's background, we may reply that the extent of Hellenistic influence Peter had in his life is not known. He lived about five miles from the region of the Greek league of ten cities known as Decapolis. We do not know whether he was bilingual or how much he learned between the Resurrection and his martyrdom. Nor do we know whether Peter had help in writing his letters. Just as today a high government official uses a speech writer, though the final product is the official's responsibility, so 2 Peter may have been drafted by an amanuensis as has been suggested under 2 above.

7. The problem of the delay of the Parousia was most certainly a first-century problem as well as a second-century one. John 21:20–23 shows that Christ's return was a live issue at the time of writing of the Gospel of John. Other texts show a similar interest at an earlier time (cf. Matt 25:1–13; Acts 1:6–11; 2 Thess 2:1–4; Heb 9:28).

8. The reference in 2 Peter 3:15–16 to Paul's letters need not refer to the complete corpus of his letters but only to those known to the writer of these verses. The collecting of Paul's letters would have begun as soon as a church or some influential person recognized their value. Paul's instruction about exchanging letters (cf. Col 4:16) and their public reading (1 Thess 5:27) would have facilitated the collection of his letters. That Luke or Timothy were traveling companions of Paul makes them likely collectors of his writings.

9. Although it is true that 2 Peter is not mentioned by name by writers in the second century, several things may account for this. For one thing, the brevity of 2 Peter, its remote destination, and the persecution of its recipients could have led to the lack of any second-century reference to it. Also we need to remember that much of the literature of the early church has not survived. For example, many, if not most, of the writings of Origen (c.185–c.254) are not extant. The odds against writings of the second century perishing were very high. Again, there is, as already has been said, some evidence of traces of 2 Peter in second-century writers. On this point, see also Bigg (pp. 199–210) and Warfield.[8]

---

[7]A.Q. Morton, *The Authorship and Integrity of the New Testament* (London: SPCK, 1965).

[8]B.B. Warfield, "The Canonicity of Second Peter," reprinted in *Selected Shorter Writings*, 2 vols., ed. by Joan E. Meeter, (Nutley, N.J.: Presbyterian and Reformed, 1970, 1973), 2:49–79.

10. The "early-Catholicism" argument, which affirms that the stress on good works and orthodoxy in the letter points to a late date, though often repeated (cf. Kelly, p. 235), entails some questionable assumptions. Why should not Peter have been concerned about the orthodox interpretation of Scripture? Why should he not have been concerned about tradition? Paul stressed tradition (cf. 1 Cor. 11:2; 15:3). The stress on good works and orthodoxy that some see as marks of "early Catholicism" appears in James, which was undoubtedly written early.

11. If, as has already been suggested, Peter wrote this letter to Christians in a remote place or an early persecution hindered its circulation, these things would have delayed its acceptance and led to doubts about it. Moreover, the existence and circulation of heretical books under Peter's name may have fed doubts about the letter and hindered its acceptance.

But there is still more to be said in favor of the Petrine authorship:

1. The book clearly claims to have been written by the apostle Peter ("Simon Peter," 1:1). It recalls how the Lord spoke to Peter about his imminent death (1:14) and refers to Peter's presence as an eyewitness at Jesus' transfiguration (1:16–18). It claims to be his second letter (3:1), a claim most commentators interpret as referring back to 1 Peter, and says that Paul is his "beloved brother" (3:15). Such indications of apostolic authorship are not easily set aside. If the book is unreliable in these statements, how can its teaching be accepted? Either 2 Peter is a genuine work of Simon Peter the apostle or it is an unreliable forgery.

2. Instead of making this choice, writers often accept 2 Peter as a pseudepigraphic work that has value for the church today (cf. Kelly, p. 225) and should be retained in the canon. Sidebottom (p. 100) justifies the acceptance of 2 Peter as pseudonymous by asserting that "the custom of a disciple writing under the name of a famous teacher or leader was well established in the ancient world . . . our conventions about copyright were not those of the first century." The last assertion is true, but what about the former one? Did the first-century Christians adopt the practices of the pagan world as to pseudonymity, or did their concern for truth cause them to repudiate it? This issue is sharply debated. Evangelical Christians have as a whole rejected the view that there are pseudonymous works in the canonical Scriptures. Baldwin concludes her study of OT pseudonymity by saying that "we contend that there is no clear proof of pseudonymity in the Old Testament and much evidence against it."[9] Guthrie argues that pseudonymity was not acceptable among Christians.[10] And Walls refers to Tertullian's statement that the presbyter who wrote the apocryphal *Acts of Paul and Thecla* pseudonymously was deposed.

> This suggests that deliberate pseudepigraphy was not, as is often stated, an established and acceptable convention. To this day, though hundreds of writings of a pseudepigraphic nature from the early Christian centuries have survived, the overwhelming majority of them are more or less affected by Gnostic or other tendentious influences, and many were clearly written to propagate such views. Most of the rest of them are works of what one might call "popular religion"—cheap

---

[9]Joyce Baldwin, "Is there pseudonymity in the Old Testament?" *Themelios* 4 (September 1978): 12.
[10]Donald Guthrie, *New Testament Introduction*, 3rd ed. (Downers Grove, Ill.: Intervarsity, 1970), pp. 671–84.

devotional literature, not intentionally deviant in theology but using expressions theologians would abhor and concentrating on the miraculous and the bizarre. The contrast with the works in the emergent canon is unmistakable.[11]

If epistolary pseudepigraphy was rejected by Christians, then who would have written this letter? Hardly a good man! If it had been a false teacher, what was his motivation? After all, the book does not seem to have any distinctive views that would require presentation under an assumed name.

3. We should also remember that pseudonymous works bearing Peter's name were circulated in the early church. The following are known to us: The Apocalypse of Peter (c. 135), The Gospel of Peter (c. 150–75), The Acts of Peter (c. 180–200), The Teaching of Peter (c. 200), The Letter of Peter to James (c. 200), and The Preaching of Peter (c. 80–140). That none of these was accepted into the canon is noteworthy. Second Peter won its way by its intrinsic worth. As Calvin (*Epistles of Peter*, p. 363) puts it: "At the same time, according to the consent of all, it [the second letter] has nothing unworthy of Peter, as it shows everywhere the power and grace of an apostolic spirit." The internal evidence of 2 Peter—viz., the quality of its teaching—should not be underestimated. In contrast to the Petrine apocrypha, one does not detect false notes in reading 2 Peter. The book rings true. The author's zeal for truth (1:12), his rejection of clever fables (1:16), and his concern for righteousness (2:7–9) are impressive.

4. The letter gives no hint of a second-century environment or of problems such as the monarchical bishop, developed Gnosticism, or Montanism.

5. The most serious problem (style) is not insuperable if we give due consideration to the use of an amanuensis (cf. Silvanus, NIV mg., 1 Peter 5:12) for 1 Peter. Selwyn (pp. 9–15) argues that Silvanus was the coauthor of the first letter. If this was so, the different style of 2 Peter might mean that Peter used a different secretary or assistant in its composition. Also, the argument from style is sometimes exaggerated (cf. Kelly, p. 236), and Green (*Peter and Jude*, pp. 16–19) cites a number of studies that show the clear limitations of style arguments.

As mentioned above, authorship and canonicity were closely related in the ancient church's decisions about canonicity. Seven NT books—Heb, James, Jude, 2 Peter, 2 and 3 John, and Rev—were recognized as canonical only after a certain amount of discussion. The other twenty books had almost universal early acknowledgment. But many other books were known and widely circulated in the early church. Some were highly regarded (e.g., The Shepherd of Hermas) but were never recognized by the church as Scripture.

Second Peter was acknowledged as Scripture by Origen (c. 240) who said, "Peter . . . has left one acknowledged epistle, and, it may be, a second also; for it is doubted."[12] Eusebius placed it among the disputed books rather than among the spurious writings.[13] By the time of Cyril of Jerusalem (c. 315–86), 2 Peter was considered canonical; and Cyril's acceptance of it as well as its acceptance by Athanasius, Augustine, and Jerome settled the issue for the early church. These leaders acknowledged 2 Peter to be Scripture because the evidence, both internal and external, showed its solid worth.

---

[11]Andrew F. Walls, "The Canon of the New Testament," EBC, 1:638–39.
[12]*Ecclesiastical History* 6.25.8.
[13]*Ecclesiastical History* 3.3.1.

2. Date

From 2 Peter 3:15–16 it is clear that the letter could not have been written until a good number of the Pauline Epistles had been written and gathered together. This means that the earliest possible date would be A.D. 60. If the reference in 3:1 ("Dear friends, this is now my second letter to you") refers to 1 Peter (though this is not entirely certain; cf. comments at 3:1), then the earliest possible date for 2 Peter would be about 63–64, i.e., around the time of the writing of 1 Peter. The latest possible date (for those who hold a non-Petrine authorship) is shortly before 135, because 2 Peter is used in the Apocalypse of Peter.[14]

If the apostolic authorship of 2 Peter is accepted and the letter was published while Peter was still alive, the date would be shortly before his death (cf. 2 Peter 1:12–15) or A.D. 64–68. Some evangelical writers view 2 Peter as "the testament of Peter" and favor a posthumous publication by one or more of the apostle's followers.[15] This would make the date about 80–90. Those who reject the letter's apostolic authorship or any connection of the letter with the apostle date it anywhere from 135 (Harnack dated it 150–75). Our conclusion is that to date the letter 64–68 is reasonable and best fits its self-witness.

3. Place of Origin

We have no reliable information for fixing the place where the letter was written, though Rome is a favorite choice because Peter is known to have been there. But since he traveled widely (Palestine, Asia Minor, Corinth [?], and Rome), it is impossible to determine where 2 Peter was written unless new information comes to light.

4. Destination

The only clues to the destination are in the letter itself. It is addressed "to those who through the righteousness of our God and Savior Jesus Christ have received a faith as precious as ours" (1:1). This contrasts with the provinces in Asia Minor mentioned in 1 Peter 1:1 and may imply that 2 Peter was written to Christians in various places. In 2 Peter 3:1 the writer says, "Dear friends, this is now my second letter to you." If this refers to 1 Peter, then the letter is addressed to Christians in Pontus, Galatia, Cappadocia, Asia, and Bithynia. But if 3:1 refers to a lost letter of Peter's (cf. 1 Cor 5:9; Col 4:16b for probable lost letters of Paul), then we have no firm information about the destination of 2 Peter. Asia Minor or Egypt have been favorite choices of commentators. From the warnings in the letter concerning the false teachers (2:1–20), it seems that their vices were more typical of Gentiles than Jews.

---

[14]So C. Maurer, "Apocalypse of Peter" in *New Testament Apocrypha*, 2 vols., edd. E. Hennecke and W. Schneemelcher (London: Lutterworth, 1963–65), 2:664.

[15]Cf. G. Barker, W. Lane, and J.R. Michaels, *The New Testament Speaks* (New York: Harper & Row, 1969), pp. 32, 349–52.

5. Occasion

The occasion for writing 2 Peter may be inferred from its contents. The immediate occasion was Peter's knowledge that his time was short and that God's people were facing many dangers (1:13–14; 2:1–3). Just as sheep are prone to wander, so Christians are prone to forget the basic truths of the faith. The gift of exhortation in the church was a means of correcting this tendency (cf. Rom 12:8). Peter himself mentions this need in his first letter (5:1 [NIV, "appeal"], 12). So 2 Peter is a reminder of the basis for Christian faith (cf. 1:12–13). Faith in Jesus as Messiah is not grounded on myths or clever stories (1:16). It is based on sure revelation from God (1:16–21). The Christian's personal faith should not be static but ever growing. Continual growth in the Christian graces gives a certainty of election to the believer (1:8–10).

Christians must beware of false teachers (2:1–22) who deny the soon return of the Lord (3:3–4) and live immoral and greedy lives. These teachers are clever and claim scriptural support from Paul's Epistles for their views of liberty, but they pervert the letters and are headed for damnation (3:15–16). The church is to be alert to error and growing in the grace and knowledge of God (3:17–18).

6. Bibliography

(See Bibliography for 1 Peter, pp. 216–17.)

7. Special Problem

There are so many similarities between 2 Peter (mainly ch. 2) and Jude that some kind of literary or oral dependence seems necessary. Mayor writes at length about this problem (pp. i–xxv, 2–15).[16]

The common material almost entirely relates to the description and denunciation of false teachers. The majority view is that 2 Peter is dependent on Jude (so Mayor, Feine, Behm). Some scholars use this apparent dependence on Jude to deny Petrine authorship.[17] But the use of Jude by the author of 2 Peter would pose a problem for Petrine authorship of the letter only if (1) the dependence of 2 Peter on Jude were conclusively proved, (2) the composition of Jude were definitely dated later than A.D. 64, or (3) it could be shown that an apostle such as Peter would not have used so much material from another writer.

Some students of 1 Peter find a large amount of catechetical material within it (cf. Selwyn, pp. 363–466). If Peter in the composition of his first letter used material common within the church, there is no reason why he should not have done the same thing in writing his second letter. However, the dependence of 2 Peter on Jude is not a certainty. Mayor (pp. i–ii) holds that 2 Peter uses Jude while Bigg (p. 218) finds that Jude borrows from 2 Peter. It is also quite possible that both letters used a common source.

Since the date of Jude is not fixed by any firm internal or external data, it might

---

[16]See also E.F. Harrison, INT, pp. 396–98.

[17]E.g., "Petrine authorship is forbidden by the literary relation to Jude" (Paul Feine and Johannes Behm, *Introduction to the New Testament*, 14th ed., ed. W. Kümmel [New York: Abingdon, 1966], p. 303).

have been written by A.D. 60. In that case Peter could have used Jude. But would an apostle of the stature of Peter make use of material by one who was not an apostle? The utilization of material by ancient authors cannot be judged by today's standards of citation in writing. Tradition played a much larger role in the thoughts of writers and speakers then than it does today. This is evident (to go back to an OT example) from parallel accounts of Kings and Chronicles and also from the synoptic gospels. To sum up, the special problem of the relation between Jude and 2 Peter or their relation to some common source remains unsolved. The adoption of a particular position— viz., Jude as prior, 2 Peter as prior, or both Jude and 2 Peter used an earlier source—does not necessarily affect the authenticity, authorship, or inspiration of these letters. Any of the three views is compatible with an evangelical theology, and conservative scholars generally leave the question open.[18]

---

[18]Cf. Guthrie, *New Testament Introduction*, pp. 925–27, esp. p. 926, n. 3.

8. Outline

I. Salutation and Blessing (1:1–4)

II. The Essential Christian Virtues (1:5–15)
1. The Efforts for Christian Fruitfulness (1:5–9)
2. The Confirmation of Election (1:10–11)
3. The Need for Reminders (1:12–15)

III. Christ's Divine Majesty (1:16–21)
1. Attested by Apostolic Eyewitnesses (1:16–18)
2. Attested by Divinely Originated Prophecy (1:19–21)

IV. False Prophets and Teachers (2:1–22)
1. Warning Against False Teachers (2:1–3)
2. Three Examples of Previous Judgments (2:4–10a)
3. The Insolence and Wantonness of the False Teachers (2:10b–16)
4. The Impotence of Their Teaching (2:17–22)

V. The Promise of the Lord's Coming (3:1–18)
1. The Certainty of the Day of the Lord (3:1–10)
2. The Ethical Implications of the Day of the Lord (3:11–16)
3. The Need to Guard Against Error and to Grow in Grace (3:17–18)

Text and Exposition

I. Salutation and Blessing

1:1–4

> [1]Simon Peter, a servant and apostle of Jesus Christ, To those who through the righteousness of our God and Savior Jesus Christ have received a faith as precious as ours:
> [2]Grace and peace be yours in abundance through the knowledge of God and of Jesus our Lord.
> [3]His divine power has given us everything we need for life and godliness through our knowledge of him who called us by his own glory and goodness. [4]Through these he has given us his very great and precious promises, so that through them you may participate in the divine nature and escape the corruption in the world caused by evil desires.

1 The author identifies himself as "Simon Peter." Some MSS have *Simōn*, which is the common Greek form of the name. The best-attested reading, however, is the Hebraic *Symeōn*, which is the more difficult spelling and is used of Peter only in Acts 15:14—a detail that supports the Petrine authorship of the letter, for a pseudonymous author would probably have used the more common spelling. *Symeōn*, an old Hebrew name, goes back to the second son of Jacob and Leah and became the tribal name of one of the twelve tribes of Israel.

The disciple *Symeōn* (Simon) also had the nickname "Cephas." This is the Greek transliteration of an Aramaic word for stone (cf. TDNT, 6:100–112) and *Petros* ("Peter") is its Greek translation. As Cullmann suggests, "In order to bring out the power of the nickname as the authors and early readers of the NT felt it, we ought perhaps to follow the NT practice and reproduce the name as Simon Rock" (ibid., 6:101). (See also Introduction to 1 Peter: Simon Peter.)

Peter gives a twofold identification of himself: "a servant and apostle of Jesus Christ." As a "servant" (*doulos*; lit., "slave"), he belongs to Jesus by right of purchase (so 1 Peter 1:18–19. "It was not with perishable things such as silver or gold that you were redeemed, . . . but with the precious blood of Christ"; cf. 1 Cor 6:19–20: "You are not your own; you were bought at a price"). As a servant of Christ, Peter is to obey his commands and do his will. The "servant" has status by virtue of the Lord he serves (cf. TDNT, 2:273–74). Moreover, as an "apostle" Peter has an authoritative commission and speaks God's words (cf. DNTT, 1:133–34).

Those whom Peter is addressing are described only in general terms that can apply to any Christian. The letter itself, however, contains a few clues concerning the people Peter is writing to. A relationship of some duration between author and recipients is implied by 1:12–15. From 3:15 we learn that Paul also wrote to them. In 3:1 Peter says, "This is now my second letter to you." Many scholars believe that the reference is to 1 Peter. If so, the recipients of 2 Peter are clearly identified in 1 Peter 1:1. But others have argued against this identification (cf. comments on 3:1) and posited a lost first letter (cf. 1 Cor 5:9 for a similar situation). If this is the case, we know practically nothing about those to whom 2 Peter was addressed.

The recipients are described as possessing "a faith as precious as ours." Is this "faith" the objective faith or "body of truth" committed to an individual? (so Schrage, Kelly,

Schelkle). Or should we take it in a subjective sense of the ability to trust God? (so Green). In favor of the latter are (1) the omission of the article before *pistin* ("faith"), (2) the fact that when faith is clearly objective (e.g., Jude 3, 20) the article is often present, and (3) that the only other use of faith (*pistis*) in this letter (cf. 1:5) is most likely subjective in sense. It is also possible that Peter combines the objective and subjective senses of faith much as we do when we sometimes speak of "our faith" (i.e., in Christ). In my judgment, the personal side of faith is clearly here. That Peter describes the faith of those he is writing to being as "precious" (*isotimon;* lit., "equally privileged") as "ours" underlines the fact that every Christian has equal access to God (Rom 5:2); every Christian has the same heavenly Father and the same prospect of glory.

The statement that those the letter is addressed to "have received" (*lachousin;* lit., "have been granted") their faith clearly implies that faith (whether objective, subjective, or both) is a gift of God. God's bestowal is through his "righteousness" (*dikaiosynē*) or, better, "justice." *Dikaiosynē* is a central biblical word, and Paul used it in stating the theme of Romans (1:1–16)—viz., justification by faith—and then in developing it. But here *dikaiosynē* means "justice," either in the sense of the impartiality of God's justice in giving all believers an equally privileged faith or in the sense of God's granting of salvation being compatible with his justice.

The phrase "of our God and Savior Jesus Christ" raises a well-known problem. Is Peter speaking of one person or two? Is Jesus called God here? The grammar leaves little doubt that in these words Peter is calling Jesus Christ both God and Savior (see Notes).

2 The first seven words of this verse are identical with 1 Peter 1:2b (see comment there), but here the words "through the knowledge of God and of Jesus our Lord" are added. As in other NT letters, the basic theme of the letter is quickly sounded. For 2 Peter it is the "knowledge" (*epignōsis*) of God. *Epignōsis* (lit., "full knowledge") also occurs in vv.3, 8 and in 2:20. The related verb *epiginōskō* occurs twice in 2:21. *Gnōsis* ("knowledge") occurs at 1:5, 6; 3:18; and *ginōskō* ("know") occurs at 1:20 and 3:3. This makes a total of eleven occurrences of these related words in this short letter (on these words, cf. Notes). The knowledge of God is a central biblical theme (cf. Jer 9:23–24; John 17:3; 1 John passim [42 occurrences of "knowing" in its 105 verses]; cf. Calvin *Institutes* 1.1). The knowledge of God was also claimed by the false teachers of the apostolic and postapostolic times. As Paul warned in Titus 1:16, "They claim to know God, but by their actions they deny him." In postapostolic times a developed "gnosticism" was the great challenge to the Christian church (cf. DNTT, 2:392–409).

3 The connection of this verse with v.2 is a problem. The English translation obscures the fact that in v.3 a genitive absolute (*dedōrēmenēs;* NIV, "has given") serves as the main verb. This either ties it to v.2 as the way in which the multiplication of the knowledge of God takes place or else it begins a new paragraph. NIV, RSV, and NEB take the latter position; KJV, RV, ASV, and NASB, the former one. Either position makes sense, but on balance the former one—namely, having vv.3–4 explain what is contained or conveyed in the knowledge of God—seems preferable.

God has called believers "by his own glory [*doxa*] and goodness [*aretē*]"—that is, God in salvation reveals his splendor (*doxa*) and his moral excellence (*aretē*), and these are means he uses to effect conversions. In bringing people to the knowledge of himself, God's divine power supplies them with everything they need for life and godliness. Probably what is in view is the work of the Spirit of God in believers, providing them with gifts and enabling them to use these gifts.

4 "Through these" refers to God's "glory and goodness" or "more generally [to] his saving intervention in the incarnation" (Kelly, p. 301). So when Jesus Christ came in his first advent, God made certain promises ("very great and precious") of the new Messianic Age (cf. 3:9, 13) to be brought in by the return of Christ. These promises of the coming Christological Age enable Christians to "participate in the divine nature."

How does this participation come about? In at least two ways, this verse implies. First, the promises themselves have a purifying effect on the believer's life (cf. 1 John 3:3). Second, conversion entails a definite break with the corruption caused by evil desire. The NIV rendering "and escape the corruption" might better be translated "since you have escaped" in order to bring out the force of the aorist participle (*apophygontes*, "have escaped"). Thus, in coming to know God through Christ, the believer escapes the corruption of sin; and Christ renews and restores the image of God in him.

Notes

1 Bigg (pp. 251–52) gives two forms of argumentation to support the view that "God" and "Savior" both refer to Jesus: grammatical and historical. The grammatical support is that (1) the use of one article with two substantives strongly suggests that these are names of the same Person; (2) if Peter intended to distinguish two Persons, it is doubtful whether he could have omitted the article before σωτῆρος (*sōtēros*, "Savior"); (3) Peter's usage of *sōtēr* is to couple it under the same article with another name (cf. 1:11; 2:20; 3:2, 18). Under historical support, Bigg finds analogous material in the NT for calling Jesus "God" (cf. John 1:1; 20:28); the doxologies addressed to Christ; the meaning of "Lord" in 1 Peter; and the language of the Apocalypse (cf. also A.T. Robertson, RHG, pp. 785–86).

2 Γνῶσις (*gnōsis*) is the noun for "knowledge"; γινώσκω (*ginōsko*) is the verb; ἐπιγινώσκω (*epiginōskō*) is the same verb with the prepositional prefix *epi*. Both verb forms are commonly translated "know," "learn," "notice," "understand." When emphasis is placed on the prepositional prefix, the meaning is "know exactly, completely, through and through" (BAG, pp. 290–91).

3–4 The vocabulary of 2 Peter contains a number of distinctive terms (e.g., θεῖος [*theios*, "divine"] and ἀρετή [*aretē*, "goodness," "virtue"]) and expressions (e.g., that "you may participate in the divine nature") that seem "unusual" for a Galilean fisherman. These "Hellenistic features" are commonly used as a major argument against Petrine authorship (cf. Werner G. Kümmel, *Introduction to the New Testament*, tr. H. Kee, rev. ed. [Nashville: Abingdon, 1975], p. 423). But we do not know how much "Hellenization" Peter was exposed to in Palestine, how much he learned after his conversion, or if he is picking up key terms in the false teachers' vocabulary and using them against them.

II. The Essential Christian Virtues (1:5–15)

1. The Efforts for Christian Fruitfulness

1:5–9

> [5]For this very reason, make every effort to add to your faith goodness; and to goodness, knowledge; [6]and to knowledge, self-control; and to self-control, perseverance; and to perseverance, godliness; [7]and to godliness, brotherly kindness; and to brotherly kindness, love. [8]For if you possess these qualities in increasing measure, they will keep you from being ineffective and unproductive in your knowledge of our Lord Jesus Christ. [9]But if anyone does not have them, he is nearsighted and blind, and has forgotten that he has been cleansed from his past sins.

5 Because of the new birth and the promises associated with it, Christians participate in the divine nature (v.4). But the new birth does not rule out human activity. Berkhof defines sanctification as "a work of God in which believers co-operate" (L. Berkhof, *Systematic Theology* [Grand Rapids: Eerdmans, 1939], p. 534). This definition fits the biblical pattern of ethical imperatives built on dogmatic indicatives (cf. Rom 6:11–14; 12:1f.; Phil 2:12–13; 1 Peter 1:13–21) and is in accord with biblical statements of how God works (cf. Rom 8:13b; Phil 2:13). So Peter urgently calls for a progressive, active Christianity. It is by faith alone that we are saved through grace, but this saving faith does not continue by itself (Eph 2:8–10). Peter's chain of eight virtues (vv.5–7) starts with faith and ends in love (cf. 1 Tim 1:5; Ignatius *To the Ephesians* 14.1: "Faith is the beginning and love is the end").

Christians are told to "make every effort to add to [their] faith." In NT times the word "add" (*epichorēgein*) was used of making a rich or lavish provision. Originally it referred to a person who paid the expenses of a chorus in staging a play. To "make every effort" (*spoudē*) requires both zeal and seriousness in the pursuit of holiness. "Goodness" (*aretē*) is an attribute of Christ himself (1:3) and therefore is to be sought by his people. It is excellence of achievement or mastery in a specific field—in this case virtue or moral excellence (cf. Phil 4:8; 1 Peter 2:9). The "knowledge" (*gnōsis*) that is to be added to faith is the advance into the will of God. The false teachers (the soon-to-come Gnostics) claimed a superior knowledge. The apostles stressed the necessity for those who know God to live a godly life (cf. 1 John 2:3–4; 5:18) and that Christ taught them the will of the Father (John 15:15).

6 The next virtue in Peter's chain is "self-control" (*egkrateia*). The concept of self-control played a great role in the philosophical ethics of classical Greece and Hellenism (TDNT, 2:340–41). But in NT ethical discussions it is not generally used, perhaps because the normal biblical emphasis is on God at work in us by the Spirit rather than on man's self-mastery. Self-control is the exact opposite of the excesses (2:3, 14, *pleonexia,* "greed") of the false teachers and the sexual abuses in the pagan world. The NT use of the noun *egkrateia* and the verb *egkrateuomai* ("control oneself," "abstain"), though limited, is instructive. Paul uses *egkrateuomai* of the unmarried— "But if they cannot control themselves, they should marry" (1 Cor 7:9)—and of his own self-discipline for the gospel (1 Cor 9:25). In preaching to Felix and Drusilla (Acts 24:25), Paul speaks of "self-control" (*egkrateia*). In the only other use of the noun besides 2 Peter 1:6, Paul lists it as one facet of the fruit of the Spirit (Gal 5:23). So while the biblical ethic does include "self-control," it sees self-control as the manifestation of the Spirit's work in man resulting in the human activity Paul speaks of in Romans 8:13.

Following self-control is patience (*hypomonē;* NIV, "perseverance"). This virtue views time with God's eyes (3:8) while waiting for Christ's return and for the punishment of sin. Perseverance is the ability to continue in the faith and resist the pressures of the world system (cf. Luke 8:15; Rom 5:3; Heb 12:2). "Godliness" (*eusebeia*) is piety or devotion to the person of God. Green defines it as "a very practical awareness of God in every aspect of life" (*Peter and Jude,* p. 70).

7 "Brotherly kindness" (*philadelphia*) and love (*agapē*) complete the list. The knowledge of God issues into the love of other believers (1 John 4:7–20). *Philadelphia* denotes the warmth of affection that should characterize the fellowship of believers. *Agapē* is the queen of the virtues (cf. 1 Cor 13) and denotes self-sacrificing action in behalf of another. This love flows from God who is himself love (*agapē* in 1 John 4:8) and reaches the world (John 3:16; 1 John 3:16). Godly people who participate in the divine nature must abound in love.

8 The knowledge of God is the beginning, the continuance, and the goal of the Christian life (cf. Phil 3:10). Peter is saying that if Christians possess in ever-increasing measure the eight virtues he has just listed, they will not be "ineffective and unproductive" (like the false teachers he describes in ch. 2). Progressive growth in the Christian graces is a sign of spiritual vitality and prevents "sloth" and unfruitfulness (Matt 13:22; John 15:1–7).

9 Not to have these virtues is to be "nearsighted and blind." In the NT "blind" (*typhlos*) is commonly used in a metaphorical as well as a literal sense (cf. John 9:39–41). The problem at this point is that in the Greek text "nearsighted" (*myōpazōn*) follows "blind." NIV solves it by reversing the order—viz., "nearsighted and blind." Perhaps the Greek construction can be taken as a causal participle—i.e., a person is blind because he is so nearsighted. Such a defect of vision (Peter is obviously speaking metaphorically) leads one to forgetfulness of cleansing from old sins. Perhaps Peter had in mind those who turn away from their commitment at baptism.

2. The Confirmation of Election

1:10–11

¹⁰Therefore, my brothers, be all the more eager to make your calling and election sure. For if you do these things, you will never fall, ¹¹and you will receive a rich welcome into the eternal kingdom of our Lord and Savior Jesus Christ.

10 In view of the dangers spoken of in v.9 and the possibility of a fruitful knowledge of God (v.8), Peter exhorts Christians "to make [their] calling and election sure." The word "make" (*poieisthai*) is in the middle voice and thus implies "to make for oneself." "Sure" (*bebaian*) is a word used of confirming something as in the legal terminology of validating a will. So a Christian by growing in grace becomes assured of having been called and elected by God. Bigg (p. 261) prefers a corporate sense of election here and in 1 Peter 1:1. In favor of a corporate or general election is the fact that "calling" (*klēsin*) and "election" (*eklogēn*) are bound together by the one Greek article (*tēn*) and that "calling" can have a general application (cf. Matt 22:14). Nevertheless, in the Pauline epistles calling and election are normally used in a particular sense (cf. Rom 8:28–30). Man responds in faith to God's gracious working. Likewise Peter's emphasis is clearly on human response. Many commentators see an influence of Paul on Peter (cf. comments on 2 Peter 3:15).

If Christians are continually advancing in the virtues mentioned in vv.5–7, they will never "stumble" or "fall" (*ptaiō*). Some have argued that "the loss of salvation" is in view here (BAG, p. 734). But the meaning of "suffer a reverse, misfortune" (TDNT, 6:884) fits the context well. Strong warnings about unfaithfulness to Christ and emphasis on the necessity of perseverance are common in the letters of Paul. See, for example, Colossians 1:22–23: "He has reconciled you by Christ's physical body through death to present you holy in his sight, without blemish and free from accusation—if you continue in your faith, established and firm, not moved from the hope of the gospel"; and 2 Timothy 2:12–13:

> If we endure,
>   we will also reign with him.
> If we disown him,
>   he will also disown us;
> If we are faithless,
>   he will remain faithful,
>   for he cannot disown himself.

11 Eschatology provides a motivation for ethics. Present difficulties are easier to go through because of bright prospects for the future, when "the kingdom of our Lord and Savior Jesus Christ" will be inaugurated. In one sense, Christians are already in the kingdom (Col 1:13). Yet, as Paul and Barnabas said, "We must go through many hardships to enter the kingdom of God" (Acts 14:22). The kingdom is seen as temporally limited in 1 Corinthians 15:24 and Revelation 20:1–6. But in this verse, Peter speaks of it as "the eternal kingdom." A kingdom is where a king exercises his rule and authority. The diversity of statements about the kingdom in the Bible reflects the many facets of the rule of the triune God over humanity (both saved and lost) and also over angels (both fallen and unfallen) (cf. Pss 22:28; 145:11–13; Dan 4:35; Acts 17:24).

Jesus Christ is now the Lord (Acts 2:36), and as such he rules. In his coming to earth, his rule or kingdom will be visibly manifested and imposed (Matt 13:40–43). This will mark the end of this age and inaugurate the earthly messianic phase of the kingdom (Rev 20:1–6), which will last for a thousand years. Yet the kingdom does not end, for God's reign is eternal (Rev 11:15); and the mediatorial kingdom becomes the eternal kingdom of the triune God. Here, then, Peter looks to the future aspects of the kingdom of Jesus Christ that the believer enters at death or at the imposition of the kingdom.

The future for the Christian who diligently pursues holiness is very bright. He will be welcomed "richly" (*plousiōs;* NIV, "receive a rich welcome") "into the eternal kingdom." He will not barely "make it" into the kingdom or "be saved, . . . only as one escaping through the flames" (1 Cor 3:15); but he will receive his Lord's "Well done, good and faithful servant!" (Matt 25:21). Green (*Peter and Jude*, p. 75) suggests that perhaps Peter's words in v.11 allude to the honors paid to winners of the Olympic games. When a winner came back to his home town, he would be welcomed by a special entrance built in the town or city wall in his honor.

3. *The Need for Reminders*

1:12-15

> 12So I will always remind you of these things, even though you know them and are firmly established in the truth you now have. 13I think it is right to refresh your memory as long as I live in the tent of this body, 14because I know that I will soon put it aside, as our Lord Jesus Christ has made clear to me. 15And I will make every effort to see that after my departure you will always be able to remember these things.

12 Truth needs to be repeated. The future hope is indeed well known to Christians. Yet reminders of it and exhortations regarding its application to life and service are essential. "So" (*dio*) links what Peter now says about reminding his readers with his statements about the need for possessing Christian virtues in increasing measure (v.8), participating in the divine nature (v.4), and the eschatological hope. Peter declares that he knows that they have a settled conviction of "the truth [they] now have" (*tē parousē alētheia*). The last statement implies a relatively fixed body of truth (cf. Jude 3: "the faith that was once for all entrusted to the saints"). This, however, is not necessarily to be taken as a sign of a late date or of "early Catholicism" since as far back as Acts 2:42 there is in the NT a body of recognizable apostolic truth.

"Firmly established" renders the perfect passive participle *estērigmenous*. Jesus used the related word *stērizō* ("establish," "strengthen") when he exhorted Simon Peter to "strengthen [his] brothers" (Luke 22:32). The teaching of the body of apostolic truth leads to spiritual strength; when one has received this teaching, he is established. But this does not obviate warnings of spiritual pitfalls, exhortations to pursue truth, and prayer for divine strengthening (1 Peter 5:10).

13-14 That Peter knows that he will not always live in "the tent of this body" (*skēnōmati*) underlines what he has been saying. The cognate word *skēnos* ("tent") was used of a body either living or dead. Paul, for example, uses it in 2 Corinthians 5:1, 4: "If the earthly tent we live in is destroyed. . . ." Although it is possible that Peter was influenced by Paul's usage, it is also possible that they shared a common linguistic and conceptual heritage. Peter knows that he will soon die and refers to a special revelation Jesus gave him (TDNT, 2:61-62). The most common interpretation links Peter's words to John 21:18-19, but this connection is uncertain. In that passage Jesus spoke of a violent death for Peter. So it is possible that Peter is speaking of some other revelation Jesus gave him.

For Christians death should hold no terrors; it is like putting off old clothes (*apothesis*) or an exit (*exodos*, v.15) from old age. According to Paul, to die is to "be with Christ" (Phil 1:23) in a new way. So in view of his approaching death, Peter wants "to refresh [his readers'] memory" (v.13). The verb rendered "refresh" (*diegeirō*) literally means "to wake up" or "arouse."

15 "And I will make every effort" translates *spoudasō* (future tense of *spoudazō*). See the use of the noun *spoudē* in v.5 and the verb in v.10. To use an educational term, Peter wants his readers to "overlearn" the basic truths so that after his death they will never forget them. Much discussion has centered around this sentence and the nature of what Peter is promising. Is he referring to the written form of his teaching or perhaps to the Gospel of Mark (so Green, *Peter and Jude*, p. 80; contra Kelly, p. 314)?

Probably Peter means that he intends to continue his ministry with all diligence until his death so as to strengthen the church. Apparently no specific writings are in view.

III. Christ's Divine Majesty (1:16–21)

1. *Attested by Apostolic Eyewitnesses*

1:16–18

> [16]We did not follow cleverly invented stories when we told you about the power and coming of our Lord Jesus Christ, but we were eyewitnesses of his majesty. [17]For he received honor and glory from God the Father when the voice came to him from the Majestic Glory, saying, "This is my Son, whom I love; with him I am well pleased."[18]We ourselves heard this voice that came from heaven when we were with him on the sacred mountain.

16 Here Peter links himself with the other apostles ("we"—cf. comment on v.18) in certifying that their message is based on their own eyewitness experience of Jesus and on hearing of God's attestation of him. Peter denies that they have followed "cleverly invented stories" (*sesophismenois mythois,* "stories," "myths"). The words refer to fables about the gods.

The NT always uses *mythos* in a negative sense and in contrast to the truth of the gospel (1 Tim 1:4; 4:7; 2 Tim 4:4; Titus 1:14). (On myth, cf. F.F. Bruce in DNTT, 2:644–47). It is likely that the false teachers claimed that the Incarnation, Resurrection, and coming kingdom the apostles spoke about were only stories. These teachers may have been men like Hymenaeus and Philetus, who said that "the resurrection has already taken place" (2 Tim 2:17–18). Apparently they denied a future aspect of eschatology or else reinterpreted it so as to lose its intended meaning.

The specific point in view was the second coming of Jesus (*tēn dynamin kai parousian,* "the power and coming"). Peter sees his preaching of the Second Coming as being based on his eyewitness observation of the transfiguration of Jesus (cf. vv.17–18 with Matt 16:28–17:5). In the return of Jesus, the kingdom will be visibly inaugurated in power. The dead will be raised, and judgment will occur. The "power" he will manifest in his coming embraces destruction of the lawless one (2 Thess 2:8) and his hosts (Rev 19:11–16), calling out the dead by his voice (John 5:28), judgment (John 5:27), and the consummation of the kingdom (Rev 11:15–18).

"Eyewitness" (*epoptai*) occurs only here in the NT. BAG (p. 305) defines it as a "t.t. [technical term] of the mysteries, to designate those who have been initiated into the highest grade of the mysteries" (cf. Kelly, p. 318; Green, *Peter and Jude,* p. 83). (Michaelis, TDNT, 5:375, denies any such usage of *epopteuō* [the related verb] here "to the usage in the mysteries.") Peter probably takes up a favorite term of some false teachers and uses their vocabulary against them. *Epopteuō* ("observe," "see") occurs in the NT only in 1 Peter 2:12; 3:2. This lends support to the view of the common origin of the two letters or of dependence of the second letter on the first one.

17 Verses 17–18 explain how and when Peter was an eyewitness of the majesty of Jesus Christ. God the Father gave honor and glory to Jesus. The "honor" is the public acknowledgment of his sonship (cf. Ps 2:6–7; Matt 3:17; Luke 3:22), and the "glory" is the transfiguration of the humiliated Son into his glorious splendor. On the Mount of Transfiguration, Jesus' face "shone like the sun," his clothes "became as white as the light" (Matt 17:1–9; Mark 9:2–10; Luke 9:28–36), a unique (*toiasde*, lit., "such as this") voice sounded from a bright cloud that covered them and said, "This is my Son, whom I love; with him I am well pleased." The scene showed Jesus as Messiah and was a preview of his glory as King.

18 Peter emphatically says, "We [*hēmeis*; NIV, 'we ourselves,' i.e., Peter, James, and John] heard this voice that came from heaven," while they were with Jesus "on the sacred mountain." It was the Transfiguration that transformed the mountain from a common one into a "sacred" (*hagios*) one. As for the place of the Transfiguration, Mount Hermon (over nine thousand feet high and near Caesarea Philippi, where the event that preceded the Transfiguration took place) or one of its spurs is the most likely choice. Traditionally, Mount Tabor, a steep eminence in the Plain of Jezreel, is identified as the Mount of Transfiguration. But its modest height makes it a less likely site than Hermon.

2. Attested by Divinely Originated Prophecy

1:19–21

> [19]And we have the word of the prophets made more certain, and you will do well to pay attention to it, as to a light shining in a dark place, until the day dawns and the morning star rises in your hearts. [20]Above all, you must understand that no prophecy of Scripture came about by the prophet's own interpretation. [21]For prophecy never had its origin in the will of man, but men spoke from God as they were carried along by the Holy Spirit.

19 By saying "And we have the word of the prophets made more certain," Peter indicates that the OT prophets spoke of the same things he did and that their words are made more certain because the Transfiguration is a foreview of their fulfillment. Green (*Peter and Jude*, p. 87) adopts the interpretation that the Scriptures confirm the apostolic witness—viz., "We have also a more sure word of prophecy" (KJV). The critical term is *bebaioteron*, which BAG (p. 137) cites as meaning in this context "we possess the prophetic word as something altogether reliable." But if this meaning is adopted, there is no point of comparison between the OT prophecies and the apostles' testimony or that of the Voice at the Transfiguration. The comparative would be used for the superlative, and Peter would merely be giving additional reasons to cling to the message. On the whole, NIV is to be preferred to KJV and BAG.

After affirming the reliability of the OT Scriptures, Peter exhorts his readers to continue to pay careful attention to the prophetic message. He compares it to "light shining in a dark place" (cf. Ps 119:105: "Your word is a lamp to my feet and a light to my path"). The "dark place" is the whole world, which has turned from God the Light (cf. Isa 9:2; Eph 6:12). Christians are to ponder and keep the word of God "until the day dawns." The "day" is the day of the Parousia (cf. Rom 13:12). The "morning star" (*phōsphoros*) appears only here in the NT, but the use of "star" for the Messiah occurs in Numbers 24:17 ("a star . . . out of Jacob"). Related expressions—"the rising sun" (Luke 1:78) and "the bright Morning Star [*astēr*]" (Rev 22:16)—support the view that Peter is referring to Christ in his advent.

The phrase "rises in your hearts" is difficult. Green (*Peter and Jude*, p. 89) suggests the possibility of reading this phrase as part of v.20 rather than v.19. But the word order in Greek is against this. The idea that the Second Coming is only subjective (that is, only "in your hearts") is clearly contrary to the eschatology of the book (cf. 3:4, 10) and to the rest of the NT (cf. Acts 1:11; 1 Thess 4:13–18; 2 Thess 2:8). The best interpretation sees "in your hearts" as the subjective results of Christ's actual coming. When he comes, an illuminating transformation will take place in believers.

20 Peter continues his exhortation with the expression "above all" (*touto prōton ginōskontes;* lit., "knowing this first"). The primary thing to be known is that the prophetic Scriptures did not come into being through the prophet's "own interpretation" (*idias epilyseōs;* lit., "of one's own unloosing"—though *epilysis* is the regular word for "interpretation"). What exactly does Peter mean by this expression? The major views are that (1) no prophecy is a matter of one's own interpretation—so either the church must interpret prophecy, the interpretation must be that intended by the Holy Spirit, or the individual's interpretation is not to be "private" but according to the analogy of faith; (2) the NIV translation, "No prophecy of Scripture came about by the prophet's own interpretation"—i.e., no prophecy originated through the interpretation of the prophet himself; and (3) *epilysis* is not to be taken as meaning the interpretation but refers to the origination of Scripture. The sense of the verse is probably that of the first view, that no prophecy of Scripture is to be interpreted by any individual in an arbitrary way. This fits the problem of the false teachers' distorting Paul's writings and other Scripture mentioned at 3:16, and the next verse clarifies that the prophecy originated with the Holy Spirit.

21 Each prophecy originated in God (*apo theou*), not in the will of man. To understand each prophecy, one must interpret it not according to one's own "private" ideas. Verse 21 is notable for the light it sheds on how Scripture was produced. Peter's statement "men spoke from God" implies the dual authorship of Scripture. This is also implied in the OT. For example, David said, "The Spirit of the Lord spoke through me; his word was on my tongue" (2 Sam 23:2); or as Jeremiah was told, "You must . . . say whatever I command you. . . . Now, I have put my words in your mouth" (Jer 1:7, 9). Men spoke, but God so worked in them so that what they said was his word. It was not through a process of dictation or through a state of ecstasy that the writers of Scripture spoke but through the control of the Spirit of God—"as they were carried along by the Holy Spirit." (For other texts on Inspiration, cf. 1 Cor 14:37; 2 Tim 3:16.)

Notes

21 NIV's "men spoke from God" follows the UBS text. The KJV "holy men" has good support but the insertion of ἅγιοι (*hagioi,* "holy") is easier to explain than its omission.

IV. False Prophets and Teachers (2:1–22)

1. *Warning Against False Teachers*

2:1–3

[1]But there were also false prophets among the people, just as there will be false teachers among you. They will secretly introduce destructive heresies, even denying the sovereign Lord who bought them—bringing swift destruction on themselves.

²Many will follow their shameful ways and will bring the way of truth into disrepute. ³In their greed these teachers will exploit you with stories they have made up. Their condemnation has long been hanging over them, and their destruction has not been sleeping.

1 Although Israel had a notable succession of true prophets, she was often plagued by false or lying prophets (cf. Deut 13:1–5; 18:20; 1 Kings 18:19; 22:6ff.; Jer 5:31; 23:9–18). "The people" (*laos*) is a common designation for Israel (cf. TDNT, 4:52–54). The church also must expect false teachers to come in (cf. Acts 20:29). They "secretly introduce" (*pareisaxousin*) or "smuggle in" their doctrines. Similar warnings occur in Galatians 2:4, concerning the entrance of false brothers into a Christian gathering, and in 2 Corinthians 11:13–15, concerning Satan's masqueraders. The "destructive heresies" are teachings that lead to darkness and damnation. The focal point of their error was christological; they were "denying the sovereign Lord who bought them." The "sovereign Lord" (*despotēs*) is Christ (so BAG, p. 175; DNTT, 2:509; TDNT, 2:48–49), as in the parallel in Jude 4.

"Who bought them" is a difficult phrase. It seems to some to raise questions about the Calvinistic doctrine of the perseverance of the saints (i.e., eternal security). The theological problem lies in the fact that persons bought by Christ appear to be lost. Clark writes, "The meaning of 2:1 is . . . that the false teachers even deny the God who delivered the Israelites from Egypt" (*II Peter*, pp. 38–39). For him the words "denying the sovereign Lord who bought them" refer to the God of the Exodus who is denied rather than to Jesus Christ and what he did on the cross for the false teachers. This requires understanding the antecedent of "them" to be "the people" in the first part of the sentence. While this is grammatically possible, it is very unlikely because of the distance between the pronoun and its antecedent noun. The natural sense of the verse is that "they" (the false teachers) deny the Lord who bought them (the false teachers).

Other solutions to the theological problem have been advanced. Among them are the following:

1. The false teachers were redeemed but fell away or lost their salvation. But to many Christians, including many who are not strict Calvinists, the idea that a redeemed person can lose his salvation contradicts clear passages that state the contrary (e.g., John 10:28–29; Rom 8:28–39). Moreover, v.2 says nothing about the application of redemption to the false teachers or their appropriation of it.

2. The word "redeem" (*agorazō;* NIV, "bought") is to be taken in the sense of "temporal deliverance" or "sovereign creation"—viz., that the word is not used soteriologically (Gary Long, *Definite Atonement* [Nutley, N.J.: Presbyterian and Reformed, 1976], pp. 67–78).

3. Some Calvinistic interpreters argue that Peter is speaking not in terms of the reality of the false teachers' faith but in terms of their profession. They profess to be those who have been bought by the blood of Christ, but they are lying.

4. Calvin, speaking of the false teachers, said, "Those who throw over the traces and plunge themselves into every kind of license are not unjustly said to deny Christ, by whom they are redeemed" (*Epistles of Peter*, p. 346).

In my judgment, v.1 asserts that Christ "bought" the false teachers; but this does not necessarily mean that they were saved. Salvation in the NT sense does not occur till the benefits of Christ's work are applied to the individual by the regeneration of the Spirit and belief in the truth. To put it in other words, Christ crucified is the propitiation for the sins of the whole world (1 John 2:2). Yet the wrath of God is on all sinners—elect and nonelect (John 3:36; Eph 2:3)—till the work of the Cross is applied to those who believe.

"Bringing swift destruction on themselves" is "not a simple extinction of existence . . . but an everlasting state of torment and death" (TDNT, 1:397). It will be "swift" because it will descend on them suddenly either at their death or at the return of the Lord.

2 The false teachers will be popular with many followers. John speaks of the same phenomenon when, speaking of the false prophets who do not acknowledge that Jesus is from God, he says, "The world listens to them" (1 John 4:5). Moreover, Peter says that the many adherents of the false teachers "will follow their shameful ways" (*aselgeiais*, "vices," "sexual debaucheries"; cf. 1 Peter 4:3; 2 Peter 2:7, 18). Their disciples will be like the false teachers and, bringing their sexual immorality into the churches, will cause "the way of truth" to be defamed. "The way" (*hē hodos*) was a common early name for the Christian faith (cf. Acts 9:2; 19:9, 23; 22:4; 24:14, 22). The thought of ungodly conduct bringing reproach on the name of God or Christ occurs in Romans 2:23–24; 1 Timothy 6:1; and Titus 2:5.

It is important to understand that the Christian faith is "the way of truth." It is not only correct thought or "truth" but it is the "way" of life that responds to and is determined by the truth. True doctrine must issue in true living. The knowledge of God should lead to a godly life.

3 Christian teachers have the right to financial support (cf. 1 Cor 9:1–14; Gal 6:6; 1 Tim 5:17–18), but their motivation in the ministry should not be mercenary. For false teachers, however, religion will be commercialized—they will "buy and sell, trade in" (cf. *emporeuomai*, BAG, p. 256) and exploit people. With fabricated stories they fleece the sheep. In the light of the commercialism of religious cults today, Peter's warning is clear enough.

The popularity and prosperity of the errorists will certainly come to an end (3b). Their judgment and doom has been announced long ago (cf. Ps 1:5–6). Destruction (*apōleia*, used twice in v.1), is now personified as "not sleeping" (*ou nystazei*). NEB translates it "perdition waits for them with unsleeping eyes." The only other NT use of *nystazo* ("become drowsy") occurs in Matthew 25:5 in the parable of the wise and foolish virgins.

2. Three Examples of Previous Judgments

2:4–10a

> [4]For if God did not spare angels when they sinned, but sent them to hell, putting them into gloomy dungeons to be held for judgment; [5]if he did not spare the ancient world when he brought the flood on its ungodly people, but protected Noah, a preacher of righteousness, and seven others; [6]if he condemned the cities of Sodom and Gomorrah by burning them to ashes, and made them an example of what is going to happen to the ungodly; [7]and if he rescued Lot, a righteous man, who was distressed by the filthy lives of lawless men [8](for that righteous man, living among them day after day, was tormented in his righteous soul by the lawless deeds he saw and heard)— [9]if this is so, then the Lord knows how to rescue godly men from trials and to hold the unrighteous for the day of judgment, while continuing their punishment. [10]This is especially true of those who follow the corrupt desire of the sinful nature and despise authority.

Syntactically, vv.4–9 are a single sentence, one of the longest in the NT. The protasis (the "if" part of a conditional sentence) is extended by the use of three examples of divine judgment. The apodosis (the conclusion) is delayed until v.9. In the NIV, the "if" (*ei*) is repeated four times (vv.5, 6, 7, 9); in the Greek text it occurs only in v.4. The cumulative examples of the first part of the sentence make the main point (v.9) stand out with force and emphasis.

4 The first example of divine judgment is that which came upon the fallen angels. The literal word order from the Greek is instructive—"For if God angels who sinned did not spare"—stressing that if angels are judged, then certainly men will also be judged. Of which judgment of angels does Peter speak? Jesus said, "I saw Satan fall like lightning from heaven" (Luke 10:18); and John in Revelation 12:7–9 describes a war in heaven after which Satan and his angels were cast down to the earth. The most common interpretation is to relate the judgment Peter speaks of with the mention of angels in Genesis 6:1–4 (where "sons of God" apparently means "fallen angels"; cf. Job 1:6; 2:1; 38:7). Another interpretation relates this judgment to the original sin of the angels. But the explanation in relation to Genesis 6:1–4 is best because (1) it was common in Jewish literature (Enoch 6:2; 1 QapGen col. 2), (2) the three examples (angels, Flood, and cities of the plain) all come one after another in the early chapters of Genesis, and (3) the angels referred to here in 2 Peter are confined to "gloomy dungeons." Apparently some fallen angels are free to plague mankind as demons while others such as these are imprisoned. The connection with Genesis 6:1–4 provides a reason for this phenomenon.

Peter uses the verb *tartaroō* ("to hold captive in Tartarus") to tell where the sinning angels were sent. "Tartarus, thought of by the Greeks as a subterranean place lower than Hades where divine punishment was meted out, was so regarded in Jewish apocalyptic as well" (BAG, p. 813). The usual translation of *tartaroō* as "sent" or "cast into hell" (so KJV, RSV, NASB, NIV, et al.) only approximates the idea of a special place of confinement until the final judgment. Though "gloomy dungeons" (*seirais zophou*) may be correct, "chains of darkness" (KJV) is an equally possible translation (cf. Jude 6). *Seira* ("a chain"), *seiros* ("a pit"), and *siros* ("a pit," "a cave") all occur in the MSS.

5 Peter's second example is the Flood. He has referred to it in his first letter (3:18–22) and will do so again in the next chapter of this one (3:5–6). Noah was the "eighth" (*ogdoos*) meaning there were seven others saved with him (wife, three sons, and daughters-in-law). They were guarded or protected by God during the Flood that wiped out the ungodly antediluvian civilization. Noah was a herald (*kēryx*) of righteousness. This could refer to his preaching activity not recorded in the OT or to the fact that his lifestyle condemned sin and proclaimed righteousness to his contemporaries (Gen 6:9).

6 The third example of judgment is the destruction of the cities of Sodom and Gomorrah. According to Genesis 19:24–28, "the LORD rained down burning sulfur on Sodom and Gomorrah—from the LORD out of heaven." The area is rich in bitumen, salt, and sulfur and has been geologically active in historical times. The Lord may have used volcanism as the means of his judgment. Peter says he "condemned" them "by burning them to ashes." The rare word *tephrōsas* means either "reduce to ashes" or "cover with ashes." This word is cited in MM (p. 632) as being used in Dio Cassius (66.1094) of Vesuvius's erupting and Lycophron's "being overwhelmed with ashes." This total destruction is an example (*hypodeigma*) to the ungodly of the things that are going to happen to them.

7–8 In the midst of God's judgment of the cities of the plain, he delivered Lot, whom Peter calls "righteous." This is puzzling because in Genesis Lot is hardly notable for his righteousness. He seems worldly and weak and had to be dragged out of Sodom (Gen 19:16). Yet Abraham's intercession in Genesis 18:16–33 may imply that he considered Lot to be righteous. Peter's characterization of Lot may reflect extrabiblical revelation or tradition such as Wisdom of Solomon 10:6, where Lot is called "the just one." It is also possible that Peter inferred Lot's righteousness from his deliverance from the destruction of Sodom and from his being "tormented" and "distressed by the filthy lives" of his fellow citizens. The contemporary application is plain. To what extent are Christians living today in a godless society "tormented" (*ebasanizen*) by what they see?

9 Peter states the main point next. It is one of abiding comfort. "The Lord knows how to rescue godly men from trials." Suffering Christians anywhere and at any time can find consolation in the fact that their Lord knows all about their plight. Furthermore, "the Lord knows how . . . to hold the unrighteous for the day of judgment, *while continuing their punishment*" (italics mine). Immediate judgment of sinners is only the beginning. Temporal judgments, death, and "being in torment" in Hades (Luke 16:23) do not exhaust the divine wrath. A great Judgment is yet future (Rev 20:11–15), followed by the "second death" (Rev 20:14)—the lake of fire.

10a God's wrath is especially certain to fall on the false teachers of Peter's day. He characterizes them as "indulging the flesh" (i.e., as "those who follow the corrupt desire of the sinful nature"). This refers to sexual profligacy. They also "despise authority." "Authority" translates *kyriotētos*, which may refer to the rejection of angelic powers (cf. Eph 1:21; Col 1:16). Most likely, however, it refers here to their rejection of the rule of the Lord (*kyrios*) Jesus Christ over them.

3. The Insolence and Wantonness of the False Teachers

2:10b–16

> Bold and arrogant, these men are not afraid to slander celestial beings; [11]yet even angels, although they are stronger and more powerful, do not bring slanderous accusations against such beings in the presence of the Lord. [12]But these men blaspheme in matters they do not understand. They are like brute beasts, creatures of instinct, born only to be caught and destroyed, and like beasts they too will perish.
> [13]They will be paid back with harm for the harm they have done. Their idea of pleasure is to carouse in broad daylight. They are blots and blemishes, reveling in their pleasures while they feast with you. [14]With eyes full of adultery, they never stop sinning; they seduce the unstable; they are experts in greed—an accursed brood! [15]They have left the straight way and wandered off to follow the way of Balaam son of Beor, who loved the wages of wickedness. [16]But he was rebuked for his wrongdoing by a donkey—a beast without speech—who spoke with a man's voice and restrained the prophet's madness.

10 The false teachers are "bold and arrogant"—i.e., presumptuous and self-willed. They respect no one, and nothing restrains them. "They are not afraid to slander celestial beings [*doxai*]." *Doxai* has been interpreted to mean (1) the imperial and magisterial power (so Calvin, *Epistles of Peter,* p. 401, but few follow this view), (2) rulers of the church (Bigg, p. 280), (3) good angels, or (4) fallen angels. As *doxai* seems highly unusual as a term for church leaders or magistrates, most interpreters think it refers to celestial beings of some kind. Because v.11 implies that these beings bring slanderous accusations in the presence of the Lord, it seems best to think of them as fallen angels. As to when they slandered or what kind of slander was involved, one can only surmise. Perhaps the false teachers were accused of being in league with Satan, and their reply was to disparage and mock him (cf. Jude 8–9).

11 In contrast to these audacious errorists, angels, even though they are stronger and more powerful, do not indict "such beings" (i.e., the "celestial beings"—perhaps the fallen angels of v.4) in the presence of the Lord. The good angels are more powerful than the fallen ones (cf. Rev 12:7–8).

12 The false teachers act like irrational animals without the restraint that angels and righteous men have. They may claim a *gnōsis* (a special knowledge), but they blaspheme out of their ignorance. Like wild beasts who are slaves to their instincts and are born to be slaughtered, they too are destined for destruction (lit., "in their destruction, they shall be destroyed").

13 "They will be paid back with harm for the harm they have done" translates three Greek words (*adikoumenoi misthon adikias*). The verb *adikeō* commonly means "to suffer injustice," which may account for the variant reading *komioumenoi* ("receiving"). Perhaps a scribe thought that the reading *adikoumenoi* implies that God was treating them unjustly. But the UBS text makes good sense and preserves a word play in Greek that is quite characteristic of Peter's style in this epistle. So the errorists "suffer harm" as a "wage" of "injury."

Normally one thinks of carousing as a nighttime activity (1 Thess 5:7), perhaps because of the shame involved. But these people carouse in broad daylight. Peter sees them as "feasting together" with the recipients of his letter. Perhaps Peter has in mind the love feasts or communal meals of the church (cf. NIV mg.). "Reveling in their pleasures" translates *en tais apatais autōn,* which literally means "reveling in their deceptions." *Apatais* in later Greek means "pleasure" or "lusts" (BAG, p. 81).

14 In the Greek text vv.12–16 are one sentence. So the vivid phrase "with eyes full of adultery" (*ophthalmous echontes mestous moichalidos;* lit., "having eyes full of an adulteress," meaning to desire every woman they see) implies that the false teachers desired to turn church gatherings into times of dissipation. They are, Peter says, "never at rest from sin" (NEB), or their eyes unceasingly look for sin. They "seduce" (*deleazō,* "lure," "bait," "entice") "unstable souls" (*psychai;* NIV, "unstable"). Here "soul" means "person" as in 1 Peter 3:20. The unstable are those with no foundation (*astēriktous*). In 1:12 of this letter Peter has spoken of his readers as being "firmly established [*estērigmenous*] in the truth," and in 3:16 he will warn them of "unstable" (*astēriktos*) people and of the danger of falling "from [their] secure position" (*stērigmos*) in 3:17 (cf. comments on 1:12).

"They are experts in greed" is literally "having a heart exercised in greed." The word "exercised" (*gegymnasmenos*) relates to athletic training (cf. our English word "gymnasium"). In biblical thought the "heart" denotes the center of human personality (cf. Prov 4:23). Deep within them, the thoughts of the false teachers are of *pleonexia* ("greediness, insatiableness, avarice, covetousness, lit. 'a desire to have more'" [BAG, p. 673]). Of them Peter exclaims, "An accursed brood!" (lit., "children of a curse"), meaning that God's curse is on them.

15-16 The false teachers resemble Balaam, the son of Beor (Bosor in most MSS), in that Balaam loved money and was willing to pursue it instead of obeying God (Num 22:5-24:25). Balaam also taught immorality (Num 31:16; Rev 2:14). So the false teachers have left the biblical way and have gone into Balaam's error—mercenary greed and sexual impurity. As Balaam went to curse the children of Israel for money (if he could) "he was rebuked for his wrongdoing by a donkey—a beast without speech." Actually, according to the account in Numbers 22:27-35, the rebuke is twofold: first from the donkey, then from the angel of the Lord. Ironically the dumb animal had more "spiritual" perception than the prophet! The utterance (*phthenxamenon*, "to utter a loud sound") restrained the prophet's "insanity" (*paraphronia*—a "hapax legomenon," [occurring only here, though a related verb is found in 2 Cor 11:23]).

Notes

---

15 Balaam is the son of Beor (Βεώρ, *Beōr;* Heb. בעור, *bᵉṣôr*) according to Num 22:5; 31:8; Deut 23:4. Yet most MSS spell his name Βοσόρ (*Bosor*) in 2 Peter 2:15. No good reason is known for this. Green (*Peter and Jude*, p. 113) suggests that *Bosor* may represent "the Galilean mispronunciation of the guttural in the Hebrew name."

---

4. The Impotence of Their Teaching
2:17-22

[17]These men are springs without water and mists driven by a storm. Blackest darkness is reserved for them. [18]For they mouth empty, boastful words and, by appealing to the lustful desires of sinful human nature, they entice people who are just escaping from those who live in error. [19]They promise them freedom, while they themselves are slaves of depravity—for a man is a slave to whatever has mastered him. [20]If they have escaped the corruption of the world by knowing our Lord and Savior Jesus Christ and are again entangled in it and overcome, they are worse off at the end than they were at the beginning. [21]It would have been better for them not to have known the way of righteousness, than to have known it and then to turn their backs on the sacred commandment that was passed on to them. [22]Of them the proverbs are true: "A dog returns to its vomit," and, "A sow that is washed goes back to her wallowing in the mud."

17 Whatever else may be said about this chapter, it is a powerful piece of writing that gains momentum as it reaches its climax. In vivid words, Peter goes on to describe the false teachers as "springs without water." Christ provides "a spring of water welling up to eternal life" (John 4:13-14), and from those who believe in him flow "streams of living water" (John 7:37–38). But the false teachers give nothing because they have nothing to give. They are "mists driven by a storm," a metaphor of their instability and transcience. The "blackest darkness . . . reserved for them" (*ho zophos tou skotous*) may refer to hell, for *zophos* is used especially of "the darkness of the nether regions" (BAG, p. 340).

18 These heretics "mouth [*phthengomenoi*, same word as in v.16] boastful [*hyperonka*, 'swollen,' 'of excessive size'] words." Kelly (p. 345) says, "In plain language, their propaganda consists of declaiming bombastic futilities (lit. 'bombastic words of vanity')." By their sensual propaganda, they ensnare (*deleazō*, same word as v.14) "people who are just escaping from those who live in error." So they take for their targets new converts to Christianity from paganism.

19 They promise "freedom," perhaps from any law or restraint of the flesh. Paul ran into similar error—"Everything is permissible for me" (1 Cor 6:12f.)—among false teachers in Corinth, and possibly in Galatia also (cf. Gal 5:14). Yet, Peter says, the very ones who speak of freedom are "slaves of depravity—for a man is a slave to whatever has mastered him." To this the best parallel is Jesus' words: "Everyone who sins is a slave to sin" (John 8:34; cf. Rom 6:16; 1 Cor 6:12b). So though the false teachers talk of religion and freedom, they do not know the Son; for as Jesus said, "If the Son sets you free, you will be free indeed" (John 8:36).

20 Of whom is Peter speaking in vv.20–22—i.e., who does the pronoun "they" refer to? Does it refer (1) to the false teachers of v.19, (2) to the unstable people of v.18, or (3) more generally to both but particularly to the false teachers (cf. Balz and Schrage, p. 140)? In my opinion, it refers basically to false teachers because (1) proximity makes the false teachers (spoken of in v.19) the normal antecedent of "they," (2) the conjunction *gar* (untranslated in NIV) in v.20 (*ei gar*, "for if ") logically connects v.20 with v.19, (3) "mastered" (*hēttētai*) in v.19 is verbally linked to "overcome" (*hēttōtai*) in v.20, and (4) the teachers are the main subject of the whole chapter. (For arguments supporting view 2, see Kelly, pp. 347–48.)

Verse 20 mentions the possibility of reverting to the old paganism after having "escaped the corruptions of the world" through knowing Jesus Christ as Lord and Savior. Is it possible, then, for Christians to lose their salvation? Many would answer affirmatively on the basis of this and similar texts (e.g., Heb 6:4–6; 10:26). But this verse asserts only that false teachers who have for a time escaped from worldly corruption through knowing Christ and then turn away from the light of the Christian faith are worse off than they were before knowing Christ. It uses no terminology affirming that they were Christians in reality (e.g., "sons of God," "children," "born again," "regenerate," "redeemed"). The NT makes a distinction between those who are in the churches and those who are regenerate (cf. 2 Cor 13:5; 2 Tim 2:18–19; 1 John 3:7–8; 2:19: "They went out from us, but they did not really belong to us. . . . but their going showed that none of them belonged to us"). So when Peter says, "They are worse off at the end than they were at the beginning," the reference is to a lost apostate.

21 This verse underlines the seriousness of apostasy. The "sacred commandment that was passed on to them" evidently refers to the authoritative, apostolic message; *paradotheisēs* ("that was passed on") is an important NT term for the transmission of the Christian faith (cf. 1 Cor 15:3; TDNT, 2:171–73). The "sacred commandment" is the whole Christian message with emphasis on its ethical demands (DNTT, 1:339).

22 Peter concludes his strong denunciation of the false teachers by citing two proverbs. The first is a biblical one (Prov 26:11); the second is extrabiblical. Both dogs and pigs were considered vile by the Jews. (For background information on "dogs" in Scripture and Jewish culture, cf. TDNT, 3:1101–4.) So the false teachers are unclean and return to the pagan corruption. Significantly, Jesus used the designations "dogs" and "pigs" in speaking of those opposed to God and his Word. Though it may be overinterpretation, many have observed that the nature of the "unclean" animals does not change. So the "dog [that] returns to its vomit" or the sow that "is washed" (*lousamenē;* lit., "washed itself," an aorist middle participle) portrays the person who has a religious "profession" or outward change without a regenerating inner change that affects his nature. Such a person soon reverts to his true nature.

Notes

---

18 The evidence in relation to ὀλίγως (*oligōs,* "scarcely," "barely"; NIV, "just") and ὄντως (*ontōs,* "really," "certainly," "in truth") is fairly evenly divided. In Gr. capitals (ΟΛΙΓΩΣ, ΟΝΤΩΣ) the readings are easily confused. *Oligōs* is a rare word and, if genuine here, this is its only NT usage.

V. The Promise of the Lord's Coming (3:1–18)

1. The Certainty of the Day of the Lord

3:1–10

> [1]Dear friends, this is now my second letter to you. I have written both of them as reminders to stimulate you to wholesome thinking. [2]I want you to recall the words spoken in the past by the holy prophets and the command given by our Lord and Savior through your apostles.
>
> [3]First of all, you must understand that in the last days scoffers will come, scoffing and following their own evil desires. [4]They will say, "Where is this 'coming' he promised? Ever since our fathers died, everything goes on as it has since the beginning of creation." [5]But they deliberately forget that long ago by God's word the heavens existed and the earth was formed out of water and with water. [6]By water also the world of that time was deluged and destroyed. [7]By the same word the present heavens and earth are reserved for fire, being kept for the day of judgment and destruction of ungodly men.
>
> [8]But do not forget this one thing, dear friends: With the Lord a day is like a thousand years, and a thousand years are like a day. [9]The Lord is not slow in keeping his promise, as some understand slowness. He is patient with you, not wanting anyone to perish, but everyone to come to repentance.
>
> [10]But the day of the Lord will come like a thief. The heavens will disappear with a roar; the elements will be destroyed by fire, and the earth and everything in it will be laid bare.

1 "Dear friends" (*agapētoi,* "beloved") is repeated in vv.8, 14, and 17 in this chapter. "This is now my second letter to you." Does this refer to 1 Peter? Most commentators say yes. But this is not certain because (1) it has not been established that the recipients of the two letters are the same, (2) 1:12, 16 may imply a personal ministry to the recipients of this second letter that 1 Peter gives no indication of, (3) the description of the two letters ("both of them as reminders") here in 3:1 does not fit 1 Peter very well, and (4) other letters of apostles have not been preserved (cf. 1 Cor 5:9; Col 4:16). None of these points is in itself very strong; yet taken together and when coupled with the lack of use of 1 Peter in 2 Peter, they raise a doubt that leaves the question open.

"As reminders to stimulate you" (*diegeirō hymōn en hypomnēsei*) is almost identical with the phrase in 1:13 that NIV translates "to refresh your memory" (*diegeirein hymas en hypomnēsei*). "To wholesome thinking" translates *eilikrinē dianoian* (lit., "pure minds"). *Dianoia* is commonly used in the LXX for "heart" (Heb. *lēb*). Behm thinks that "in 2 Pt. 3:1 the [*eilikrinēs dianoia*] which the author seeks to maintain in his readers through the epistle is a 'pure disposition'" (TDNT, 4:967).

2 In the Greek text, v.2 continues the sentence begun in v.1 and is notable for the succession of words in the genitive case. NIV smooths out the rough construction by reversing the order of words. The sense is fairly plain, but a few points need clarification. The "words spoken in the past" are the prophetic oracles with special reference here to the day of the Lord. The "commandment" is a way of referring to the moral demands of the Christian faith (cf. 2:21 and comments there) and primarily to the command of love.

Kelly claims that "the expression *your apostles* could not of course have been penned by the historical Peter; it inadvertently betrays that the writer belongs to an age when the apostles have been elevated to a venerated group who mediate Christ's teaching authoritatively to the whole church" (p. 354). Kelly's claim, however, is unfair. If Peter had written "my command" or "from us," the same objection would doubtless be raised. The premise on which Kelly's claim rests is that the apostles were not so conscious of their authority as v.2b implies. If this premise is adopted, the apostolicity of many sections of the NT must be rejected, for they claim more than Peter does here (cf. Rom 1:1, 5; 1 Cor 14:37; 1 John 1:1–5; 4:6; Rev 22:18). To place the prophets and apostles on the same level is not "postapostolic" (cf. Eph 2:20) but it is simply to recognize that the Spirit used them both.

3 Peter next states a primary thing to be remembered from the prophetic and apostolic deposit: the appearance of scoffers in the last days, who deny biblical truths and live in an ungodly way (cf. Dan 7:25; 11:36–39; Matt 24:3–5, 11, 23–26; 1 Tim 4:1ff.; 2 Tim 3:1–7; Jude 17–18). The "last days" are the days that come between the first coming of the Messiah and his second coming. The "scoffers" are the false teachers of chapter 2 who deny a future eschatology. Bertram suggests that they were "possibly Gnostic libertines" (TDNT, 5:636). On the subject of mockery, see TDNT, 5:630–36, for the antithesis between the mockers and the righteous in the biblical revelation (cf. Ps 1:1, 6).

4 Part of the early church proclamation was the announcement of the return of Jesus to complete the work of salvation and to punish the wicked (cf., e.g., Matt 24:3ff.; John 14:1–3; Acts 1:11; 17:31; Rom 13:11; 1 Cor 15:23; 1 Thess 4:13–18; 5:1–11; 2 Thess 1:7–10; Heb 9:28; Rev 1:7). The false teachers ask, "Where is this 'coming' he promised?" Mocking the faith of Christians, they support their own position by claiming, "Ever since our fathers died, everything goes on as it has since the beginning of creation." Who are the persons Peter calls "our fathers"? Kelly (p. 355) and Schelkle (p. 224) argue that they were first-generation Christians. But Bigg (p. 291) and Green (*Peter and Jude*, p. 128–29) consider this unlikely. "Fathers" are much more likely to be OT fathers as in John 6:31, Acts 3:13, Romans 9:5, and Hebrews 1:1. This is the normal NT usage, and the other view requires a clumsy forger to have missed so obvious a blunder. "Our fathers died" (lit., "fell asleep") is a lovely metaphor for the death of believers (cf. Acts 7:60; 1 Thess 4:13–14). The argument of the false teachers is essentially a naturalistic one—a kind of uniformitarianism that rules out any divine intervention in history.

5–6 But they "deliberately [*thelontas*, 'willingly'] forget" the great Flood, when God intervened in history by destroying the antediluvian world. What they forget is not only the Flood but also God's prior activity by his word—the existence of the heavens and the watery formation of the earth (Gen 1:2–10). It seems unlikely that Peter is seeking to affirm that water was the basic material of creation, though many commentators claim this. He does not use the verb *ktizō* ("create") but says that "long ago by God's word the heavens existed [*ēsan*] and the earth was formed [*synestōsa*] out of water and with water." In Genesis the sky (firmament) separates the waters from the waters by the word of God and the land appears out of the water by the same word.

At the beginning of v.6, NIV renders the Greek *di' hōn* ("through which," a plural form) as "by water." The antecedent may be "water," "waters," "word" and "water," or "heavens." Probably both water and the word are to be understood as the agents for destroying the former world (v.6), as the word and fire will be the destructive agents in the future (v.7). "The world of that time" translates the Greek *ho tote kosmos*. The globe was not destroyed, only its inhabitants and its ordered form.

7 Peter's reference to a future conflagration to destroy the present cosmos is highly unusual. Some, indeed, would contend that it shows the influence of Stoic or Iranian (Persian) eschatology (TDNT, 6:928–52). Yet the OT speaks of fire in the day of the Lord (Ps 97:3; [possibly Isa 34:4]; Isa 66:15–16; Dan 7:9–10; Mic 1:4; Mal 4:1). And Matthew 3:11–12 speaks of the future baptism of fire by the Messiah in which he will destroy the "chaff" (cf. 2 Thess 1:7). Peter argues that just as in the past God purged the then-existing *kosmos* by his word and by waters, so in the future he will purge the *kosmos* by his word and by fire. Whether this will take place before the Millennium or after, Peter does not say. Matthew 3:11–12 supports the former, while the sequence of Revelation 20–21 puts the new heaven and new earth after the thousand years (cf. 2 Peter 3:13).

8 Peter's second argument against the false teachers' scoffing at the "delay" of the Lord's coming stems from Psalm 90:4: "For a thousand years in your sight are like a day that has just gone by, or like a watch in night." They overlooked God's time perspective. The admonition "Do not forget" is addressed to believers and uses the same word (*lanthanō*) that is used in v.5 of the false teachers' deliberate forgetfulness. Christians must be careful lest the propaganda of the scoffers distort their thinking.

9 The third argument against the scoffers grows out of the second one. God's "delay" is gracious; it is not caused by inability or indifference. The scoffers argued that God was slow to keep his promise of the new age, and evidently some Christians were influenced by this ("as some understand slowness"). God's time plan is influenced by his patience (*makrothymei*), an attribute prominent in Scripture (cf. Exod 34:6; Num

14:18; Ps 86:15; Jer 15:15; Rom 2:4; 9:22). In Romans 9:22 Paul says that God "bore with great patience the objects of his wrath." Here in v.9 God's patience is directed *eis hymas* ("to you"—NIV, "He is patient with you"). Other MSS read "to us" (*eis hēmas*) or "because of you" (*di' hymas*).

With whom is God patient and whom does he desire to come to repentance? This verse has been a battleground between some Arminian and some Calvinistic interpreters. One of the latter argues, "It is not his [God's] will that every man without exception should repent. . . . Peter therefore is saying simply that Christ will not return until every one of the elect has come to repentance" (Clark, *II Peter*, p. 71). This view, if rigorously applied, is obviously incompatible with premillennialism, whose adherents normally teach that some will be saved during the millennial period following Christ's return.

Calvin's comment shows his moderation and exegetical wisdom: "*Not willing that any should perish*. So wonderful is his love towards mankind, that he would have them all to be saved, and is of his own self prepared to bestow salvation on the lost" (italics his) (*Epistles of Peter*, p. 419). Thus the "you" is addressed to mankind and the "not wanting" (*mē boulomenos*) is of his "desirative" will, not of his decretive will (cf. ibid., pp. 419-20 and Ezek 18:23; 1 Tim 2:4).

10 Peter's fourth argument against the false teachers reaffirms the early church teaching—viz., the day of the Lord will come suddenly. Jesus taught that his coming would be as unexpected as the coming of a thief (Matt 24:42-44). This analogy is commonly repeated in the NT (cf. Luke 12:39; 1 Thess 5:2; Rev 3:3; 16:15). The "Lord" in these texts is Jesus in his exaltation and should so be understood here in 2 Peter. In that catastrophic day "the heavens will disappear with a roar." The "roar" (*rhoizē-don*, only here in NT) is an adverb related to *rhoizos*, "the noise made by something passing swiftly through the air" (BAG, p. 744). Revelation 6:14 says, "The sky receded like a scroll, rolling up," and 20:11 portrays the earth and sky as fleeing from the presence of God.

"The elements" (*stoicheia*) could be stars (heavenly bodies) or the basic materials that make up the world (cf. TDNT, 7:666-87). The "elements" commonly thought of in NT times were air, earth, fire, and water. It is possible that in this verse Peter is looking at three realms (the heavens, that of the heavenly bodies, the earth); so the "heavenly bodies" (*stoicheia*) affected would be those mentioned in other eschatological passages (Joel 2:10; Mark 13:24-26; Rev 6:12-13). Some have seen the splitting of the atom or atomic fusion in this verse, but that is certainly eisegesis. On "the earth and everything in it will be laid bare," see note below.

Notes

10 Ἔργα εὑρεθήσεται (*erga heurethēsetai*, "everything in it will be laid bare") is very uncertain and the meaning difficult. (1) It could mean that all human products will be destroyed (if κατακαήσεται [*katakaēsetai*, "shall be burned."] is accepted). (2) It could mean that all that man does will be known in the judgment (1 Cor 3:13-15). (3) Kelly translates it, "And the earth and the works it contains—will they be found?" (pp. 364f.). NIV (v.11) accords with the first view.

2. The Ethical Implications of the Day of the Lord

3:11–16

> ¹¹Since everything will be destroyed in this way, what kind of people ought you to be? You ought to live holy and godly lives ¹²as you look forward to the day of God and speed its coming. That day will bring about the destruction of the heavens by fire, and the elements will melt in the heat. ¹³But in keeping with his promise we are looking forward to a new heaven and a new earth, the home of righteousness.
>
> ¹⁴So then, dear friends, since you are looking forward to this, make every effort to be found spotless, blameless and at peace with him. ¹⁵Bear in mind that our Lord's patience means salvation, just as our dear brother Paul also wrote you with the wisdom that God gave him. ¹⁶He writes the same way in all his letters, speaking in them of these matters. His letters contain some things that are hard to understand, which ignorant and unstable people distort, as they do the other Scriptures, to their own destruction.

11 Peter here makes the impending disintegration of the universe the ground for a personal challenge to his readers. The present tense of *lyomenōn* (NIV, "destroyed") may be taken either as emphasizing the certainty of imminent destruction or as implying the process of disintegration (cf. 1 John 2:17) "in this way" (i.e., as in v.10). In view of what is in store for the world, Peter asks his readers, "What kind of people ought you to be?" Since the day of the Lord will soon come to punish the wicked and reward the righteous, believers should live "holy and godly lives." Holiness entails separation from evil and dedication to God; godliness relates to piety and worship.

12 Another element of godly living is expectation of the future day. Peter relates this to the idea of "speed[ing] its coming." But how can Christians hasten what God will do? Peter would probably answer by saying that prayer (Matt 6:10) and preaching (Matt 24:14) are the two principal means to bring people to repentance. To the crowd that gathered after the healing of the lame beggar at the Beautiful Gate in Jerusalem Peter proclaimed, "Repent, . . . so that your sins may be wiped out, that times of refreshing may come from the Lord, and that he may send the Christ" (Acts 3:19–20). Once more Peter describes the coming as a fiery disintegration of the very heavens (cf. comment on v.10). Again, the "elements" probably refers to the "celestial bodies" on fire. *Tēketai* ("melt") occurs in the LXX (mg.) of Isaiah 34:4.

13 Through his prophets God promised righteousness. Jeremiah sees the Righteous One bringing in righteousness, and his name is "The LORD Our Righteousness" (23:5–7; 33:16; cf. Ps 9:8; Isa 11:4–5; 45:8; Dan 9:24). This promise of righteousness will be fulfilled ultimately in the new heavens and the new earth of which Isaiah spoke (65:17–25) and which Peter refers to here. John also saw "a new heaven and a new earth" in which there was nothing impure (Rev 21:1, 8, 27).

14 Since there will be perfect righteousness in the new heaven and new earth, Christians must now be righteous in their lives. "So, then" (*dio*) makes the transition to their conduct. "Make every effort" (*spoudasate*) is a favorite word of Peter's (cf. 1:10, 15 and the related noun in 1:5). Christians are to make intense efforts to be morally pure ("spotless, blameless") like Christ. The two words *aspiloi* and *amōmētoi* used here occur in reverse order in 1 Peter 1:19 ("without blemish or defect"), where they refer to Jesus. Their appearance in both letters, though pointing to a connection between the letters, does not prove anything regarding their common authorship. In 2:13 Peter has called the false teachers "blots and blemishes" (*spiloi kai mōmoi*). When the Lord comes, all will appear before him. Believers should aim to live so as "to be found . . . at peace with him"—i.e., having the peace that results from their efforts to please the Lord. In Revelation 2:16, the risen Christ warns the church to repent or he will "fight against them with the sword of his mouth." Those who are "found at peace with him" have put out of their lives the things he hates.

15-16 Again Peter stresses the purpose of the Lord's "patience" (*makrothymia*, "longsuffering," KJV)—that it is designed for salvation. Some confuse the divine patience with slackness. But Christians should esteem (*hēgeisthe*—the same verb occurs in v.9) it as salvation.

"Just as our dear brother Paul also wrote you" is very significant in the light of Paul's rebuke of Peter (Gal 2:11-14). Peter had recognized the ministry of Paul and Barnabas to the Gentiles. But what did Paul write to the recipients of 2 Peter? It is impossible to answer that question. Nor is it necessary to do so in view of Peter's general statement: "He [Paul] writes the same way in all his letters." Green (*Peter and Jude*, p. 145) suggests that Peter may have alluded to a copy of Romans sent out as a circular letter. In Romans 2:4 Paul says that "God's kindness leads you toward repentance." Many commentators (e.g., Kelly, p. 370) argue that vv. 15-16 reveal clearly that the apostolic age is past and that the writer is trying to pass himself off as an apostle but fails to do so. The presuppositions one brings to these verses are determinative. If one accepts the Petrine authorship, they make good sense.

Peter affirms that Paul's letters contain "some things that are hard to understand" (*dysnoēta*). This word is found only here in the NT, twice in the classics (so LSJ, p. 459), and a few times in the patristic writings (cf. G.W.H. Lampe, *A Patristic Lexicon* [Oxford: Clarendon, 1961], p. 393). The difficulty in Paul's letters stems from the profundity of the God-given wisdom they contain. Apparently false teachers were seeking to use Pauline support for their opposition to Peter. Paul's letters contain things—e.g., slogans and arguments—that can be given meanings far beyond what Paul intended. (For examples of this, see esp. Rom 3:8; 5:20-6:1; 7:25; 1 Cor 6:12-13; 8:4.)

The unlearned (*amatheis*; NIV, "ignorant") are those who have not learned the apostolic teaching (Acts 2:42) nor have they been taught by the Father (John 6:45). They are "unstable" (*astēriktoi*) because they are without a foundation (cf. comments on 2:14). They "distort" the things in Paul's letters as they do the "other Scriptures." The word "distort" (*strebloō*, "twist," "torment") is used in the papyri of torture. Like Satan, the false teachers and their followers can quote Scripture out of context for their purpose (cf. Matt 4:6).

Does Peter's expression "the other Scriptures" (*tas loipas graphas*) imply that Paul's writings were already considered Scripture by this time (c.A.D. 64)? This is the normal understanding of the Greek (BAG, p. 481; cf. Introduction: Authorship and Canonicity). Bigg (pp. 301-2) cites some evidence that the expression could be translated "the Scriptures as well" or "the Scriptures on the other hand," but his NT example from 1 Thessalonians 4:13 is not parallel because it contains a distinguishing phrase ("who have no hope"). That Paul's writings should be considered "Scripture"— authoritative writing—is not surprising, for from the moment of composition they had the authority of commands of the Lord through his apostle (Rom 1:1; 1 Cor 14:37; Gal 1:1).

Twisting the Scriptures leads to "destruction" (*apōleia,* cf. comments at 2:1, 3) because it is the rejection of God's way and the setting up of one's own way in opposition to God (cf. Rom 8:7). In a time when the Christian church is plagued by heretical cults and false teaching, Peter's warning about the irresponsible use of Scripture is important. Correct exegesis must be a continuing concern of the church.

3. *The Need to Guard Against Error and to Grow in Grace*

3:17–18

> ¹⁷Therefore, dear friends, since you already know this, be on your guard so that you may not be carried away by the error of lawless men and fall from your secure position. ¹⁸But grow in the grace and knowledge of our Lord and Savior Jesus Christ. To him be glory both now and forever! Amen.

17–18 With an affectionate reference to his readers—"Therefore, dear friends" (*hymeis oun agapētoi;* lit., "You, therefore, beloved")—Peter begins his conclusion. These two verses touch on the main themes of the letter and summarize its contents. First, there is the reminder for his readers to watch out lest the false teachers lead them astray. Second, there is the exhortation to grow in Christ. The dominant motivation for writing this letter was Peter's love and concern for the flock (cf. the repeated use of *agapētoi*). Since he has told the believers beforehand about the false teachers, they are able to be on guard.

The "lawless" (*athesmoi*) men will attempt by their error to shift the believers off their spiritual foundation. The noun *stērigmos* ("secure position," NIV) occurs only here in the NT, but the related verb and adjective are important in Peter's life (cf. Luke 22:32 of Jesus' command to Peter) and also in this letter (cf. 2:14; 3:16). The Christians' guarding against false teachers includes (1) prior knowledge of their activities, (2) warning against their immoral lives (2 Peter 2; Matt 7:16: "By their fruit you will recognize them"), (3) reminders of the historicity of the apostolic message (2 Peter 1:16–18), (4) the prophetic teaching of the past (2 Peter 1:19; 3:1–2), and (5) the warning of judgment, e.g., the Flood.

Now Peter speaks positively: "But grow in the grace and knowledge of our Lord and Savior Jesus Christ." In 1:3–11 he has already stressed the necessity for progress in Christian living. Green (*Peter and Jude,* p. 150) says, "The Christian life . . . is like riding a bicycle. Unless you keep moving, you fall off!" John says that the knowledge of God and Christ is "eternal life" (John 17:3). But as Paul says, Christians never in this life attain all there is in Christ; so their goal is to know Christ in a fuller, more intimate way (Phil 3:10–13; cf. Eph 1:17).

The closing doxology is notable for its direct ascription of "glory" (*hē doxa;* lit., "the glory") to Christ. For a Jew who has learned the great words in Isaiah 42:8—"I am the LORD; that is my name! I will not give my glory to another"—this doxology is a clear confession of Christ (cf. John 5:23: "that all may honor the Son just as they honor the Father"). This supreme honor belongs to Jesus Christ today ("now") and "forever" (lit., "unto the day of the age"). So Peter finally points his readers to the new age, "the day of the Lord," when Christ will be manifested in all his glory.

1 JOHN

Glenn W. Barker

1 JOHN

Introduction

The Epistles of John are foundational to what is known in the NT as Johannine Christianity. Even as his gospel account is distinct from the others in content, structure, and theological emphasis, so John's epistles differ in style and content from the other NT letters. Although numbered among the Catholic or General Epistles, John's epistles have little in common with them. His are not concerned with the problem of institutionalizing the Christian Movement, nor do they fit easily into any historical reconstruction of the growth and development of the Christian church in the world.

If John's epistles address the problem of heresy, they do so in unconventional terms. They insist that true Christian faith requires knowing that Jesus the Christ came in human flesh, lived a human life, and died in the flesh. But the evidence of that faith is measured by the genuineness of one's Christian lifestyle, not so much by what one "knows." The knowledge that God is light is tested by whether one walks in that light and obeys God's commands. The knowledge that God is righteous is tested by whether one lives righteously as befits one born of God. The knowledge that God is love is tested by whether one loves fellow believers even as one loves God. The single but radical requirement for love and obedience in the Johannine Epistles recalls the simplicity of Jesus' own teaching and the radical response he required of those who would follow him. The ability of these letters to recall to the church its origins and cause it to hear afresh the word of him who came in the flesh has preserved a special place for them in the life and devotion of the church.

1. Background

Establishing the background for the Johannine Epistles is at best speculative. Whereas for the Pauline Epistles we have the Book of Acts with its treatment of the origin of the church, the conversion of the apostle, and a record of his subsequent journeys to provide background for understanding his epistles, we have nothing similar for the Johannine material. While Paul's epistles fairly bristle with historical allusions that we can readily identify from other sources, those of John contain almost no references to known persons or places. Nonetheless, traditions relating to the origin of these writings did develop in the church. And since there are no alternatives, it is these traditions that have been largely responsible for providing the historical background for interpreting these letters. Traditions that existed uncontested from the third to the eighteenth centuries connected them and the fourth Gospel with the apostle John, recognized Asia as the place of their publication, and identified Cerinthianism as the heresy troubling the Johannine churches.

The tradition concerning authorship is preserved in the writings of Irenaeus and in the Muratorian Canon. The assumption is that 1 John and John's Gospel have a common origin. Irenaeus quotes copiously from 1 John and attributes it to John the disciple of the Lord.[1] The Muratorian Canon includes the following testimony:

> The fourth of the Gospels, that of John, [one] of the disciples. When his fellow disciple and bishops urged him, he said: Fast with me from today for three days, and what will be revealed to each one let us relate to one another. In the same night it was revealed to Andrew, one of the apostles, that whilst all were to go over [it], John in his own name should write everything down. . . . For so he confesses [himself] [in 1 John 1:1] not merely an eye and ear witness, but also a writer of all the marvels of the Lord in order.[2]

Regarding John's Epistles, the Muratorian Fragment testifies that two are received by the Catholic Church. Whether 1 John is omitted because of its previous inclusion in the missing opening portion of the Fragment, as Gregory maintained, is not of great significance. All agree that the Muratorian Canon certainly meant to testify to the full authority of 1 John and that it clearly supports Irenaeus's view of its authorship.

Asia as the place of the epistle's publication finds support from two lines of tradition. First, there is the direct statement of Irenaeus: "Afterward John, the disciple of the Lord, who also had leaned upon his breast, himself published his gospel, while he was living at Ephesus in Asia" (*Contra Haereses* 3.1.1). Second, the earliest-known references to the epistle are by church leaders from Asia. Polycarp of Smyrna appears to have been depending on 1 John when he asserted that whoever does not confess that Jesus Christ has come in the flesh is antichrist. Polycarp likewise urges a return to the message handed down from the beginning.[3] Eusebius testifies that Papias of Hierapolis quoted from 1 John.[4]

The tradition identifying Cerinthus as the opponent of 1 John also depends on Irenaeus. He preserved a description from Polycarp of an encounter between the apostle and Cerinthus in a public bathhouse, which John hurriedly left so that he would not have to bathe in the same place with such an enemy of the truth.[5] Irenaeus also described in some detail the heresy of Cerinthus.[6] Cerinthus, he said,

> represented Jesus as having not been born of a virgin, but as being the son of Joseph and Mary according to the ordinary course of human generation, while he

---

[1] *Contra Haereses* 3.16.5, 8.
[2] E. Hennecke and W. Schneemelcher, *New Testament Apocrypha*, trans. R. McL. Wilson et al., 2 vols. (London: Lutterworth, 1963–65), vol. 1, *Gospels and Related Writings* (1963), pp. 941–42.
[3] *To the Philippians* 7.1–2; cf. 1 John 2:24; 3:8; 4:2–3.
[4] *Ecclesiastical History* 3.39.
[5] *Contra Haereses* 3.4.
[6] Ibid., 1.26.1.

nevertheless was more righteous, prudent and wise than other men. Moreover, after his baptism, Christ descended upon him in the form of a dove from the Supreme Ruler, and that then he proclaimed the unknown Father, and performed miracles. But at last Christ departed from Jesus, and that then Jesus suffered and rose again, while Christ remained impassible, inasmuch as he was a spiritual being.[7]

Traditional critics see strong evidence that Cerinthus was the opponent of the apostle in the insistence in 1 John that Jesus was the Son of God; that he came as the Christ in the flesh; and that his baptism, his suffering, and his dying make up the redemptive event.

The conclusions Westcott drew from this traditional material, and which have been followed by many of the earlier exegetes, are that (1) the Epistle is "addressed primarily to a circle of Asiatic Churches, of which Ephesus was the centre" (p. xxxii), (2) the false teaching with which John is involved "is Docetic and specifically Cerinthian" (p. xxxiv), and (3) the false teaching was a "condensed moral and practical application of the gospel" (p. xxx).

While there remains some general support for the reconstruction advanced by Westcott among the modern exegetes, there are also some significant departures from it. Asia continues as the clear choice of modern scholars for the place of publication. Comparison of the problems presented in 1 John with the more complete description of the heresies of the second century now available from recent finds provides additional support for Asia as the place where 1 John originated.

It is not absolutely certain, however, that Cerinthus was the opponent of John or that the heresy in view in the Epistle resulted from a Gnostic theological movement that had infiltrated the church. The internal evidence strongly suggests that the heresy arose within the church and was propogated by respected and able teachers in the community who had defected from the true faith and fellowship (2:19). Indeed, the seriousness of the situation probably derived from the fact that past leaders had become "false prophets," teaching untruths and becoming embodiments of Antichrist. That they were able to lead the community astray (2:26; 3:7) gives strong support to the idea they were secessionists, not intruders. Moreover, while they held some ideas in common with Cerinthus, it is clear that they also differed from him in significant ways. There is no reflection in 1 John of Cerinthus's distinctions between the supreme God and the series of divine emanations proceeding downward to the aeon who was Christ and who created the material universe. (For further discussion on Gnosticism, see introduction to commentary on Colossians in EBC, 11:166–67.) Furthermore, the false teachers in 1 John appear to draw theological conclusions that have no parallels in Cerinthian Gnosticism. The espousal of sinlessness (1:8, 10), their claim to know God through inspiration (2:4; 4:1–3), their loss of "fellowship" with God (1:6), and their life in the light (2:9) seem to be independent of Cerinthus's teaching. The attempt to identify the false teachers with Cerinthus or his followers is therefore dubious.

Alternate suggestions for the identity of the false teachers have lacked scholarly consensus. Schnackenburg (pp. 20ff.) suggests that a better case can be made for the Docetic heretics attacked by Ignatius. They were known for resisting belief in the validity of Jesus' suffering and for denying the reality of his flesh. Moreover, they are

---

[7]Ibid., 28.1.

described as being without love or compassion for the oppressed and afflicted. Yet Schnackenburg acknowledges that the false prophets of 1 John differ at numerous points from the Docetics of Ignatius and concludes that it is impossible to identify the heretics in 1 John with any who are known to us historically.

Marshall (p. 21) identifies the opponents with Christians

> who felt that they had moved beyond the elementary stages of orthodox theology to a new position which called affirmations into question. . . . Relying on their belief that they were inspired by the Spirit and claiming a direct knowledge of God, they thought that they no longer needed Jesus or his teaching. Under the influence of Docetism they argued against a real incarnation of the Son of God in Jesus, and probably adopted a view like that of Cerinthus or Basilides, that the Christ or Son of God inhabited Jesus only for a temporary period.

Although Marshall's reconstruction is essentially acceptable, it does leave unanswered the question of how the heresy happened to develop in such a distinctive form within the church and why it grew into such a powerful movement.

At this point Dodd's theory provides some help. He sees the root of the problem in the confrontation of Christianity with the "evangelistic and pietistic religious movements" developing within the "higher paganism" characteristic of the Hellenistic world but especially present in Asia. When the missionaries of the Christian faith first came into contact with the representatives of these movements, they undoubtedly received, at least initially, a warm welcome. The eclectic character of these advocates of "higher paganism" would make sure that they would be prepared "to adopt Christianity as they had already tried to adopt Judaism" (pp. xvi–xvii).

As Dodd shows, the Johannine community already reflected some of the language style of this world. He believes therefore that one could expect the Johannine community to be unusually successful in its missionary effort among such persons. Converts from this particular milieu would inevitably bring philosophical and religious verbiage with them into the community that would require an extensive theological response by the teachers. The Gospel of John may in itself represent not only a missionary document for these persons but some response to the questions raised by the converts. Inevitably, however, a significant number of the faithful would prove vulnerable to pagan reinterpretation that borrowed from Christian categories.

In his First Epistle John seems to recognize this pull and seeks to help those trying not to fall back into non-Christian speculation. On the other hand, as Dodd points out, the community would inevitably contain some "enthusiastic but ill-informed converts to Christianity," who would be eager to reinterpret their new found faith "in terms of modern thought" (ibid., p. xvii). The false teachers who previously had been in the community and had then departed, proving that they had not really belonged to the community, may well have been representatives of such a movement. They would be presenting themselves as preserving the best of both traditions.

Furthermore, the false teachers' motive, at least in the beginning, may have been prompted only by the desire to translate the gospel into the terms of another culture. Their enthusiasm would likely blind them to the fact that their reinterpretation would ultimately lead to the dissolution of what was central to the Christian faith: Jesus as the Son of God through whose death the bonds of sin had finally been destroyed. If this reconstruction is valid, it would help explain why these new "false teachers" had such a strong position in the community. Originally they had belonged to those who had been most involved in the missionary activity of the community. That they no longer were true to the faith and were to be classed as antichrists would certainly be hard for some of the community to accept.

2. Occasion and Purpose

It is clear from the internal evidence of 1 John that a developing schism within the Christian community led to its writing. The difficulty had already reached a point where some members, including teachers, had separated themselves from the others and were in the process of setting up their own community (1 John 2:19). Although the breach was complete, the dissidents continued to keep in touch with the rest of the membership and were actively trying to entice them to join the new group (2:26). With the breach of fellowship, there came also a breach in understanding the faith. What earlier may have been hypothetical questions now became tenets of the rival community, identified in John's epistles primarily by what the false teachers denied. They denied that Jesus was the Christ, the Son of God (2:22; 5:1, 5). They denied that the Christ had come in the flesh (4:2; 2 John 7). They denied authority to Jesus' commands (2:4). They denied their own sinfulness (1:8, 10). They denied salvation through the work of Christ (2:2). They denied the absolute demand that believers love one another (2:9). They denied righteous conduct as a requirement of fellowship with God (1:6; 2:29; 3:6, 10). They denied the responsibility to live as Jesus had lived (2:4, 6; 3:7). They denied the nature of the company of believers as a community of fellowship with the Father, with his Son, and with one another (1:3; 2:11). They denied the authority of the writer of the Epistles as the proclaimer of the message that had been from the beginning (1:5; 3 John 10). They denied that the members of the community who did not follow them were in the truth (2:20–21).

It is harder to reconstruct the points at which the false teachers agreed with the community of faith. Apparently they believed in God as light (1:5). They seemed to have believed that the truth of the gospel released them from the power of sin (1:8). They also seemed to have believed in the Christ as a philosophical concept, though denying his existence in the flesh (4:2). They believed in the mission to the world (2 John 10). They apparently held to the anointing of the Spirit (2:27). They probably believed in the devil as an anti-God (3:8–10; 4:2–3).

The writer responded to the false teachers by recognizing them as a supreme danger threatening the very life and faith of the community. He saw that what was called for was a positive reaffirmation of the cardinal doctrines of the faith that have been from the beginning and a clear and explicit exposure of the heresies the dissidents were promoting. He also sensed the need for reassuring the faithful. So he gave his letter a strong pastoral flavor. Its contents are marked by strong affirmations and words of encouragement for the community—viz., that the nature of the fellowship is one of love and righteousness (1:3, 7), that its origin is from the beginning (1:1), that in the community there is genuine forgiveness of sins (1:9) and a walk of obedience not unlike Jesus' own example (2:6), that walking in the light is living in love (2:10), that members of the community will not be ashamed at Jesus' coming (2:28), and that they may have complete confidence in his answering their prayers (3:22). Warnings are addressed to the community against the seduction of the world (2:15), against the present antichrist, (2:18), and against false spirits and false prophets (3:22; 4:1–2). Reminders to the members of their anointing (2:20) as being sufficient to enable them to remain in God (4:13) are provided as well as promises that belong to them as the children of God (3:1). Jesus Christ as the epitome and example of love to the community becomes a critical theme (3:16–18) just as the proclamation that God himself is love (4:16), that love derives from him, and that the Christian life is lived in him (4:12–13) are also critical themes. Again and again the letter returns to the primary confession that Jesus is the Christ, the one who has come in the flesh and has overcome the world. He is the true God and eternal life (5:20).

3. Structure

The development of the Epistle is fascinating. In some places it seems intricately structured; in others it seems rambling and disconnected. Outlines offered by various commentators reflect this.[8] R. Law represents those who see the Epistle as significantly structured. He is impressed with its recurring themes and thinks the ideas develop in the form of an ascending spiral. His outline is as follows:

Prologue. 1:1–4
1. First Cycle. 1:5–2:28. The Christian life as fellowship with God (walking in the Light), tested by righteousness (1:8–2:6), love (2:7–17), and belief (2:18–28).
2. Second Cycle. 2:29–4:6. Divine sonship tested by righteousness (2:29–3:10a), love (3:10b–24a), and belief (3:24b–4:6).
3. Third Cycle. 4:7–5:21. Closer correlation of righteousness, love, and belief.

P.R. Jones also sees the Epistle as significantly structured but thinks the structure develops from statements about the nature of God.

Prologue. 1:1–4.
  I. God is light. 1:5–2:27.
    1. Communion with God and confession of sin. 1:5–2:2.
    2. Communion with God and obedience. 2:3–11.
    3. Attitude toward the world. 2:12–17.
    4. Warning against the antichrists. 2:18–27.
  II. God is righteousness. 2:28–4:6.
    1. The righteous children of God. 2:28–3:10.
    2. The righteous love of the children of God. 3:11–18.
    3. Confidence before God. 3:19–24.
    4. Warning against the spirit of antichrist. 4:1–6.
  III. God is love. 4:7–5:12.
    1. The nature of true agape. 4:7–21.
    2. Cruciality of faith in Jesus. 5:1–12.
Epilogue. 5:13–21.

On the other hand, Marshall represents those who see the Epistle as primarily unstructured. He thinks the organization of the Epistle is "governed by association of ideas rather than by a logical plan."

---

[8]The following three outlines are from Marshall, pp. 22–26.

Prologue—the Word of life. 1:1–4.
Walking in the light. 1:5–2:2.
Keeping his commands. 2:3–11.
The new status of believers and their relation to the world. 2:12–17.
A warning against antichrists. 2:18–27.
The hope of God's children. 2:28–3:3.
The sinlessness of God's children. 3:4–10.
Brotherly love as the mark of the Christian. 3:11–18.
Assurance and obedience. 3:19–24.
The spirits of truth and falsehood. 4:1–6.
God's love and our love. 4:7–12.
Assurance and Christian love. 4:13–5:4.
The true faith confirmed. 5:5–12.
Christian certainties. 5:13–21.

In the outline presented in section 8, the writer of this Epistle is seen as following a somewhat structured approach without being bound by it. He is quite willing to depart from the structure in order to allow room for the introduction of divergent themes as well as overlapping ones. As the exposition will show, the writer of the Epistle deals with the problems raised by the schismatic actions of the "false teachers." He does this within the context of a general exposition that focuses on the nature and life of the community of God. His deepest concern is pastoral. He desires to reassure, protect, alert, and teach the faithful members about their life together as the people of God. To accomplish this the writer shows that "from the beginning" the basis of the believing community is Jesus Christ. He is the one through whom fellowship with the Father and with the members of the community becomes possible. This fellowship is further defined as life in him and as eternal life.

The writer asserts that the fellowship of believers draws its character from God, who is light, righteousness, and love. It is these attributes of God, shown by Jesus our example, that in turn become criteria for the standard of conduct expected of the children of God. Obedience to him thus becomes a primary obligation of the community.

The writer makes clear that the fellowship is exclusive. It consists of those born of God who are committed to obedience to his Son's commands and example; who confess Jesus as the Christ, the incarnate Son of God; and who depend on him for forgiveness and for overcoming the evil one. So the writer provides tests by which the false teachers can be exposed and the faithful members of the community reinforced in their own confidence that they truly are the children of God. Over and over he stresses the fact that the test of true faith and practice for those born of God is to love one's brother. This becomes the final test for walking in the light, living in truth and righteousness, and loving God. Into all this the writer also weaves his pastoral concern for the flock entrusted to his care.

4. Authorship

The author of 1 John never identifies himself in the Epistle. Apparently his identity was so well known to his "children" that he knew they would recognize him by what he wrote. We do get an ambiguous clue in 2 and 3 John when he uses the title "elder" to address them. The fourth Gospel is likewise unidentified as to authorship except that in the epilogue there is the enigmatic statement about "the disciple whom Jesus loved" (21:20; cf. 13:23): "This is the disciple who testifies to these things and who wrote them down" (21:24).

For those who recognize common authorship for the Gospel of John and John's epistles, it is possible through a process of elimination to identify the "beloved" disciple as John the son of Zebedee. Since this identity is also attested by the universal witness from the traditions of the church from the end of the second century forward, a large number of critics have accepted Johannine authorship for both the Gospel of John and the Epistles. A more detailed presentation of this evidence is given by Merrill C. Tenney in the Introduction to his commentary on the Gospel of John in volume 9 of this Commentary. See also Morris's comprehensive treatment.[9]

Strong objections to this identification have been made by critical investigators. Many modern exegetes eliminate the apostle John as author on stylistic and linguistic grounds ("The Gnostic language of the Johannine Jesus discourses make impossible the composition of John by an apostle") and because the Gospel "was able to make its way along so slowly and against opposition" into the mainstream of the church.[10]

These objections, however, are largely based on a reconstruction of events that see the Gospel and the Epistle written in response to "Gnostic" influence. These events have traditionally been located outside Palestine and generally assigned a date in the second century. But the Qumran writings certainly indicate that what has been called "Gnostic" language was already in use in Palestine before Jesus' birth. For a gospel to use this kind of language does not necessarily prove it to be non-Palestinian.

Second, Gnosticism may owe its later development—rather than its origin (cf. Brown, pp. 145–46)—to those who seceded from the Johannine community. If that is so, it is easy to see why the Johannine writings would cause difficulty for the main body of the church. That the fourth Gospel was known and cited by the defectors, that they used thought forms similar to those in the Gospel and in the Johannine Epistles, would cast a shadow on these writings. There would certainly be reluctance on the part of the church to cite them in debate with the Gnostics and their predecessors lest the church appear to concede the argument. Nevertheless the church was able to distinguish the two bodies of literature, accepting the Johannine literature as belonging to the apostolic witness, while rejecting the Gnostic materials. On balance and in view of what is now known, the best answer to the question of the authorship of the fourth Gospel and the Johannine Epistles is that the apostle John wrote them.

5. Date

The date for the Epistles of John is at best very problematic. It depends largely on our ability to reconstruct the history of the Johannine community. This community

---

[9]Leon Morris, *The Gospel According to St. John,* NIC (Grand Rapids: Eerdmans, 1971), pp. 8–30.
[10]Paul Feine and Johannes Behm, *Introduction to the New Testament,* ed. W. Kümmel (Nashville: Abingdon, 1966), p. 174.

may have begun about the same time as the church at Antioch. Persecution may have finally driven the leaders from Jerusalem, and John may have gathered with some of the Samaritan converts along with the former followers of the Baptist. They probably located somewhere in southern Palestine and continued their mission to the Jews.

Sometime before A.D. 70 (Brown thinks closer to 80), perhaps as a result of increased hostility from the Jews, the Johannine community migrated to Asia Minor and initiated what became a very successful mission to those Gentiles whose religious orientation was in the direction of "higher paganism."

The need for a gospel that would double as a missionary document for these converts became evident, and the Gospel of John was published somewhere around A.D. 75–80 to meet this challenge. It expresses its own purpose clearly: "These are written that you may believe that Jesus is the Christ, the Son of God, and that by believing you may have life in his name" (20:31).

The heretical developments discussed elsewhere in this Introduction took place during the next ten years and finally resulted in the secession of some members of the community in order to found a rival one. First John was written as a response to this crisis somewhere around 85–90. That it was written to reassure the faithful is also clear from its author's own testimony: "I write these things to you who believe in the name of the Son of God so that you may know that you have eternal life" (5:13). The letter is addressed to a single community but probably was meant to circulate throughout the geographical area where Johannine churches had been established.

The Second and Third Epistles of John are brief letters written to what appear to be member churches in other places. These churches also appear in danger of problems created by the secessionists. So the two letters were apparently written in anticipation of these problems.

The perspective of 1 John is clearly reflected in 2 John. The community addressed in it has been faithful to "the truth" (i.e., the gospel) as the "elder" has proclaimed it (v.4). He warns, however, against traveling missionaries whom he expects to visit this locality soon (v.10). Evidently they will present themselves as emissaries of the secessionists and continue to spread their false teaching (v.7). The elder warns the church neither to extend hospitality to such emissaries nor even to welcome them into the community (v.11). Second John was probably written not long after 1 John.

The background of 3 John is more obscure, despite its personal references. It seems best to consider that the situation was the same for 3 John as for 1 and 2 John. If so, still another community is addressed—a community in which there appear to be several groups of Christians in "house" churches as well as one larger group or church led by one Diotrephes (v.9). The smaller house churches, one led by Gaius and another apparently led by Demetrius, have remained faithful to the elder. They remain "in the truth" and "in love." They have received missionaries from the elder's faithful community and have shown them the proper hospitality (vv.5–8). But the elder complains against Diotrephes, the description of whom shows that he has been affected by the secessionists. He "gossips" maliciously against the elder and refuses to receive his message. He even goes so far as to throw out of the church anyone who welcomes the faithful "brothers" from the elder's community (v.10).

There would appear to be an interval of time between 2 John and 3 John. The situation has grown decidedly worse in the place where Gaius ministers than in that where the "chosen lady" is. Probably one would do well to think of an interval of a year or more between the two Epistles. Their date may be placed around A.D. 90.

6. Relation to Other Writings

With a few notable exceptions, modern critics agree that the evidence points to a common author for 1, 2, and 3 John. They also concur that there is a strong connection between 1 John and the Gospel of John, though they do not all agree as to the best explanation of this connection.

Historically, the relationship between the Gospel and the First Epistle has been explained in accord with tradition—viz., on the basis of common authorship. Internal evidence strongly supports this conclusion. Among modern critics, Brooke (pp. i–xv) best presents this view. He includes the lists originally developed by Holtzmann with even a more complete citing of the parallel passages from the Greek text. His material provides graphic evidence of the relationship between the two writings. He demonstrates their common vocabulary, similar style, overlapping ideas, a singular point of view, and a shared theology. Though he raises the question of imitation, he shows that the nature of the relation between the Gospel and the First Epistle makes common authorship a far more likely possibility than imitation.

Nevertheless, a significant number of modern critics dissociate themselves from that conclusion. The relationship they propose is not one of literary dependence but common style and vocabulary resulting from membership in a common or Johannine school. Thus they surmise a coterie of teachers who lived, taught, and ministered within a common theological heritage. Members of this coterie traced their roots to the apostle John and remained within their particular theological milieu. They were responsible for the different layers and development of sources associated with the Gospel of John as well as for certain redactional activity connected with that writing. The sources for the Gospel of John and its redactions, the Epistles of John, and the bulk of Revelation are believed by these critics to owe their existence to members of this Johannine school. The only external evidence, however, for someone other than the apostle John as author is drawn from this difficult-to-interpret testimony of Papias, quoted by Eusebius:

> If anyone came who had followed the presbyters, I was accustomed to inquire about the sayings of the presbyters, what Andrew or what Peter had said, or Philip or Thomas or Jacob or John or Matthew or any other of the Lord's disciples, and what Aristion and the presbyter John, the disciple of the Lord, say.[11]

Papias's statement certainly allows the possibility that there were two disciples named John. However, it does not establish beyond all doubt that the presbyter John whom he identifies as a disciple of the Lord may not also have been one of the Twelve. The link with Aristion may indicate that Aristion and the presbyter John were "personal disciples" of the Lord other than the Twelve. Nevertheless, Papias's chief intention was to distinguish between what had been said by disciples (known to others) and what these two disciples were saying. In either instance, according to Papias's statement, we are dealing only with persons who were historical disciples of the Lord. Thus the eyewitness factor is not changed, nor does the age of the persons enter into the question. Moreover, we have no historical evidence connecting the writing of either the Gospel of John or 1 John with any John other than the son of Zebedee.

---

[11]*Ecclesiastical History* 39.4.

The most extensive argument based on internal evidence for different authors of the Epistle and the Gospel was worked out by Dodd. As evidence for his hypothesis, he lists linguistic differences—viz., omission of key words, phrases, or ideas; words or phrases used in different ways or with different meanings; and altered theological perspectives.[12] Other modern supporters for different authors include Bultmann, Haenchen, Conzelmann, G. Klein, and, more recently, R.E. Brown and Schnackenburg.

Supporters for common authorship maintain that the difference between John's Gospel and the First Epistle can be accounted for on the ground of differing purposes and an interval of time between the two publications. They argue that none of the differences requires a different author and say that the likenesses are so indisputable that they require the hypothesis of a complex Johannine school for which no historical evidence exists.

On balance and on the basis of present evidence, single authorship appears to be the simpler explanation of the data. As Kümmel points out, "There hardly exists adequate reason to suppose another author."[13] But if another author is proposed, this requires a person with a viewpoint so similar to that of the author of the Gospel that it makes little difference in the end whether one holds to one or two authors.

7. Bibliography

Books

Alexander, J.N.S. *The Epistles of John*. Torch Bible Commentaries. London: SCM, 1962.

Barclay, William. *The Letters of John*. Daily Study Bible Series. Philadelphia: Westminster, 1976.

Barker, Glenn; Lane, W.L.; and Michaels, J.R. *The New Testament Speaks*. New York: Harper & Row, 1969.

Boice, James Montgomery. *The Epistles of John*. Grand Rapids: Zondervan, 1979.

Brooke, A.E. *A Critical and Exegetical Commentary on the Johannine Epistles*. ICC. Edinburgh: T. & T. Clark, 1912.

Brown, R.E. *The Community of the Beloved Disciple*. New York: Paulist, 1979.

Bruce, F.F. *The Epistles of John: Introduction, Exposition, and Notes*. Grand Rapids: Eerdmans, 1970.

Brunner, Emil. *The Misunderstanding of the Church*. Translated by H. Knight. Philadelphia: Westminster, 1953.

Bultmann, Rudolf. *The Johannine Epistles*. Hermeneia Series. Translated by R. Phillip O'Hara, et al. Philadelphia: Fortress, 1973.

Dodd, C.H. *The Johannine Epistles*. MNT. London: Hodder and Stoughton, 1946.

Haas, C.; deJonge, M.; and Swellengrebel, J.L. *A Translator's Handbook on the Letters of John*. Helps for Translators, *Volume XIII*. London: United Bible Societies, 1972.

Harrison, E.F. *Introduction to the New Testament*. Grand Rapids: Eerdmans, 1964.

Houlden, J.L. *A Commentary on the Johannine Epistles*. Black's New Testament Commentaries. London: Black, 1973.

Johnston, G. "I, II, III John." *Peake's Commentary on the Bible*. Edited by Matthew Black and H.H. Rowley. New York: Nelson, 1962.

---

[12]C.H. Dodd, "The Johannine Epistles" BJRL, 21 (April 1972), ix.

[13]Feine and Behm, *Introduction to the NT*, p. 312.

Law, R. *The Tests of Life: A Study of the First Epistle of St. John.* Edinburgh: T. & T. Clark, 1914.

Marshall, I.H. *The Epistles of John.* NIC. Grand Rapids: Eerdmans, 1978.

Marxsen, Willi. *Introduction to the New Testament: An Approach to its Problems.* Translated by G. Buswell. Philadelphia: Fortress, 1968.

Morris, Leon. "1 John, 2 John, 3 John." *New Bible Commentary Revised.* Edited by D. Guthrie, et al. Grand Rapids: Eerdmans, 1970.

O'Neill, J.C. *The Puzzle of 1 John.* London: SPCK, 1966.

Ross, A. *The Epistles of James and John.* NIC. Grand Rapids: Eerdmans, 1954.

Ryrie, C.C. "Commentary on 1, 2, 3 John." *Wycliffe Bible Commentary.* Edited by C.F. Pfeiffer and E.F. Harrison. Chicago: Moody, 1962.

Schnackenburg, R. *Die Johannesbriefe.* Herders Theologische Kommentar zum Neuen Testament. Freiburg: Herder, 1973.

Stott, J.R.W. *The Epistles of St. John.* TNTC. Grand Rapids: Eerdmans, 1964.

Wengst, K. *Häresie und Orthodoxie im Spiegel des ersten Johannesbriefes.* Gutersloh: Mohn, 1976.

Westcott, B.F. *The Epistles of St. John: The Greek Text with Notes and Essays.* London: Macmillan, 1883.

Articles

Feuillet, A. "The Structure of First John. Comparison with the Fourth Gospel. The Pattern of Christian Life." *Biblical Theology* 3 (1973), 194–216.

Filson, F.V. "First John: Purpose and Message." *Interpretation* 23 (1969), 259–76.

Funk, R.W. "The Form and Structure of II and III John." *Journal of Biblical Literature* 86 (1967), 424–30.

Horvath, T. "3 John 11b: An Early Ecumenical Creed?" *Expository Times* 85 (1974), 339–40.

Hunter, A.M. "Recent Trends in Johannine Studies." *Expository Times* 71 (1960), 164–67, 219–22.

Minear, P.S. "The Idea of Incarnation in First John." *Interpretation* 24 (1970), 291–302.

Moody, Dale. "The Theology of the Johannine Letters." *Southwestern Journal of Theology* 13 (1970), 7–22.

Ward, R.A. "The Theological Pattern of the Johannine Epistles." *Southwestern Journal of Theology* 13 (1970), 23–39.

8. Outline

I. Preface (1:1–4)

II. Requirements for Fellowship With God Who Is Light (1:5–2:28)
1. Walking in the Light (1:5–2:2)
2. Obeying His Commands (2:3–11)
3. Knowing the Father and Abiding Forever (2:12–17)
4. Warnings Against Antichrists (2:18–28)

III. Requirements for Fellowship With God Who Is Righteous (2:29–4:6)
1. Doing What Is Right (2:29–3:10)
2. Loving One Another (3:11–24)
3. Warning Against the False Spirits (4:1–6)

IV. Requirements for Fellowship With God Who Is Love (4:7–5:12)
1. Brotherly Love (4:7–12)
2. Living in God and Living in Love (4:13–16)
3. Love Displaces Fear (4:17–18)
4. Love Summarized (4:19–21)
5. Love for the Father and Faith in the Son (5:1–5)
6. The Spirit, the Water, and the Blood (5:6–12)

V. Concluding Remarks (5:13–21)

Text and Exposition

I. Preface

1:1–4

> [1]That which was from the beginning, which we have heard, which we have seen with our eyes, which we have looked at and our hands have touched—this we proclaim concerning the Word of life. [2]The life appeared; we have seen it and testify to it, and we proclaim to you the eternal life, which was with the Father and has appeared to us. [3]We proclaim to you what we have seen and heard, so that you also may have fellowship with us. And our fellowship is with the Father and with his Son, Jesus Christ. [4]We write this to make our joy complete.

1 The unusual nuance of feeling and thought present in the Greek of this Preface to the letter is difficult to catch in translation. Even to untangle its syntactical structure takes special effort. The four verses represent a single periodic sentence in Greek. But the main verb and subject "we proclaim" (*apangellomen*), which controls the whole sentence, does not appear until v.3, though in the NIV the translators have introduced it at the end of v.1 in order to help the English readers. Instead the Preface opens with the object of the verb. This consists of four relative clauses—"That which was from the beginning, which we have heard, which we have seen with our eyes, which we have looked at"—and is followed by a parenthesis in v.2 enlarging on "the Word of life." Only then are the subject and main verb introduced, with a restatement of the object "what we have seen and heard." Two purpose clauses, indicating the direction of the author's thinking—"that you also may have fellowship with us" and "to make our joy complete"—conclude the Preface.

This grammatical tangle should not lead us to infer that the author is careless in his written expression. Actually it is the main instance in the Epistle where such complexity occurs. What does confront us here is the intensity of the author's feeling when he reflects on the nature of the Christian message in the light of its very beginnings. Although the events the message is founded on occurred many years earlier, the immensity of their implication and the abiding mystery they represent retain the power to overwhelm his thinking and extend his literary skills as he witnesses to them. This first paragraph could be described as the author's language of ecstasy.

The reader is clearly pointed back to John 1:1—"In the beginning was the word"—and from there to Genesis 1:1—"In the beginning God"—with this difference: The Gospel deals with the "personal word" (*ho logos*), of his eternity and his entrance into time. The Epistle centers on the life heard and in turn proclaimed (cf. Acts 5:20; Phil 2:16). This message, the gospel, is from the beginning because it is of God. It precedes creation, time, and history. NEB perhaps strikes the right note in saying, "It was there from the beginning." But in God the message of life also draws near to humanity and finds its culmination in Jesus. In him the Word of life becomes incarnated, manifested, and hence can be seen, touched, and even handled.

According to Dodd (*Johannine Epistles*, p. 5), the author's stress is twofold. He is stating what has always been true about the gospel. His witness, unlike that of his opponents, represented neither innovation nor afterthought. Moreover his witness was based on the immediate evidence of the senses. It does not represent "airy speculation or *fabricated fable*" (emphasis his).

The use of the pronoun "we" assures the reader that the message is being proclaimed by those who had heard the gospel with their own ears and who had touched him with their own hands (perhaps a reference to the Resurrection appearances—Luke 24:39, John 20:24–29—but see Notes). Already the writer is mounting his polemic against the heretics who denied that Christ came in a human body.

2 Because this is the nub of John's argument, he takes pains to restate it: The life to which he bears witness, the life that was with the Father, is precisely the life manifested in the historical person of Jesus. That is why John can say he has seen it (*heōrakamen*), can bear personal witness to it (*martyroumen*), and can make an apostolic declaration concerning it (*apangellomen*). Westcott (p. 9) says, "The three verbs give in due sequence the ideas of personal experience, responsible affirmation, authoritative announcement, which are combined in the apostolic message." The phrase "eternal life" underscores the divine character of the life described, not its length.

3 This verse introduces the purpose of the Epistle: "that you also may have fellowship with us. And our fellowship is with the Father and with his Son, Jesus Christ." The Greek word rendered "fellowship" (*koinōnia*) occurs here and in v.6. It is not easily put into English. It has been translated "fellowship," "communion," "participation," "share a common life," and "partnership"; its root meaning is "common" or "shared" as opposed to "one's own." Hellenistic literature uses it to describe partners in business, joint owners of a piece of property, or shareholders in a common enterprise. In the NT it refers to Christians who share a common faith (Philem 6), who share possessions (Acts 2:44; 4:32), or who are partners in the gospel (Phil 1:5).

Koinōnia, with its derivatives, occurs over sixty times in the NT in reference to the supernatural life that Christians share. This supernatural life is disclosed in the incarnate Christ. It is the eternal life that comes from the Father and becomes the life shared individually and corporately by the company of believers. It is what causes the oneness of faith. "The Koinonia ('fellowship') is the union in common faith brought about by the proclamation" (Bultmann, p. 12). Brunner (p. 12) says of this "fellowship" that it is its combining of the vertical with the horizontal, "the divine with the human," that constitutes its "utterly unparalleled life."

That the words "fellowship with us" precede in the text the words "fellowship is with the Father and with his Son, Jesus Christ" may be significant. Westcott (in loc.) sees here a reminder that there can be no fellowship with the Father or with the Son that is not based on apostolic witness. So John stresses "fellowship with us" as having priority in time. Brunner (p. 11) states it this way: "Therefore the community as bearer of the Word and Spirit of Christ precedes the individual believer. One does not first believe and then join the fellowship: but one becomes a believer just because one shares in the gift [the Holy Spirit] vouchsafed to the fellowship."

4 The author links his concern for his readers to his own standing as an apostolic witness. Their obedience will result in the completion of joy in him, and therefore also in them and in the whole fellowship. The joy he refers to is mentioned in his gospel: "I have told you this so that my joy may be in you and that your joy may be complete" (John 15:11). "Now is your time of grief, but I will see you again and you will rejoice, and no one will take away your joy. In that day you will no longer ask me anything. . . . Ask and you will receive, and your joy will be complete" (John

16:22–24). "I say these things while I am still in the world, so that they may have the full measure of my joy within them" (John 17:13).

Clearly this joy is inseparable from the salvation that is present in the Son, but it is directly bound up with the person of the Son, who is himself present in the fellowship. Joy is a gift of the Father, even as the Son is a gift of the Father, and is present wherever the fellowship truly appears. But joy can never be perfectly known or fully complete because the fellowship itself, though real, is imperfectly realized. The present joy in the fellowship is a token of the ultimate expression of joy, which depends on the final revelation of the Son. In the Gospel, this final revelation required Jesus' "going away" so that he may "come again" (cf. John 16:16).

Notes

1 Bultmann's dating of the Johannine literature makes its composition by an eyewitness impossible. His first alternative in dealing with the "we" is to distinguish contemporaneity with the historical event from contemporaneity with the eschatological event. The "we" of 1 John is for Bultmann those who were "eschatological contemporaries" of Jesus. Though the verbs used in the text indicate sense perception, Bultmann sees them as used against the gnosticizing Christians who sever the present eschatological relationship from the historical. But would this not place the writer in an impossible position? Would his enemies allow him to represent himself as an eyewitness to an event of which he himself had no more information than they did?

Bultmann's second alternative has more merit, though it is equally difficult. Those who bore witness, he says, are the "bearers of the tradition," and as such they have personal authority over the congregation. But if there is no correspondence between the author's claim to being an eyewitness and the facts of history, would the author's enemies allow him this platform from which to launch an attack? Would they permit him to describe himself as an eyewitness? The better explanation still appears to be that the author is building his case on the fact that he is one who bears the tradition precisely *because* the manifestation of the truth of the gospel included him! (For Bultmann's interpretation, see pp. 7–13 of his commentary.)

2 "Thus one cannot enter into His self-revelation merely by believing in a dogma, but only insofar as one has communion with Him through the Son, and therewith ceases to be an isolated individual. Insofar as one learns to know God, who gives Himself for us and wills to dwell with us, inasmuch as one learns to know Him in such wise that to know Him and to dwell with Him are one and the same, one is brought into the life of self-impartation for and communion with, mankind. Fellowship with Christ and fellowship with men are correlative, the one cannot exist without the other" (Brunner, p. 14).

II. Requirements for Fellowship With God Who Is Light (1:5–2:28)

1. *Walking in the Light*

1:5–2:2

⁵This is the message we have heard from him and declare to you: God is light; in him there is no darkness at all. ⁶If we claim to have fellowship with him yet walk in the darkness, we lie and do not live by the truth. ⁷But if we walk in the light, as he is in the light, we have fellowship with one another, and the blood of Jesus, his Son, purifies us from all sin.

⁸If we claim to be without sin, we deceive ourselves and the truth is not in us. ⁹If we confess our sins, he is faithful and just and will forgive us our sins and purify us from all unrighteousness. ¹⁰If we claim we have not sinned, we make him out to be a liar and his word has no place in our lives.

²:¹My dear children, I write this to you so that you will not sin. But if anybody does sin, we have one who speaks to the Father in our defense—Jesus Christ, the Righteous One. ²He is the atoning sacrifice for our sins, and not only for ours but also for the sins of the whole world.

If the readers are to have fellowship with the Father and with the Son (v.3), they must understand what makes this possible. They must know who God is in himself and, consequently, who they are in themselves as creatures of God. So the author first describes the moral character of God in terms of light (v.5) and then goes on to deny three claims made by those who falsely boast of their knowledge and fellowship with God. The false positions are (1) moral behavior is a matter of indifference in one's relationship to God (v.6); (2) immoral conduct does not issue in sin for one who knows God (v.8); and (3) the knowledge of God removes sin as even a possibility in the life of the believer (v.10). True "tests" or evidence of fellowship with God or walking in the light are (1) fellowship with one another (v.7), with subsequent cleansing by the blood of Christ; (2) confession of sin, (v.9) which brings both forgiveness and cleansing; and (3) trusting that if we sin we have Jesus Christ as an advocate and sacrifice for our sins (2:2).

5 John begins his exposition by referring to the message "heard from him," that is, from Jesus. The allusion is probably not to a specific word of Jesus (though it may include reference to the sum of his teaching) but to Jesus himself as the one sent, the Son in whose life and death the Father manifested himself. Again, in contrast to the false teachers he opposes, the author shows the authority that lies behind his own apostolic witness.

The message that "God is light" needs to be compared with the declarations elsewhere by John that "God is spirit" (John 4:24) and that "God is love" (1 John 4:8). All three stress the immateriality of God and the "Godness" of God—viz., God in his essence. Light emphasizes especially the splendor and glory of God, the truthfulness of God, and his purity.

Certain OT ideas dominate the Christian concept of "light" as a description of God. Light stresses the self-communicative nature of God. It is his nature to impart himself without limit. It stresses the action of God for man and for his salvation. The psalmist catches this with such utterances as "In your light we see light" (Ps 36:9) or "The LORD is my light and my salvation" (Ps 27:1). John expounds this in vv.5–7 (cf. John 1:9).

Light also accents God's empowering activity. God as light not only shines downward for man's salvation but enables him to walk in the light. Jesus said, "I am the light of the world. Whoever follows me will never walk in darkness, but will have the light of life" (John 8:12; cf. also 12:35). Likewise, in Ephesians 5:8–14, Paul exhorts believers to live as children of light. John similarly encourages his readers to walk in the light. Light, then, is the presence of God's grace.

God's light also has the character of a demand. That is certainly the meaning here in vv.5–6. Light defines the mode of human existence. If men turn from the light or love darkness rather than light, it is because their deeds are evil (John 3:19–21). In the world of first-century religious thought, the word "light" described ultimate realities. But there the weight was on the metaphysical implications. John is far removed from that type of speculation. He is concerned with the goodness of God and also the goodness of man. The heretical form of Christianity that prospered later showed all too clearly the folly of dividing moral seriousness from philosophic or theological speculation.

Even some pagans had a greater sensitivity to the ethical than did some expressions of the Christian faith. But as Dodd says, "There is no religion in the Christian sense of the word unless it includes moral endeavour and the criticism of conduct. . . . [Christians] believing in a God of pure goodness, accept the obligation to be good like Him" (*Johannine Epistles*, p. 20; cf. Matt 5:48). The latter part of v.5—"in him [i.e., in God] there is no darkness at all"—is a negative corollary specially emphasizing the statement that God is light. As darkness has no place in God, so all that is of the darkness is excluded from having fellowship with God. This idea stands out as the author approaches the behavior pattern of his opponents.

6 John introduces the first of three antithetic tests of Christian faith by the clause "If we claim." He apparently uses this device to refer to "boasts" made by the false teachers. The first false claim—to have fellowship with God and yet to walk in darkness—probably belongs, as Bultmann asserts (p. 17), to Gnostics who, as John describes them, have no love for one another (v.7), hate their brothers (2:9, 11), claim sinlessness (v.8), and deny that Jesus came in the flesh (2:22). To "walk in the darkness" is the same as "abiding" in darkness or "living in darkness." In each case the meaning is that of allowing darkness to define one's life.

It is not to be assumed that the opponents agreed with the author that they did indeed walk in darkness. Far from it! They claimed to walk in the light while they practiced the deeds of darkness. This is what made their actions so pernicious. Inevitably they, like all persons in similar situations, began to call their "darkness" light and to claim righteousness without becoming righteous or doing righteousness. In such situations, the author says, we lie and do not live by the truth. He also links lying to the life of darkness (cf. note on v.2).

"Do not put the truth into practice" translates *ou poioumen tēn alētheian* (lit., "we do not the truth," or "we do not live out the truth"). For the author the test of truth is not belief—though that is not excluded—but action, deeds, and conduct. As Brooke (p. 14) says, "'Speaking' the truth is only one part of 'doing' the truth and not the most important. To 'do the truth' is to give expression to the highest of which one is capable in every sphere of his being. It relates to action, and conduct and feeling, as well as to word and thought."

7 The positive test of knowing God is to live (*peripateō*, "walk") in the light as he himself is in the light. It would not be different if he had said here, as he did in v.5, "as he is the light" (cf. Bultmann, p. 20, n. 21). He is simply reiterating the fact that light is God's sphere. It is his nature, and he wills that it should become ours.

The consequence of obedience is to have fellowship with one another. Although life with God should indeed have wholesome effects on our relationship with all human beings, Bultmann wrongly sees this as the primary meaning of the text. Those who walk in the light are also those who have fellowship with one another. The author is combating the heresy that boasts of knowledge of and communion with God but neglects fellowship with other Christians. As Westcott (p. 20) states, "True fellowship with God comes through men. Love of the brethren is the product of the love of God: fellowship with the brethren is the proof of fellowship with God."

A second consequence of walking in the light is that the blood of Jesus keeps on cleansing us from every defilement due to sin. The language is, as Westcott has shown, ritualistic and reminds us of the OT sacrificial system, as well as of the interpretation of Christ's death given us in the Epistle to the Hebrews. The present tense of the verb stresses Christ's work as an ongoing provision against present and future contingencies. Without it enduring fellowship would be impossible, for the guilt resulting from sin destroys fellowship. The cleansing John speaks of results in forgiveness, restoration, and the reestablishment of love. Stott's summary is excellent: "What is clear is that if we walk in the light, God has made provision to cleanse us from whatever sin would otherwise mar our fellowship with Him or each other" (p. 76). Similarly, the use of the singular "sin" reminds us that the emphasis is not on sinful acts but on the work of God in Christ that meets and deals with the sin principle itself.

8 The second denial is against the false assertion that a Christian has no sin. The opponents probably did not claim that they had never committed wrong (sinful acts), but they denied that the sin principle (*hamartian echein*, "to have sin") had lasting power over them or even had a presence in them. It is not surprising that Gnostics, whether Christian or otherwise, should have denied sin. No human being, ancient or modern, wishes to understand his existence under that rubric.

The Gnostic rationalization, though ingenious, was not unique. Some, according to Dodd's reconstruction, held that

> Christians have been given a new nature superior to that of other men. . . . Christians are already sinless beings; or if not all Christians, at least those who have attained to superior enlightenment. They have no further need for moral striving: they are already perfect. . . . if the enlightened do things which in other men would be counted sinful, they are not sinners. Their mystical communion with God in itself removes them from the category of sinful men (*Johannine Epistles,* pp. 21–22).

Law (in loc.) has argued that the phrase *hamartian echein* pertains especially to the guiltiness of the sin. This would certainly pertain to the Gnostics since they evidently chose to accept no responsibility for moral action.

Others may have argued, like some in Corinth, that sin was a matter of the flesh and had nothing to do with the spirit, or that since they possessed the spirit, they were beyond the categories of good and evil and therefore moral principles no longer applied to them.

Whatever the shape of the argument, and regardless of whether it is an affirmation from the ancient world or a modern restatement, it remains true that whenever the principle of sin is denied as an ongoing reality, there follows a denial of responsibility for individual actions. Gossip, defiling of persons, hatred of the brethren, jealousy, and boasting become sanctioned as non-sins; walking in the light is denied; and the fellowship to which we are called is never permitted to exist.

The implications of the denial of the sin principle are momentous. First, there is the matter of personal responsibility. Brooke (p. 18) points out that the fact that we have deceived ourselves "emphasizes the agent's responsibility for the mistake. The evidence is there; only willful blindness refuses to accept it." Bultmann (p. 21), commenting on the same phrase, says that "self-deception does not mean a simple mistake, but rather that misdirected self-identity which is not aware of its nothing-ness."

Second, we recognize that the truth is simply not in us or with us. When the principle of sin is denied, truth as an inner principle of life cannot exist. The futility and irony of our predicament then becomes evident: In God's name, we make God's presence and power an impossibility.

9 In what follows we are confronted with our second definite test of obedience. Walking in the light is demonstrated not by the denial of sin but by confessing and abandoning it. This action links us to God's mercy. " 'He who confesses and condemns his sins,' says Augustine, 'already acts with God. God condemns thy sins: if thou also dost condemn them, thou art linked on to God' " (Ross, p. 146). And we can confess our "sins" (note the plural) to God and before man fearlessly and in confidence because God is both faithful and just.

The plural "sins" makes clear that we affirm our sinfulness by "confessing our sins." The forgiveness that comes is related to God's faithfulness and justice. God is faithful in himself, that is, to his own nature (cf. 2 Tim 2:13), and faithful to his promises (cf. Rom 3:25; 1 Cor 10:13; Heb 10:23; 11:11). Everywhere he promises forgiveness to his children—e.g., "I will forgive their wickedness and will remember their sins no more" (Jer 31:34; cf. Mic 7:19–20). And in keeping this promise, God reveals his faithfulness and justice.

Commentators disagree as to the force of *dikaios* ("just") in v.9. Does it point to the Cross (Stott, Ross), to the covenant (Brooke), to God's eschatological rule (Bult-mann), or to the attributes of God from which forgiveness flows (Dodd)? Probably the use ought not to be forced in any single direction. And certainly God's mercy must not be set against his justice. The phrase "he is faithful and just" includes all those things. It is a corollary of the fact that God is light and love.

The word the author uses for forgiveness (*aphiēmi*) has at its roots the idea of the "cancellation of debts" or the "dismissal of charges." The verb used for purification is *katharizō*. It pictures an act of cleansing from the pollution of sin so that a new life of holiness may begin. The sinner is perceived as cleansed from moral imperfections and from the injustices that separate him from God.

10 The third and final false claim begins with the assertion "If we claim we have not sinned." But is this a different assertion from that in v.8 or just a restatement of the same issue with an even more dramatic conclusion: "We make him [God] out to be a liar and his word has no place in our lives"?

In favor of the former possibility is the change in the verbal construction of *hamar-tian ouk echomen* ("we have no sin," present tense) (v.8) to *ouch hēmartēkamen* ("we have not sinned," perfect tense) (v.10). To be sure, the latter statement is more inclusive. The persons involved could be saying, "Whatever is true about the sin principle in others, we as Gnostic believers have transcended it all. We do not sin! We have not sinned! Sin has gained no foothold in us." Probably we should under-stand that both statements had their adherents among the Gnostic believers. Some may have said it one way, some the other. Some may have claimed that through their "knowledge" derived from the Christian proclamation they were removed from the possibility of sin. Others may have boasted that they had entered a sinless state through "knowledge" before the gospel had even come to them.

Although the assertions made in v.8 and v.10 are more alike than unlike, the latter statement is far more blatant and defiant. It makes a mockery of the gospel. It states that the reason God acted in grace and mercy toward us for the sake of our sins is false, that God first deceived us about ourselves and then becomes himself the Deceiver. The author's statement "his word has no place in our lives" means that the Word proclaimed, the tradition received, or the witness from the OT Scriptures has no place in those who deny their sin. The most elemental presence of the Word of God in the heart and conscience has been denied. Consequently the possibility of hearing a redemptive Word is denied. The ability to live by the Word is removed (see note on v.10). The possibility of receiving the forgiveness offered by God is lost.

2:1 As John resumes his discourse on sin and forgiveness, we see a striking change of mood. Whereas earlier he was focusing on his opponents and their false teaching, now he specifically speaks about these things as they affect his followers. The note of endearment—"my dear children"—in no way minimizes the seriousness of the discussion. Lest any conclude from his previous statements that sin must be considered inevitable in the life of the believer and not a matter of urgent concern since forgiveness is present by confession and the blood of Christ, John hastens to add, "I write this to you so that you will not sin." There is no question at all in his mind that sin and obedience to God are irreconcilable. Sin is the enemy. It removes the believer from the light. It prevents fellowship with God and it destroys fellowship with the children of light. The principle of sin as the power of darkness must be excluded from the believer's life, and individual acts of sin must be resisted. Where failure occurs, the sin must be confessed before the body and the Lord and then abandoned. And always the intent of the believer remains the same—not to commit sin!

If any of his children should fail and commit sin, the author is anxious that they neither deceive themselves about it nor lie about their action nor give up walking in the light. The answer to lapsing into sin is not self-deceit but the forgiveness of God made available through Jesus Christ. He has been designated the believer's advocate, the counsel who speaks in our defense. His worthiness to perform this function rests on the fact that even as God is righteous (1:9), so Jesus Christ also merits the title "The Righteous One."

2 The advocate does not maintain our innocence but confesses our guilt. Then he enters his plea before the Father on our behalf as the one who has made "atoning sacrifice for our sins." The word describing this activity is *hilasmos*. It is used elsewhere in the NT only in 4:10 (cognates appear in Luke 18:13; Rom 3:25; Heb 2:17; 9:5).

Notes

6 Περιπατεῖν (*peripatein*, "to walk"), which describes the manner of one's life, is a standard expression in the Johannine writings (cf. John 8:12; 11:9; 12:35; 1 John 1:6–7; 2:11; 2 John 4, 6; 3 John 3–4).

Concerning ψευδόμεθα (*pseudometha*, "lie") Conzelmann says, "In accordance with the Johannine meaning of ἀλήθεια . . . the lie is not just error but an active contesting of the truth, i.e., unbelief. . . . The demand that we do the truth and not lie is based on the statement that God is light. . . . Lying is also a denial of the confession, 2:21f. The liar is a historical manifestation of antichrist" (TDNT, 9:602).

10 Westcott (p. 26) says, "The word, like the truth, can be regarded both as the moving principle which stirs the man and as the sphere in which the man moves. The word abides in him (John v.38, comp. viii.37), and conversely he 'abides in the word' (John viii.3)."

2:2 The normal use of the word ἱλάσκομαι (*hilaskomai*, "propitiation") in Greek literature carries the idea of an offering made by a guilty person in order to placate or appease the person (God) who has been offended. The English word "propitiate" is used to render this meaning. But Westcott argues, and Dodd agrees, that "the scriptural conception . . . is not that of appeasing one who is angry . . . but of altering the character of that which from without occasions a necessary alienation, and interposes an inevitable obstacle to fellowship" (Westcott, p. 85; cf. C.H. Dodd, "*Hilaskomai*, Its Cognates, Derivatives, and Synonyms in the Septuagint," JTS 32 [1931], 352–60). If this is the correct emphasis, then the word is better rendered by the English word "expiation."

Modern translations reflect the difficulty; there is no clear consensus. NEB offers the translation "remedy for defilement," which suggests the idea of expiation. TEV reflects a related stance with its "means by which our sins are forgiven," as does JB in "the sacrifice that takes our sins away." In support of NIV's "atoning sacrifice," Marshall (p. 18) argues that "both concepts—propitiation and expiation—must be included . . . The one action has the double effect of expiating the sin and thereby propitiating God."

Surely the text makes clear that God is not over against man as the opponent since God is the one who sends the Son in order that as Father he may grant forgiveness to the confessor. It is sin that is the offense. It must be atoned for so that the just punishment due the sinner can be averted. The blot of the sin must also be removed so that the believer will not rest under the burden of guilt and defilement. Both actions are necessary for the restoration of the child to the Father.

The sacrifice is "also for the sins of the whole world." This statement asserts two things: Christ's sacrifice is sufficient for all, and it is necessary for all.

---

2. Obeying His Commands

2:3–11

> ³We know that we have come to know him if we obey his commands. ⁴The man who says, "I know him," but does not do what he commands is a liar, and the truth is not in him. ⁵But if anyone obeys his word, God's love is truly made complete in him. This is how we know we are in him: ⁶Whoever claims to live in him must walk as Jesus did.
> ⁷Dear friends, I am not writing you a new command but an old one, which you have had since the beginning. This old command is the message you have heard. ⁸Yet I am writing you a new command; its truth is seen in him and you, because the darkness is passing and the true light is already shining.
> ⁹Anyone who claims to be in the light but hates his brother is still in the darkness. ¹⁰Whoever loves his brother lives in the light, and there is nothing in him to make him stumble. ¹¹But whoever hates his brother is in the darkness and walks around in the darkness; he does not know where he is going, because the darkness has blinded him.

The first section (1:1–2:2) dealt with fellowship, primarily fellowship with God. Three false claims made by the opponents were denied (vv.6, 8, 10), and each false claim was used as an occasion for the presentation of what are true "tests" or evidences of living in fellowship with God. The second section (2:3–11) is concerned with knowledge of God. Again the false claims to knowledge by the opponents are stated first, this time introduced by the clause "he who says" (cf. vv.4, 6, 9). Each of these claims is again denied and the evidence or "tests" of the true knowledge of God is set forth: obeying his commands (v.5), walking in his likeness (v.6), and loving one's brother (v.10).

3 There appears to be a break in subject matter with what precedes as the author now turns to the topic of knowing God. For him to know God is, however, a natural corollary to the idea of walking in the light and of having fellowship with God. It is simply another way of speaking of the reality of God. In this instance the language probably is a response to the opponents for whom knowledge (*gnōsis*) was a key term. These "Gnostic" opponents, though not sharing the full-blown ideas reflected among the second-century Gnostics, naturally shared some of their essential thoughts. Knowledge of God, they said, came through "mystical insights" or by a "direct vision of God." *Corpus Hermetica* 10.5–6 is an example of Gnostic thought:

> Not yet are we able to open the eyes of the mind and to behold the beauty, the imperishable, inconceivable beauty, of the Good. For you will see it when you cannot say anything about it. For the knowledge of it is divine silence and annihilation of all senses. . . . Irradiating the whole mind, it shines upon the soul and draws it up from the body, and changes it all into divine essence (cited in Dodd, *Johannine Epistles*, p. 30).

Such thinking is clearly devoid of interest in moral conduct and unconcerned about human behavior. For the Hebrew or Christian mind, however, knowledge of God is not separable from the experience of righteousness. Consequently there is no greater claim one can make in knowing God than to obey him. "We can be sure we know him," the author says, "if we obey his commands." For John, therefore, the test of knowledge of God is moral conduct (cf. also Titus 1:16). It is keeping God's commandments. Bultmann (p. 25) appropriately observes that " 'keeping the commandments' (like fellowship with one another, 1:7) is not the condition, but rather the characteristic knowledge of God. There is no knowledge of God which as such would not also be 'keeping the commandments.' "

4 In v.3 the author dealt with the general question of how we may have assurance that we know God. Here he deals with those who claim that they know God but at the same time break his commandments. For John knowledge of God is clearly not perceived as academic, theoretical, or speculative but as practical and experiential. It is "a relationship to God, in which the one knowing is determined in his existence (and thus also in his 'walking,' his conduct) by God" (Bultmann, p. 25). To claim to know God and at the same time to be disobedient to his commandments is, the author asserts, to lie and be devoid of all truth.

5 Next John states the positive side of knowledge. He who "obeys his word" (a way of speaking of the gospel that is more comprehensive—including the promises as well as the commandments) finds God's love "made complete" in him. The true knowledge of God does not end with speculative ideas, as for the Gnostics, but with obedience to the moral law and with the presence of God's love in the believer. The term "made complete" (*teleioō*) carries with it the idea of continuous growth and development.

It describes both state and process. As obedience is practiced, so also God's love matures in us.

6 "To live in him" ("abideth," KJV) introduces another way the opponents described their relationship to God. What they claimed by this experience we do not know; probably they boasted of mystical experiences, visions of the light, and the like. What they did not claim was any new ethical seriousness as a consequence of their life in God. The author's comment is direct and forceful: "Whoever claims to live in him [either the Father or the Son, but in the context the Father is more likely] must walk [live] as Jesus did." The uniqueness of Christian ethics comes again to the surface. Relationship to God requires moral behavior worthy of God. And as the revelation of God in Christ is accepted as the high point of divine self-disclosure, so the human life of Jesus becomes the measuring stick of true moral and ethical behavior. The author is not claiming that the walk of Jesus can be perfectly imitated but that there is a divine imperative—which must be taken seriously—for believers to live according to the way Jesus lived. Also included is the true test for those who want to know whether their life in God is real or mere fantasy: To claim a relationship to God necessitates a commitment to moral standards expressed positively (to love as God himself loves) and negatively (to obey commandments and not to sin).

7 The introduction of the affectionate term "dear friends" (*agapētoi*, "beloved") reminds us that the author is looking in two directions at once. On the one hand, he is setting forth tests that will expose the false teachings and claims of his opponents; on the other hand, he is providing tests by which his own spiritual children will know they are walking in the light.

In addition, John may be dealing with a serious charge against his own teaching. The opponents may have claimed that he has in fact distorted the gospel by adding to it. For his opponents the knowledge of God available in the gospel was itself the end of the religious quest. The knowledge was freedom from the world. To the author, the gospel is fulfilled in the knowledge of God that is revealed in Jesus, and this in turn requires obedience to his commands and results in a new relationship with God expressed in a life of love. The point of view reflects Jesus' words as recorded in John's gospel: "A new command I give you: Love one another. As I have loved you, so you must love one another" (John 13:34). The new command John speaks of here in v.7 sums up what it means to "walk in the light" and to "walk as Jesus did." Thus it stands at the heart of the gospel. Moreover, what John was proclaiming to his "dear children" was not "a new command but an old one" they had had since the beginning." So he denies that there ever was "a message" that did not have this command at its heart, despite his opponents' claims.

8 In view of v.7, how can the author assert that this command is also at the same time "a new command"? Its newness lies at the point of its realization and fulfillment. Jesus lived a life of divine love. He also extended this life to his disciples as a new command. But certainly for them this requirement had to be received in an eschatological framework, as a command yet to be fulfilled in them (John 15:12ff.). After Jesus' death and resurrection, however, they discovered that as they obeyed his commands, his promise found fulfillment. What had been true in Jesus' own life now became part of the reality of their lives. They too began to know what it was to "love." Luke and Paul also experienced this realized eschatology. For Paul the old had passed away;

in Christ all had become new (2 Cor 5:17). For Luke the gift of the Holy Spirit marked the beginning of fulfillment of the promise (Acts 2). Here in v.8 John expresses the realized fulfillment by simply saying that "the darkness is passing and the true light is already shining." Paul also used this imagery of light (cf. Eph 5:8–14; 1 Thess 5:4–8).

9 This verse brings us to the third false claim that the author denies. Whereas obedience to the new command leads to love among the brethren, among the opponents who claim to "be in the light" there is hate. This hate for one's brother shows that the light they follow is nothing but darkness.

How does John understand hate? Does he think in conceptual terms or concrete ones? Undoubtedly the answer for him lies primarily in what one does. Hate is the absence of the deeds of love. To walk in the light is to love one's brother, and God's love will express itself in concrete actions. If these are missing, it is not because love can be neutral or can exist unexpressed. Love unexpressed is not love at all. Love has no neutral capabilities. When it is absent, hate is present.

In this instance, then, hate is the failure to deny oneself, the unwillingness to lay down one's life for a brother (John 15:13). It considers its own plight first (1 Cor 13:5); disregards the robbed and afflicted (Luke 10:30–37); despises the little ones (Matt 18:10); withholds the cup of cold water from the thirsty (Matt 25:42); and makes no effort to welcome the stranger, clothe the naked, or help the sick (Matt 25:43). Whenever a brother has need and one does not help him, then one has despised and, in fact, hated his brother.

Does the word "brother" refer here to one's neighbor or to one who belongs to the community of faith? In this instance it probably refers to a member of the community of faith. It is not that John lacks concern for those outside the faith; rather, in this letter he has the community of believers in view. Moreover, if a believer cannot love his brother, it is doubtful whether he can love his neighbor.

10 The author now gives us a positive test of living in the light. Unlike his opponents, his concern is with deeds, not claims. "Whoever loves," he says, is "in the light." Conversely, it follows that one who does not live "in the light" will not manifest God's love.

The uncertain antecedents of the Greek pronouns leads to some ambiguity in the rest of the sentence. The pronouns could be rendered in the following ways: "There is nothing in him to make him [his brother] stumble" or "There is nothing in him to cause his [own] stumbling" or "There is nothing in it [the light] to cause him to stumble" or "There is nothing in it [the light] to cause him [his brother] to stumble." In view of the author's aim, it is probable that he is saying that the one who loves and abides in the light will never cause the offense the opponents do.

11 Now the author picks up the concept of darkness from 2:9 and gives it a final elaboration and conclusion. He who "hates his brother" is not simply "in the darkness" but is condemned to walk or spend his life in darkness. Though he has eyes, he can see nothing. And the darkness so blinds his eyes that he has no idea "where he is going." Life is a search, but for him it is without direction. He never knows whether he is closer or further from his destination. The only certainty is that he is without hope of reaching it. So hate destroys any window for light from God. To live without loving one's brother is, for the author, to live in total meaninglessness, denying oneself the presence of God and the reality of fellowship with the brothers.

Notes

3 "Knowledge" is a characteristic concept in this Epistle. Two verbs for "knowing" are used in the Greek for the concept: οἶδα (oida) and γινώσκω (ginōskō). The latter, a common word in the Johannine Epistles (twenty-five times), emphasizes knowledge by experience; the former, that which is immediate and absolute.

Αὐτόν (auton, "him"), though ambiguous here, probably refers to God the Father. When Jesus is referred to, the writer generally uses ἐκεῖνος (ekeinos) (cf. Schnackenburg, p. 75).

5 The author develops this idea in 4:12, 17–20. "In this" most likely refers to obeying the commandments (v.3) and keeping God's word (v.5). Whether "the love of God" is to be understood as a subjective genitive, "the love that God gives" (so NIV, Bultmann, Houlden, Westcott), or as an objective genitive, "our love for God" (so RSV, Brooke, Bruce, Dodd, Marshall, Ross, Stott), or as a descriptive or qualitative genitive, "God's kind of love" (so Schnackenburg), is disputed. NIV is probably correct because (1) generally in the NT ἀγάπη (agapē, "love") is followed by a subjective genitive; (2) it is certainly a subjective genitive in 1 John 4:9; (3) the subjective idea is what dominates the author's mind (cf. 1 John 3:1: "The Father has given to us love"; cf. also 4:7, 16); (4) it agrees best with the context (see Westcott, p. 49).

Τελειόω (teleioō, "perfected") is a favorite Johannine word (cf. John 4:34; 5:36; 17:4; 19:28, 30).

6 Μένειν (menein, "abide"; NIV, "live in him") occurs twenty-four times in 1 John, three times in 2 John, and forty times in the Gospel of John. Bultmann points out that "abide" always contains a negative implication: Do not yield, Do not leave, Stay where you are (p. 26, n.9). In 1 John and the Gospel of John, "abide" means "faithfulness" and reciprocity (cf. John 15:1–17). (For an extended treatment of "abide," see Schnackenburg, pp. 105–10.)

7 Ἀγαπητοί (agapētoi, "beloved") also occurs in 3:2, 21; 4:7, 11. The singular form occurs in 3 John 2, 5, 11 (cf. Rom 12:19; 2 Cor 7:1).

8 "Its truth" does not refer to the truthfulness of the new command but to the fact that there is something that must "properly" and "truly" be understood as a new command (cf. Marshall, p. 129; for a different position, see Westcott, p. 53).

"True" as applied to "light" (cf. John 1:9; 1 John 1:5–7; 5:20) should be understood in contrast to the "false" light in which the Gnostic opponents walk. The adjective ἀληθινός (alēthinos, "true") is common in Johannine literature; it occurs four times in 1 John, nine times in the Gospel of John, and ten times in Revelation.

10 Σκάνδαλον (skandalon) occurs twenty-five times in the NT, but only here in John. It means literally "trap" or "snare" (cf. Westcott, p. 56). (For a different conclusion, see Brooke, p. 39; Bultmann, p. 28; Schnackenburg, p. 115.)

11 Σκοτία (skotia, "darkness") is an important theme in the Gospel of John (see 8:12; 9:39–41; 11:9–10; 12:35–36, 40).

Ἀδελφός (adelphos, "brother") is consistently used in the NT to refer to a member of the church, Bultmann's opinion (p. 28) notwithstanding (see Westcott, p. 55).

---

3. Knowing the Father and Abiding Forever

2:12–17

12I write to you, dear children,
   because your sins have been forgiven on account
      of his name.
13I write to you, fathers,
   because you have known him who is from
      the beginning.

I write to you, young men,
    because you have overcome the evil one.
I write to you, dear children,
    because you have known the Father.
14I write to you, fathers,
    because you have known him who is from
        the beginning.
I write to you, young men,
    because you are strong,
    and the word of God lives in you,
    and you have overcome the evil one.

15Do not love the world or anything in the world. If anyone loves the world, the love of the Father is not in him. 16For everything in the world—the cravings of sinful man, the lust of his eyes and the boasting of what he has and does—comes not from the Father but from the world. 17The world and its desires pass away, but the man who does the will of God lives forever.

The first part of the Epistle (1:5–2:11) involved untrue assertions made by the author's Gnostic-type opponents and provided "tests" for exposing the false claims as well as for assuring those who walked in the light. The next section is in two parts. The first (2:12–14) contrasts the position of the believer who walks in the light with that of the Gnostics who walk in darkness. The second part (2:15–17) warns the believer not to fall into the trap of worldliness, as the false teachers did.

The first section is rhythmical, almost lyrical. Two sets of three statements introduced by the words "I write" and "I have written," or "I wrote" (NIV does not bring out this distinction) are addressed in turn to "children," "fathers," and "young men." We do not know why the author changes tenses. Most commentators agree that the change is stylistic and is added for emphasis. Nor do we know the significance of the various forms of address. It is possible that John's intention was to address his entire congregation from two standpoints—that of chronological age ("children," "young men," "fathers") and that of spiritual age (novices in the faith, those whose faith is vigorous and who are responsible for the work of the gospel, and those whose knowledge and experience in the faith are the foundation on which the community exists).

The alternative suggestion that the categories of "children," "young men," and "fathers" represent offices in the Johannine community comparable to those of deacons, elders, and bishops (if indeed the last two are to be distinguished) in the Pauline church is attractive but speculative (cf. Houlden, pp. 70–71). What is clear in any instance is that John wanted to speak representationally to the entire church. As members of the new covenant, their sins are forgiven, they know the truth, and they have overcome the world.

12 "Dear children" (teknia) is the author's favorite term for the congregation of believers as a whole. Under this rubric he offers the most basic and universal words of assurance he can give: "Your sins have been forgiven on account of his name" (see Notes). They have confessed their sins (1:9) and, on account of his name, or by faith in his name (3:23; 5:13), or by faith in him (5:1, 5)—the meaning is the same—forgiveness that was bought through the covenant of his blood (1:7) has become their possession. In this knowledge they may stand firm. Because they are forgiven, they may also have fellowship with God and true knowledge of him (13c). Whether the

author is speaking to new converts or to old ones is unimportant. Knowledge of God begins with conversion in which sin, known and confessed, is forgiven.

13a "Fathers" is an unusual form of address for senior members of a congregation. According to Jewish custom, it would refer to those who had responsibility for authority. Many times it is used to refer to the leaders of the past, the fathers of Israel, the patriarchs, etc. If it refers to members of the congregation who were mature both in years and in faith, it was indeed a solemn designation, one entailing assumption of responsibility in the community of believers. The secondary address to the "fathers" in v.14—"because you have known him who is from the beginning"—is peculiarly appropriate to older members of the community. It stresses the historic origins of the faith and the growth of the personal knowledge of Christ that comes only with experience.

Although the pronoun "him" is ambiguous and could refer to God (so Bruce, Stott), it is more likely in view of the reference to the Father in 13c that here it refers to Christ. In any instance, it looks back to 1:1-3, where both God and Christ are equally represented, and reminds the readers that they have come to know Jesus as the One who is and who was from the beginning. Dodd (*Johannine Epistles*, pp. 36-37) points out that this "knowing" God and the Son that looms so large in the Epistle and the Gospel of John reflects a special interest of the prophets: "Isaiah (xi.1-9) forecasts the reign of a Messiah, upon whom rests the spirit of knowledge," as one in which the earth shall be full of the knowledge of God. Isaiah says, "Therefore my people will know my name; therefore in that day they will know that it is I who foretold it" (Isa 52:6). Jeremiah (31:34) says, "They will all know me, from the least of them to the greatest. . . . For I will forgive their wickedness and will remember their sins no more."

13b The description of the community as "young men" who "are strong" (14b) and "have overcome" adds a new dimension. Believers are to see themselves as not only in conflict with the enemy but as having perceived the victory in Christ's name and by his power. The victory obviously was gained through Christ's death, and now his followers have the task under his leadership of establishing his reign over the world and the devil (14b). This victory, seen as already realized, does not promise that believers shall be removed from the heat and peril of the battlefield. But it does assure them that if they are faithful they will overcome the "evil one." As Christ has been victorious over the evil one, so they too may commit themselves to the conflict without fear (cf. John 16:33; Rom 8:31-39; Col 2:15; 1 John 3:8). This idea will be expanded on in 4:4 and 5:4-5. It is clear that "the evil one" is but another way to refer to the devil (3:12; 5:18; cf. John 17:15; Eph 6:16; 2 Thess 3:3).

13c This time the "children" are addressed as *paidia*. If a difference in emphasis is intended, the use of *teknia* emphasizes more the relationship, the dependence or weakness of the infant, while *paidia* stresses the immaturity (subordination) of the child, the need to be under instruction or direction. The author is saying that as children under teachers or instructors in the faith his readers have come to know God as the Father. Second only to forgiveness in importance for the new community of faith is the relationship to God as Father that came through the gospel of Jesus Christ.

14 After referring again to the "fathers," the author concludes by addressing the young men as those in whom "the word of God lives." They were indeed "strong" as the children of faith, but the author reminds them that their strength ultimately depends on one fact alone—the Word of God abiding or living in them.

Six times the author uses the perfect tense (rendered by "have" in NIV) to describe the action expressed in the subordinate clauses. In each instance, what is described has been initiated or established in the past (i.e., the Cross and/or their conversion) and continues to be true into the present.

15 Having assured the believers of their position before God—viz., their sins are forgiven, they know the Father, and they have overcome the evil one—John moves to application. He warns them not to love the world and gives two reasons: Love of the world precludes love for the Father, and the investment of love in the world is without meaning because the world is passing away (v.17). The love of the world versus the love of the Father provides yet another "test" of walking in the light.

The word for world (*kosmos*) occurs six times in vv.15–17. It obviously means something quite different here than in John 3:16. There the Father's love of the world is apparently based on God's having willed the world into existence. It is his creation; he created it to be good, beautiful, and worthy of giving glory to him. Likewise those who live in the world are his creatures; he created them, loves them, and, even in their desperate state of living in darkness and the shadow of death, remains constant in desiring to rescue them from eternal death.

Here, however, the world is presented as the evil system totally under the grip of the devil (cf. 1 John 5:19; John 12:31; 14:30). It is the "godless world" (NEB), the world of "emptiness and evil" (Bultmann, p. 33), the world of enmity against God (James 4:4).

Love also means something different in this passage. Here it is not the selfless love for one's brother (cf. 2:10) but the love that entices by evil desire or base appetite that is forbidden (John 3:19; 12:43). It is the world's ability to seduce the believer, to draw him away from love of the Father, that concerns John. "Anything in the world" is not a reference to "natural" phenomena, as v.16 makes clear.

16 What love for the world or worldliness entails is now spelled out by John in a memorable triad: "the cravings of sinful man, the lust of his eyes and the boasting of what he has and does." The phrase "the cravings of sinful man" (lit., "the desire of the flesh [*sarkos*]") describes the principle of worldliness from which love of the world flows. "Flesh" refers to "the outlook orientated towards self, that which pursues its own ends in self-sufficient independence of God" (DNTT, 1:680) and in self-sufficient independence of one's fellow man. The "flesh" not only becomes the basis for rebellion against God and for despising his law but also connotes all that is materialistic, egocentric, exploitative, and selfish. It is at the root of racism, sexism, love of injustice, despising the poor, neglecting the weak and helpless, and every unrighteous practice.

The "lust of the eyes," according to Bultmann (p. 34), "can refer especially to sexual lust, but can also mean everything that entices the eyes." Marshall (p. 145) sees it as "the tendency to be captivated by outward, visible splendor and show, but more probably the basic thought is of greed and desire for things aroused by seeing them." Stott (p. 100) gives "Eve's view of the forbidden tree as 'a delight to the eyes,' Achan's covetous sight among the spoil of a 'goodly Babylonish garment,' and David's lustful looking after Bathsheba as she bathed" as obvious examples. Law sees it as "the love of beauty divorced from the love of goodness" (cited in Stott, p. 100).

The key term in the third phrase, "pride of life," is *alazoneia;* it occurs only here and in James 4:16. The corporate adjective *alazōn* is used in Romans 1:30 and 2 Timothy 3:2. It describes a pretentious hypocrite who glories in himself or in his possessions. He is a person of ostentatious pride in "his own non-existent importance." (Barclay, in loc.). Bruce (p. 61) says, "If my reputation, my 'public image,' matters more to me than the glory of God or the well-being of my followers, the 'pretentiousness of life' has become the object of my idol-worship."

"Pride of life" will be reflected in whatever status symbol is important to me or seems to define my identity. When I define myself to others in terms of my honorary degrees, the reputation of the church I serve, my annual income, the size of my library, my expensive car or house, and if in doing this I misrepresent the truth and in my boasting show myself to be only a pompous fool who has deceived no one, then I have succumbed to what John calls the pride of life.

The following is an ancient caricature of the self-important fool, the *"Alazon"*:

> The *Alazon* is the kind of person who will stand on the mole and tell perfect strangers what a lot of money he has at sea, and discourse of his investments, how large they are, and what gains and losses he has made, and as he spins his yarns he will send his boy to the bank—his balance being a shilling. If he enjoys company on the road, he is apt to tell how he served with Alexander the Great, how he got on with him, and how many jewelled cups he brought home; and to discuss the Asiatic craftsmen, how much better they are than any in Europe—never having been away from Athens. He will say that he was granted a free permit for the export of timber, but took no advantage of it, to avoid ill-natured gossip; and that during the corn-shortage he spent more than fifteen hundred pounds in gifts to needy citizens. He will be living in a rented house, and will tell anyone who does not know the facts that this is the family residence, but he is going to sell it because it is too small for his entertainments (Plutarch's *Characters*, quoted in Dodd, *Johannine Epistles*, p. 42).

17 All the vanity of this evil world with its devices is passing away. It has already begun to putrify. It is a corpse not yet buried. But the person who really does the will of God has the breath of eternal life.

Notes

12 For the origin and use of the expression "his name," see Ezek 20:8–9; 36:22; in the NT see Matt 10:22 (Gk.); Luke 24:47; Acts 4:12, 30; 13:38; 1 Cor 1:10. Elsewhere in Johannine literature, see John 20:31; 1 John 3:23; 5:13.

12–14 The change from the present tense, γράφω (*graphō*, "I write"), in vv. 12–13 to the aorist tense, ἔγραψα (*egrapsa*, "I wrote"), goes unnoticed in NIV. Schnackenburg (pp. 125ff.) says that *egrapsa* can be used to describe something being written in the present as well as of the past (cf. 1 John 2:21; Gal 6:11; Philem 19, 21). Brooke (p. 41) prefers to think that the writer used the aorist tense in referring to that part of the letter already finished. The possibility that these are epistolary aorists, in which the writer has projected himself forward to the readers' time, for whom the event would already be past, does not seem to offer any real value here. Most likely the author changed tenses for the sake of emphasis.

15 In the choice between "love for the Father" or "the kind of love manifested in the Father," I would take the former (cf. Bultmann, p. 33; Marshall, p. 143).

4. Warnings Against Antichrists

2:18–28

¹⁸Dear children, this is the last hour; and as you have heard that the antichrist is coming, even now many antichrists have come. This is how we know it is the last hour. ¹⁹They went out from us, but they did not really belong to us. For if they had belonged to us, they would have remained with us; but their going showed that none of them belonged to us.

²⁰But you have an anointing from the Holy One, and all of you know the truth. ²¹I do not write to you because you do not know the truth, but because you do know it and because no lie comes from the truth. ²²Who is the liar? It is the man who denies that Jesus is the Christ. Such a man is the antichrist—he denies the Father and the Son. ²³No one who denies the Son has the Father; whoever acknowledges the Son has the Father also.

²⁴See that what you have heard from the beginning remains in you. If it does, you also will remain in the Son and in the Father. ²⁵And this is what he promised us—even eternal life.

²⁶I am writing these things to you about those who are trying to lead you astray. ²⁷As for you, the anointing you received from him remains in you, and you do not need anyone to teach you. But as his anointing teaches you about all things and as that anointing is real, not counterfeit—just as it has taught you, remain in him.

²⁸And now, dear children, continue in him, so that when he appears we may be confident and unashamed before him at his coming.

In the first three sections of his letter, the author has been directly presenting his followers with "tests" by which they could know they were truly in union with the Father. At the same time, he was dealing with his opponents by showing that they failed each of these tests of discipleship. In this section he reverses his method. He no longer uses indirection against his opponents but now confronts them and their teaching by openly labeling them for what they are: antichrists (vv. 18–19). He exposes their method: they lie and deny Jesus as Christ (vv. 20, 23). He teaches his followers how to cope with this: they are to remain in what they were taught (vv. 24–26); and, finally, he assures his followers of their power to overcome: "His anointing teaches you" (vv. 27–28).

18 The reference to the transitoriness of the world—viz., "it is passing away" (v. 17)—provides the link to what has preceded. One of the signs of the end of this transitory world is the appearance of false teaching and of the Antichrist. What the apostles warned of is now being fulfilled. The spirit of antichrist is present in the world, evidenced by the fact that many antichrists have already appeared. This is no surprise, however, but only further confirmation that the company of believers are living in the last hour, an hour that draws its significance from the appearance of the true Christ in the flesh.

The term "last hour" occurs only here in the NT. Like the similar terms "the last days" and "the last times," it owes much to OT expectations (cf. Joel 2:28; Mic 4:1) and later Jewish speculation. Jesus called the present age an evil age and looked forward to the age to come, which would be ushered in by God's own intervention. Some Jewish theologians believed this "golden age" would be inaugurated by a special personage, namely God's Messiah.

The NT writers thought of the "last days" in two ways. Theologically they connected this period to the new age that they associated with the advent of Jesus. In the Gospel of John this new age is designated by the statement "the hour is come" and is marked

117

by Jesus' death and resurrection (John 4:23; 5:25). In Acts the new age is referred to as the "days to come" and is signaled by the pouring forth of the Spirit (2:17) and salvation through calling on the name of the Lord (2:21). The NT writers did not believe the new age had completely come. They recognized it as being present provisionally in Christ and in the Holy Spirit. But because of this dawning of the new age, they saw the present age as already doomed and passing away.

They also used the term "last days" eschatologically to designate the last days before Christ's return (cf. 2 Tim 3:1ff.; 2 Peter 3:3). In the Gospel of John, the last day refers to the last resurrection and judgment (cf. 6:39–40, 44, 54; 11:24; 12:48).

How should the term "last hour" in 1 John be understood? The majority of commentators see it eschatologically, indicating "the last period of the interval between the first and second coming of Christ" (Brooke, p. 51; cf. Dodd, *Johannine Epistles*, pp. 48ff.). Some commentators therefore conclude that the author was mistaken.

Westcott (p. 68) translates the Greek literally—"it is a last hour"—and observes that, since no definite article is used with "last hour," the term describes "the general character of the period" rather than its temporal nature. Stott (pp. 108–9) agrees that it refers to "the last hours of the last days," which the author could say on theological grounds "had struck." He understands, however, that the words involve no chronological or temporal assertions.

Against any exclusively eschatological interpretation stands the Gospel of John, which uses "hour" theologically to indicate the fulfillment of time, the time of redemption and salvation (John 2:4; 4:21; 7:30; 8:20; 12:23).

19 The "departure" may have had a greater effect on the congregation than the reason for it. The early church obviously had severe debates with significant differences of opinion being expressed. Yet as far as we know, no one thought that "separation from the congregation" was an option for anyone professing belief. Departure, like Judas's going out from the community of disciples, pointed to betrayal, denial of faith, and separation from God's grace. That is why John acknowledges that those false teachers he now designates as antichrists had been regular members of the congregation. "They went out from us," he says, but hastens to add, "they did not really belong to us." Like Judas, they had been nominal members of the community and had never truly shared its fellowship.

John now goes on to teach the congregation the significance and abiding nature of life in the community. "If they had belonged to us, they would have remained with us." Those who have actually been a part of the divine life will without fail persevere in the community. But in order that the true nature of the false teachers might be exposed, "they went out from us," so that the community might know that "none of them belonged to us" (cf. Matt 24:24).

Expulsion from the Christian community for misdeeds is a serious act, and hopefully it lasts only so long as to allow for repentance and restoration (cf. 1 Cor 5:2–5; 2 Cor 2:5–11). The case at hand is unique; apparently the going out was neither expulsion nor excommunication but the voluntary departure of those involved. Yet their departure is taken as absolutely serious. It shows that they were never truly one with the community. If they had been true disciples, their nonperseverance with the community would never have occurred. Here Stott (pp. 105–6) cites Calvin: "Future and final perseverance is the ultimate test of a past participation in Christ (cf. Heb iii.14). 'Those who fall away,' on the other hand, 'have never been thoroughly imbued with the knowledge of Christ but only had a slight and passing taste of it.'"

20 The author now returns to the heretical claims of his opponents. They probably claimed superior knowledge because they had received an exclusive ritual anointing that gave them knowledge (*gnōsis*). Dodd (*Johannine Epistles*, p. 61) suggests that their attitude may have been similar to that of the " 'Gnostic' sect known as Naassenes," who much later also boasted of a special sacrament of anointing: " 'We alone of all men are Christians, who complete the mystery at the third portal, and are anointed there with speechless chrism' (*Philosophumena* V. 9.121–2)." Schnackenburg (p. 152, nn. 3 and 4) also refers to the Gnostic ritual of anointing with oil.

The author combats his opponents' claim by reminding his readers: "But you have an anointing from the Holy One, and all of you know [because all of you received it] the truth." This is probably an allusion to the coming of the Holy Spirit as set forth in the Gospel of John: "But when he, the Spirit of truth, comes, he will guide you into all truth" (16:13; cf. also 14:17; 15:26). The early Christians connected this with their baptism. Although "anointing" is used only infrequently in the NT, both Luke and Paul do use it with reference to the Holy Spirit (Luke 4:18; Acts 10:38). "He anointed us, set his seal of ownership on us, and put his Spirit in our hearts as a deposit, guaranteeing what is to come" (2 Cor 1:21–22).

The messengers of God proclaimed the gospel, but God himself by his Spirit taught the heart, from which true knowledge was then manifested. When this divine teaching was truly recognized, Christians were genuinely protected against false teaching or unbelief. Paul has this same emphasis in his epistles: "Now about brotherly love we do not need to write to you, for you yourselves have been taught by God to love each other" (1 Thess 4:9); "I myself am convinced, my brothers, that you yourselves are full of goodness, complete in knowledge and competent to instruct one another" (Rom 15:14).

The statement "you have an anointing from the Holy One" may refer to God, but it more likely refers to Christ (cf. John 6:69).

21 Lest there be any doubt among the faithful as to John's perception of their understanding and orthodoxy, he says that he has not written because they did not know the truth—he is not providing new information or teaching—but because they know it so certainly. They know the character of truth, and therefore they know that "no lie comes from truth." The author aims his remarks precisely at the innate knowledge of the gospel that he knows his followers possess. Lies cannot come from God. The antichrists and their followers, the false teachers, are liars. So they do not come—in fact, cannot come—from God who is the truth.

22 "Who is the liar?" v.22 asks and then rhetorically answers by pointing to those antichrists who promulgate the particularly pernicious falsehood that Jesus is not the Christ. This falsehood should not be linked to the Jewish opponents who denied that Jesus was the Messiah but rather to the Gnostic opponents who denied that Christ came in the flesh. (For more explicit references, see 1 John 4:2–3 and 2 John 7.)

The exact kind of Gnostic denial in view is uncertain. Commentators have traditionally favored a Gnosticism like that of Cerinthus, who held that "after Jesus' baptism, the Christ, coming down from that power which is above all, descended upon him in a form of a dove. . . . In the end, however, the Christ withdrew again from Jesus. . . . The Christ, being spiritual, remained unable to suffer" (Brown, p. 112).

However, since the opponents came out of the Johannine community, it is more likely that their Christology would not be as extreme as that of Cerinthus. Yet it probably did include the ideas that the true Christ, who was preexistent, merely appeared in human form to bring eternal life, that his human existence was without real significance, and that his human presence was not essential to his true being. The revelations he brought came not through any of his actions as Jesus of Nazareth or through any of the events connected to his life—especially not through his sufferings or his death on the cross. It was not in his human life as Jesus of Nazareth that eternal life came but in his divine glory as the preexistent and eternal Christ.

Obviously such a denial of Jesus' humanity struck at the very heart of the Incarnation. Denying Jesus' true sonship, these opponents of John denied the Father as well. Because they denied Jesus' human life, they rejected the community of love he established. It is likely that the false teachers in the name of orthodoxy and purism mocked the commands of Jesus as taught by the apostles. Little wonder that John designates them "antichrists." They rejected Jesus. They rejected their own sinfulness, their need of forgiveness, the life of love, and the "fellowship" with the Father and the Son.

23 The statement "No one who denies the Son has the Father; whoever acknowledges the Son has the Father also" makes clear the singular dependence of the Christian faith on the reality of God available through the Son. Those who claim they have a Father but exclude the Son have neither the Father nor the Son. Consequently, when Jesus is acknowledged as the Son and as the eternal Christ, the Father has also truly been lifted up, known and honored, confessed and possessed. The words "has the Father" probably are meant to stress this relationship. John is not talking about having a creed but possessing a person. A person is confessed or believed when we accept or acknowledge our relationship to him. So also we deny God by denying him his proper relationship with us.

24 At this point John shifts his attention to his readers. They, in contrast to the antichrists, are exhorted to make certain that what they heard "from the beginning," that is, the true apostolic declaration concerning Jesus as Son and Christ, "remains" in them. If it "remains" in them, they may be assured that they will also "remain" in the Son and in the Father.

The use of the special Johannine word "remain" (*menō*, "abide") gives weight to the warning. The Word of the gospel must not only be heard but it must be given a vital place in one's life. The power of the gospel depends on the freedom permitted it. The Word is not present simply as a matter of course but only where a person is committed to receive it and unite with it. Marshall (p. 161) says, "It is not enough merely to have heard it and assented to the message in time past. The message must continue to be present and active in the lives of those who have heard it. They must continually call it to mind and let it affect their lives."

If the gospel "abides" in them, Christians may be assured they will also "abide" in the Son and in the Father. While the exhortation is clearly to faithfulness to the Word, it is an exhortation with an assured promise of fulfillment. Where the Word abides, there also the Son and Father abide. Fellowship with the Father and the Son, which is of such concern to the author, is assured those in whom the Word of God abides. The Word is not the goal of the fellowship but rather a means through which the fellowship with the Son and the Father occurs. The listing of the Son before the Father may emphasize the fact that access to the Father becomes possible only through the

Son (John 10:10; 17:2; 20:31). This is why denial of the Son has such fearful consequences.

25 What is promised in the gospel is the everlasting knowledge of Father and Son (John 17:3). It is a promise the community has already received. Eternal life has begun, but its eschatological fulfillment is also promised. What dimension this fellowship with the Son and the Father will assume in the "life to come" is yet unknown (3:2). But the hope is certain. All that is now known about it is only a foretaste of the glory that will be revealed. If the author shows concern about emphasizing the present possibilities of fellowship with the Son and the Father, he does not do so at the expense of the future.

26–27 The author concludes his attack on the false teachers with a warning and a word of encouragement for his followers. He has identified the heretical beliefs of those who have deserted the community of believers (v.22). He has properly labeled his opponents antichrists (v.18) and has described them as "those trying to lead you astray" (cf. 4:6; 2 John 7). This description is the more significant because it reveals the actual intent of those who have deserted the community. Not only have they forsaken the true faith, but they intend to lead many of the faithful astray. Their aim is to assume leadership over the community. They are enemies who are not content to spread new teaching but "invaders" and "deceivers" who seek to win the whole community over to their position.

Against their threat, John once more expresses his supreme confidence in the power of the divine anointing. The Son's gift of the Spirit, who accompanied the apostolic word "from the beginning," abides in them (cf. John 14:16). If they abide in the teaching and in the anointing, they need neither new teaching nor new teachers. Since they have received their "teaching" from the Son through those who were his witnesses from the beginning and have his "anointing," they have in fact no need for anyone more to teach them, not even John himself. Does he think of this letter as "teaching"? Probably not. He is simply reminding them to keep to the teaching they received from the beginning. His opponents are, however, false teachers, antichrists, deceivers, because they teach that which was not from the beginning. This definition of teachers differs from that found in the Pauline epistles, but the result is much the same. Though teaching in the Pauline church is a gift of ministry, what is taught can only be what was received from the beginning (Gal 1:6; 1 Tim 6:3; 2 Tim 1:13; 4:3–5; Titus 1:9; cf. also 2 Peter 3:2).

The last part of v.27 summarizes the threefold reason to trust the anointing already received from Jesus (2:20). First of all, his anointing teaches all things. "All things" seemingly means everything necessary and possible for them to know concerning the Word of Life. He does not mean to advance the idea, perhaps favored by some of his opponents, that the Spirit will add new revelation to what has already been given.

Second, this anointing is real (true) and not counterfeit (cf. John 15:26; 16:3), a reference to the gnosticizing opponents who claim as the source of their teaching a special anointing not commonly received by the company of believers. But the test of the anointing is its fidelity to that which is from the beginning. Since the opponents' teaching fails precisely at this point, their anointing is exposed as false or "counterfeit."

Third, the community has in its history experienced the teaching from the anointing

—i.e., they have known the confirming work of the Spirit in their lives. The gospel has taken root in them and has brought forth its fruit (cf. 2:12–14). Therefore John concludes with his most important word to them: "Remain [abide] in him [Christ]."

28 This verse makes the transition from concern about false teachers to concern for the children of God. It joins the admonition developed in the previous paragraph ("remain in him") to the confidence and unashamedness that should be the possession of the children of God when Christ appears. In some sense, John now explains what it means to remain or abide in Christ by the tests he now develops. *Mē aischynthēnai* can be either middle ("to be ashamed") or passive ("to be put to shame," "to be disgraced") in sense.

Parrhēsian ("confidence") in Acts and in Paul's writings especially denotes the boldness given through the Spirit for witnessing. It is also a favorite word of John's to describe the freedom that belongs to the Christian before God in prayer (3:21; 5:14; cf. Heb 4:16; 10:19) and at Christ's coming. "Confidence" is too weak a word to translate the Greek, but there is no suitable alternative.

Parousia ("coming") occurs only here in 1 John and not at all in John's Gospel. The combination of *phanerōthē* ("appears"), used in 1:2 to describe Jesus' historical appearance in the flesh, with *parousia*, the technical term to refer to Jesus' second coming, makes it certain that the author held in common with other early Christians that Jesus would return in visible splendor. Historically *parousia* was used to describe the festivities attendant on a monarch's arriving for a state visit. The early Christians anticipated the Lord's return as being no less joyous and majestic.

Notes

19 It is inescapable that the false teachers not only went out to establish their own teaching but also physically departed from fellowship with the community. Although Bultmann (p. 36) sees them as still claiming membership in the community, the language of "leaving and remaining" seems to imply a final separation.

20 The object of οἴδατε πάντες (*oidate pantes*, "you all know") is to be supplied from v.2, where *oidate* occurs again, followed by the object ἀλήθειαν (*alētheian*, "truth"). The author draws again on the innate knowledge his followers have as Christians. Lies cannot come from God. The antichrists are liars. Therefore they do not come from God who is the truth.

21 "Because" renders ὅτι (*hoti*) in the text. It may be understood as a simple causal dependent on ἔγραψα (*egrapsa*, "I wrote"; so NIV) or as an explanatory conjunction dependent on οἴδατε (*oidate*, "you know") (so RSV), which is far preferable. RSV reads "and know that no lie is of the truth" (italics mine).

27 The Greek allows the verb μένετε (*menete*) to be either indicative ("you abide") or imperative ("abide"). In view of the context, however, the imperative seems to be correct.

The Greek pronoun αὐτῷ (*autō*) here can mean either "in him" (the Father, the Son, or the Holy Spirit) or "in it" (the "anointing," which may be a reference to what has been taught). Again, the context seems to support "in him."

III. Requirements for Fellowship With God Who Is Righteous (2:29–4:6)

The main theme of this second main division of the epistle is to provide assurance that even as the believers "continue in Jesus" they can know they are the children of God. The "tests" for knowing this are (1) doing what is right (2:29–3:10), (2) loving one another (3:11–24), and (3) testing the spirits (4:1–6). Obedience will guarantee confidence before Jesus at his coming (2:28) and before God in prayer (3:21).

1. Doing What Is Right

2:29–3:10

29If you know that he is righteous, you know that everyone who does what is right has been born of him.
3:1How great is the love the Father has lavished on us, that we should be called children of God! And that is what we are! The reason the world does not know us is that it did not know him. 2Dear friends, now we are children of God, and what we will be has not yet been made known. But we know that when he appears, we shall be like him, for we shall see him as he is. 3Everyone who has this hope in him purifies himself, just as he is pure.
4Everyone who sins breaks the law; in fact, sin is lawlessness. 5But you know that he appeared so that he might take away our sins. And in him is no sin. 6No one who lives in him keeps on sinning. No one who continues to sin has either seen him or known him.
7Dear children, do not let anyone lead you astray. He who does what is right is righteous, just as he is righteous. 8He who does what is sinful is of the devil, because the devil has been sinning from the beginning. The reason the Son of God appeared was to destroy the devil's work. 9No one who is born of God will continue to sin, because God's seed remains in him; he cannot go on sinning, because he has been born of God. 10This is how we know who the children of God are and who the children of the devil are: Anyone who does not do what is right is not a child of God; neither is anyone who does not love his brother.

John begins this section with a promise of future likeness to Jesus (2:29–3:3), followed by a warning that a life of sin is not compatible with a life of fellowship with God but evidences the presence of the devil. Christ came to destroy the devil's work, prominent in which is hatred of one's brother.

29 There is a clear break in thought and a new topic—"tests for knowing the children of God"—introduced here. Attention naturally focuses on the Father (3:1) and the significance of being "born of him." Since John never speaks of being "born of Jesus," it makes more sense to conclude that the subject from the beginning of v.29 is the Father and that John depended on his readers to get the meaning from the total context.

Neither God's righteousness nor that of the Son appears to be the subject of dispute between John and his opponents (cf. 1:5; 2:1, 20; 3:7) but rather the significance of this righteousness. For John, who reflects the teaching that is "from the beginning," to be born of God and to become his child means to accept as the standard for Christian conduct the Father's righteousness as revealed through the Son (2:6; 3:7; cf. also Matt 5:48). Therefore, one must keep Jesus' commands, foremost of which is the command to love, which also becomes the test for distinguishing who is truly born of God. Those who obey his commands, who do his righteous will, should know (imperative force)

123

that they have been born of him. Righteous conduct is not a condition for rebirth but a consequence of it.

On the other hand, the opponents of the author, who presumably also claimed rebirth, apparently thought of it not in ethical or moral terms but in terms of nature (*physis*). They may have said that because they possessed the divine nature they could not sin (1:8) and were consequently removed from any obligation to the commandments (2:3–4). For them the proof that they were born of God or had fellowship with God lay in their new teaching, which freed them from commandments; in their knowledge, which enabled them to reject the fact that Christ had come in the flesh; and in their exclusivism, which allowed them to hate their brothers (3:17–20), forsake the community (2:19), and deny the commandment to love (3:10).

From the tone of the epistle, we conclude that the denial of the necessity to keep the commandments had not yet led to flagrant immoral conduct among the dissidents but that the implications of their theological method were seen by John as allowing—if not encouraging—that possibility. The willingness of the antagonists to destroy the community, to refuse the admonition of love, and to deny the significance of the message heard from the beginning certainly gave him no reason for optimism about the future.

3:1 The phrase "born of him [God]" (2:29) leads the author to marvel at the wonder of God's redemptive activity. See how great the gift of his love really is! Why he has identified us as being his very own children! And this is exactly what we have become through his acts. We have really been born of him. Clearly the author means to encourage his readers by reminding them of the grace of God they have received through the lavishness of God's own love. Such grace and love are missing from his opponents' lives. Love appears to be of no concern to them. They fail to recognize God's love and feel no obligation to express it. But apart from love, there would have been no children of God.

Because the believers are the children of God, the author warns them that the world is unable to recognize them or relate to them. That should not surprise them because neither did the world recognize God. The failure of the world to know God is one of the basic themes of the Gospel of John (5:37; 7:28; 16:3). Those who belong to the world live in darkness. They cannot come to the light but must inevitably hate it. This "belonging to the world" becomes also a matter of their choice; i.e., they refuse to acknowledge God in their hearts.

The author wants his readers to know that approval by the world is to be feared, not desired. To be hated by the world may be unpleasant, but ultimately it should reassure the members of the community of faith that they are loved by God, which is far more important than the world's hatred.

2 Though they are now God's children, the unveiling of their identity or the complete revelation of their nature still lies in the future. Moreover, "has not yet been made known" probably means that it is a "mystery" to be revealed only at the last time. The author encourages no speculation in these matters. His concern is to reiterate the "tradition" from which the promise comes. He (Jesus) will appear. We will see him as he truly is; his full glory will be revealed (cf. John 17:1, 5, 24). We will become like him. That the author is once more presenting the teaching shared in the church "from the beginning" seems clear from its similarity to Paul's teaching: We shall "be conformed to the likeness of his Son" (Rom 8:29; cf. 1 Cor 15:49); we are being transfigured into his likeness—from one degree of glory to another; and with unveiled face we will behold the glory of the Lord (2 Cor 3:18; Col 3:4).

3 All who have their hope in Jesus, i.e., their hope of being like him (3:2) when he appears (2:28), will also be committed to keeping themselves from sin. They will put away every defilement; they will aim to be like him in purity and righteousness. Once more we have the pattern of the incarnate Jesus being held up as an example to believers (cf. 2:6; 3:7, 16; 4:17). Those who claim likeness to him must be conformed to his earthly life, even as they wait for his coming. To live in sin or disobedience to his commands is to abandon any hope in him. It is the pure in heart who will see God (cf. Matt 5:8).

4 Here John uses two words to describe sin: *hamartian* and *anomian* (translated here "lawlessness"). In the OT as well as the NT, these two words are used frequently as synonyms (cf. Pss 32:1; 51:3; Rom 4:7; Heb 10:17). In John's community, however, they were used apparently with different meanings. "Sin" (*hamartian*) was used to describe the transgression of the law, the breaking of the commandments of God. "Lawlessness" (*anomian*) defined sin as rebellion against God and was connected with Satan's rebellion against God. This latter concept had its origin early in the teaching of the church (Matt 7:22; 24:11–13; 2 Cor 6:14–16; 2 Thess 2:1–12). Apparently the false teachers and John agreed that "lawlessness" was incompatible with being born of God. What they did not agree on was that sin, defined as transgression of the moral law, was "lawlessness." Indeed, as those "born of God" they claimed themselves "morally" to be sinless, or guiltless. Either they believed that they were by nature incapable of violating the law or that sinful deeds done in the flesh were of no concern to God, and they were therefore "sinless" in his sight.

John decries such a dichotomy. That his opponents hate their brothers (2:11) shows that their claim to sinlessness is a lie, which along with their failure to love stems from one source, their lawlessness. And their lawlessness shows that they do not belong to God but to the devil (3:10). They are part of the evil soon to be revealed (2:18).

5 In this verse John turns again to the teaching received "from the beginning" in order to raise two additional arguments against sin as a principle of life. First, not only is sin lawlessness (v.4), but Jesus appeared in history in order to remove it (cf. John 1:29; Heb 9:26). Second, Jesus lived a sinless life (cf. 2:1; 3:3; 2 Cor 5:21). In this latter statement the author probably is looking in two directions. Because Jesus was sinless, the devil had no hold on him (cf. John 14:30). Therefore Jesus was able to destroy the works of the devil, one of which is sinning (3:8).

But in addition, Jesus' sinlessness reveals what kind of lifestyle is proper for those who abide in him. John uses the present tense ("in him is no sin") to emphasize that sinlessness is characteristic of Jesus' eternal nature. He was sinless in his preexistence, in his life in the flesh, and in his eternal position as Son.

6 This verse seems to contradict 1:8, 10. However, as we have reconstructed the situation (see comment on 3:4), the author simultaneously faced two different problems with these precursors of Gnosticism. There were those who apparently claimed to be sinless by nature; i.e., they were unable to sin because they were "born of God."

There were others who claimed a standing with God apart from a life of righteousness. They believed that the commandments had no authority over them, i.e., over their flesh, and taught that it was a matter of indifference to God whether they sinned or not. Therefore they could hate their brothers without guilt or concern (cf. Dodd, *Johannine Epistles*, p. 80; Stott p. 126).

In opposition to the latter opponents, the author states that those who "live" in the "sinless one" will, like him, live a life of righteousness. They commit themselves not to sin. And if they sin, they will confess it as lawlessness and abandon it.

John acknowledges the life of righteousness, or sinlessness, as being possible only in Christ. By "living" in him, in his "sinlessness," one can expect conformity to his righteousness. On the other hand, those who continue to sin make it certain that they have never had their eyes opened spiritually to see him, nor have they ever known him (cf. John 5:37–38; 8:19; 14:7, 9; 3 John 11).

7 The warning "do not let anyone lead you astray" appears to have been directed against the false teachers in the community. The author, by using the address "dear children" (cf. 2:1), places his own position in the community on the line.

8 There is clearly a progression in the author's thought on sin in this section. He begins with the "sinfulness" of sin—viz., "it is lawlessness," rebellion against God (v.4). Next he shows its incompatibility with Christ: "He appeared so that he might take away our sins" (v.5). Then he shows its incompatibility for anyone who lives in Christ: "No one who lives in him keeps on sinning" (v.6). Now he shows the diabolic nature of sin—its source is the devil who "has been sinning from the beginning" (v.8). The statement that the Son of God appeared "to destroy the devil's work" is an elaboration of what John said in v.5.

John sees the enmity of God against the devil as absolute. It lies at the heart of God's commitment to rescue man from the devil's clutches. It is a battle without quarter. God will destroy the devil and all his works, including those children of the devil who accept sinning as a way of life. The statement "the devil has been sinning from the beginning" probably refers to the Genesis account of the Fall and includes an identification of the devil with the serpent. He was, from the beginning, evil. "He was a murderer from the beginning, not holding to the truth" (John 8:44). The force of the statement is that the character, the very being of those like the false teachers, derives from the devil. His desires become their desires (John 8:44). Like him they become liars and seducers. Those who continue in sin prove themselves to be the children of sin and the children of the devil (3:10).

9 John summarizes what he has said. In v.6 he stated that no one who "lives in him" can practice a life of sin. Here he adds that "no one who is born of God" or has "God's seed" in him can "continue to sin." Both elements are necessary for understanding John's theology of community. The believers must abide or "live" in him. The Father in turn must dwell in the believers (3:24; 4:12; cf. John 14:20; 17:21–23). If we live in him, "we are removed" from "life in the world," or life under the dominion of Satan. If he lives in us, then our life will be his life in us and we will live even as he lived.

10 This verse reveals the heart of the entire section and furnishes a transition to the next one. It is not a theoretical consideration of the nature of sinfulness or the possibility of sinlessness that occupies the author but the issue of the community. How are the children (community) of God to be recognized and how are the children (community) of the devil to be discerned?

"Anyone who does not do what is right is not a child of God." And what is the "right" he does not do? He "does not love his brother." "Love for one's brother" is the true test of righteous behavior. This requirement of love helps explain the absolute requirement that those who are born of God "cannot go on sinning" (vv.6, 9). For if God is love, and if God lives in us and we in him, then love for the brethren will occur as an expression of righteousness without exception. Bruce (p. 93) comments on this connecting of love with righteousness: "For him, righteousness and love are inseparable; since they are inseparable in the character of God and in His revelation in Christ, so they must be inseparable in the lives of His people."

"Righteousness involves the fulfillment of all law, of relation to God and to man, both personally and socially. The love of Christian for Christian, resting on the sense of a divine fellowship (cf. 1:3) carries forward to its loftiest embodiment the righteousness which man can reach" (Westcott, p. 106).

The author, then, is not stressing absolute moral conformity or "sinless perfection" but the one requirement by which all other requirements are measured—love for one's brother. For this there is no substitute, its violation allows for no excuse, its application permits no compromise. Here there are no gray areas, no third possibilities. One either loves his brother and proves he is God's child or does not love his brother and proves he belongs to the devil.

Notes

29 Γινώσκετε (ginōskete, "know") has the same Greek form in the indicative and the imperative. Γεγέννηται ἐξ αὐτοῦ (gegennētai ex autou, "born of him") is a favorite concept of the author (cf. 3:9; 4:7; 5:1, 4, 18; cf. also John 1:13; 3:3–8).

3:1 Bultmann (p. 41) notes that in the Gnostic literature "there is no mention of brotherly love."

3 The phrase "everyone who has" is used characteristically by John to refer "to someone who had questioned the application of a general principle in particular cases" (Westcott, p. 98). In this situation his opponents probably claimed likeness to God for themselves though they refused to be obedient to the commandments, especially the commandment of love.

The *Translator's Handbook* gives the following helpful analysis for hope: "There are to be distinguished four main semantic components which combine in various ways to represent the concept of "hope." These are (1) time, for hope always looks to the future; (2) anticipation, for there is always some goal to the time span; (3) confidence, namely, that the goal hoped for will occur; and (4) desire, since the goal of hoping is a valued object or experience" (Haas, deJonge, and Swellengrebel, p. 79).

7 Note the interchangeable character of certain key words in this context. The author can say "that everyone who does what is right has been born of him" as in 2:29, or that everyone "who does what is right is righteous." (For the phrase "just as he is righteous," see comments on 2:6, 29; 3:3).

9 The use of "seed" to describe the divine life in believers is common in the later Gnostic literature. John clearly means the term figuratively. It may refer to the Spirit (cf. John 3:6; so Schnackenburg), his offspring (so Moffatt), Jesus as the Word (John 1:12), the Word of God (cf. Luke 8:11; 1 Peter 1:23, 25; so Dodd), or God's nature (Goodspeed). In any instance, it is not the means of the divine presence that is the issue but the fact of that presence.

2. Loving One Another

3:11–24

> [11]This is the message you heard from the beginning: We should love one another. [12]Do not be like Cain, who belonged to the evil one and murdered his brother. And why did he murder him? Because his own actions were evil and his brother's were righteous. [13]Do not be surprised, my brothers, if the world hates you. [14]We know that we have passed from death to life, because we love our brothers. Anyone who does not love remains in death. [15]Anyone who hates his brother is a murderer, and you know that no murderer has eternal life in him.
>
> [16]This is how we know what love is: Jesus Christ laid down his life for us. And we ought to lay down our lives for our brothers. [17]If anyone has material possessions and sees his brother in need but has no pity on him, how can the love of God be in him? [18]Dear children, let us not love with words or tongue but with actions and in truth. [19]This then is how we know that we belong to the truth, and how we set our hearts at rest in his presence [20]whenever our hearts condemn us. For God is greater than our hearts, and he knows everything.
>
> [21]Dear friends, if our hearts do not condemn us, we have confidence before God [22]and receive from him anything we ask, because we obey his commands and do what pleases him. [23]And this is his command: to believe in the name of his Son, Jesus Christ, and to love one another as he commanded us. [24]Those who obey his commands live in him, and he in them. And this is how we know that he lives in us: We know it by the Spirit he gave us.

As the knowledge of God is tested by conduct—whether one walks in the light (1:5–2:11)—so being "born of God" (2:29) is tested by righteous action and love of the brethren. The command to love the brethren was first introduced in 2:9–11 as a test of whether one was walking in light, i.e., had true knowledge. Here it is the sum of the new life in God. In the former instance it was primarily leveled as a charge against the heretics. Here it is addressed to the community of faith both for encouragement and for admonition. It is likely that the disregard for the principle of love by the heretics had caused a lessening of the emphasis of love within the community. The author's procedure is to present the case for love first by the negative example of Cain (vv.12–15) contrasted with the positive example of Jesus (v.16).

11 The admonition that "we should love one another" is highlighted by the return to the critical formula "This is the message you heard from the beginning," an almost identical reminiscence of 1:1 and 1:5. Since the nature of God as light is the foundation of the gospel that was received from the beginning, so the command to "love one another" has the same origin. Love is not the application of the "message" but the goal established "from the beginning." As Westcott (pp. 100–101) says, "The whole aim of the gospel is the creation and strengthening of love. . . . The words ['love one another'] do not simply give the content of the message, but its aim, its purpose."

12 The mention of Cain points back to 3:8 and reminds us that hatred is also from the beginning. The choice between the children of God and the children of the devil, between "hatred and love, life and death, murder and self-sacrifice," stems from the earliest moment of man's existence (Stott, p. 139). It also probably points to John 8:37–47, where some Jewish opponents of Jesus had exhibited the same kind of hatred toward Jesus that Cain expressed toward Abel (8:59). There Jesus says to them, despite their claim to be Abraham's children: "As it is, you are determined to kill me. . . . If God were your Father, you would love me. . . . You belong to your father, the devil, and you want to carry out your father's desire. He was a murderer from the beginning, not holding the truth" (John 8:40, 42, 44). The overlap of language and ideas between the two passages supports Dodd's contention that John 8 was probably in the author's mind when he wrote this section.

The sequence of thought in this section of 1 John is probably significant. It is not that Cain by murdering his brother became the child of the devil; but, being a child of the devil, his actions were evil and culminated in the murder of his brother. The reason given for the murder is that his brother's acts were righteous. Righteousness draws hatred from the devil and hatred from the children of the devil. Darkness cannot tolerate light; immorality, morality; hatred, love; or greed, sacrifice. All the words of darkness are shown to be what they really are by the light; hatred that can lead to such brutality as Cain's slaughter of Abel. *Sphazō*, the verb for "murder" (used twice in v. 12), has the meaning of "butcher" or "slaughter" (BAG, p. 803). This verse is the only direct reference to the OT in the epistle.

13 The hatred of the world for the community of faith must not surprise the believers. The author does not say that the world always hates believers. It did not always hate Jesus. But whenever the community of faith acts so as to expose the greed, the avarice, the hatred, and the wickedness of the world, it must expect rejection; and if it should go so far as to interfere with its evil practices, as Jesus did in the temple, it may expect suffering and brutal death (cf. John 15:18–19, 25; 17:14).

"Brothers" (*adelphoi*) occurs only here in 1 John. At this most critical point, the author appears to step past his relationship to them as "little children" and to openly proclaim them his peers. Perhaps they have already experienced persecution with him. Or perhaps he associates himself with them this way because he knows that if they receive his letter and obey it, persecution will soon come because they have identified themselves with him rather than with his opponents.

14 This verse looks back to v. 10 and answers the question How do we know who have been "born of God"? or Who are the children of God? by saying, "We know that we have passed from death to life, because we love our brothers" (cf. John 5:24). This conviction is not based on self-judgment or self-justification but on the certainty that love is the basis for life in the believing community. As Bultmann (p. 55) observes, "The arrogant 'we know' makes the congregation aware of its real character, against which each individual member is to measure himself. In this sense, therefore, v. 14 is also an indirect admonition as was the case of v. 6a. The question is therefore posed for each individual, whether he belongs to the Christian congregation." Love will not cause the passage to spiritual life but will give evidence of it. Conversely, to be unable to love means that a person is without life from the Father and remains in death.

15 Here John links hatred with murder. We are reminded of Matthew 5:21–22, where Jesus made the two equivalent. In the heart there is no difference; to hate is to despise, to cut off from relationship, and murder is simply the fulfillment of that attitude. Cain, because he murdered his brother, was cut off from the covenant community. He received no promise. So no murderer is within the community, nor anyone who "hates his brother." He has no life of God, no rebirth, no fellowship with the faithful.

16 The test of true love is identified as willingness to sacrifice one's life for one's brother. The demonstrative "this" that begins the statement points backward to the negative example of Cain and forward to the positive example of Christ (cf. Westcott, p. 110). Love is used absolutely and its reference point is Christ's death. The demand for love thus arises from his command, and the meaning of love is found in his example.

In the Greek "we know" (*egnōkamen*) is in the perfect tense. It shows that the knowledge that is involved belongs to the historical event of Jesus Christ. It was the same knowledge that was transmitted through those who saw it and heard it from the beginning (1:1; 3:11). *Agapē* ("love") cannot be derived from some intuitive grasp of an idea but is known in the historical event in which Jesus Christ laid down his life for us. His sacrificial death thus distinguishes *agapē* love from all other loves by its costliness, its unconditional acceptance of another, and its "accomplishment." Its costliness is expressed in the Gospel of John by the image of the Good Shepherd who lays down his life for his sheep (John 10:11).

The personal commitment of Christ is expressed in the words of John 15:12–13 (cf. 13:1): "Love each other as I have loved you. Greater love has no one than this, that one lay down his life for his friends." Its accomplishment as a "for us" kind of love is reflected in Jesus' work. "I give them eternal life" (John 10:28). It is clear that Jesus understood his death as an effectual, accomplishing act—the only method open to him to fulfill his Father's will (cf. John 10:11–18; 27–30; 15:9–18; 17:19). (That John's understanding is held in common with early apostolic witness is shown by Mark 10:45; Rom 5:8; Gal 1:4; Titus 2:14; 1 Peter 3:18.)

Since *agapē* love is grounded in Jesus' death "for us," it is clear that knowledge of it can be received only where his "death" is appropriated into our experience. Bultmann points out that only when we have "experienced" love can we know love. "From his love for us we learn what love is" (p. 55).

The dramatic conclusion we are irresistibly led to is this: "And we ought to lay down our lives for our brothers." We are to do this not simply because that is what Jesus did, but because that is what Jesus revealed to be the demand of *agapē* love. Love is denial of self for another's gain. It is doing what Jesus himself would do.

17 Again John's penchant for providing practical "tests" of the validity of one's faith comes to the fore. How can we know whether we would sacrifice our life for a brother? We can know by being compassionate toward him in his present need. If we are unable or unwilling to sacrifice material advantage for the sake of our brother, we know the love of God is not in us. What are the conditions for our involvement with our brother? If we are in a position to see (*theōreō*) with our own eyes his need, as, for example, the good Samaritan did, and can offer help, then we cannot do otherwise than act. To withhold help from a brother in need, to shut off compassionate action, is to deny the presence of God's love in one's own heart. As Dodd says, "If such a minimal response to the law of charity, called for by such an everyday situation, is absent, then it is idle to pretend that we are within the family of God, the realm in which love is operative as the principle and the token of eternal life" (*Johannine Epistles,* p. 86).

18 The vocative "little children" gives this admonition the tone of a spiritual father pleading for the heart-felt response of his children. Love requires more than idle talk or exalted theology. It demands simple acts, which anyone can see, that meet the needs of brothers and sisters in distress. Any expression of love that fails here is not only empty but blasphemous. "Suppose a brother or sister is without clothes and daily food. If one of you says to him, 'Go, I wish you well; keep warm and well fed,' but does nothing about his physical needs, what good is it?" (James 2:15; cf. 1 Cor 13:1).

19–20 John began this section (2:29–4:6) by addressing the question How may we be confident and unashamed at Christ's coming? (cf. 2:28). The answer expressed in the phrases "continue in Jesus" and "doing what is right" (2:29; 3:7, 10) is tested by our love for our brothers. Now the author addresses the question of assurance—i.e., confidence before God. How may "we know that we belong to the truth" (3:19) and how do we deal with our own condemning hearts (3:20–21)? The anxious note in the first part of the question should probably be attributed at least in part to the unrelenting attack of opponents on the "teaching" and "beliefs" of the Christian community. The whole section, however, may also simply be explaining the nature of "fellowship" with the Father (1:3).

The passage itself is complex in the Greek and allows several translations and interpretations. "This" (v.19) may be taken to point backward to the absolute demand of love introduced in 3:14ff. If we know that we love truly, with actions and not mere words, that knowledge will not only assure us "that we belong to the truth" but will also act to "set our hearts at rest in his presence whenever our hearts condemn us."

It is possible, however, in the Greek text to make a full stop after "presence" and then read v.20 as follows: "If our hearts should condemn us, God is greater than our hearts, and he knows everything."

Another possibility is that the "this" in v.19 points not only backward to 3:14ff. but forward to v.20b. The meaning would be as follows: There are two ways we know that we "belong to the truth": First, because we love in deed; second, God himself assures us that we belong to the truth—he "is greater than our hearts, and he knows everything." The latter possibility is preferable because it allows a more connected argument.

In any instance, what is stressed is *agapē* love, which always expressed first in deeds, is reassuring evidence that we are of God. Why our hearts should condemn us is not discussed by the author. Apparently it is not important. His readers, like all others, know how easily the conscience can render us ineffective. Doubt, guilt, and failure are never far from any of us. Sometimes our misgivings are the result of our own actions or inactions. Sometimes it is the "accuser" who seizes our weaknesses and shortcomings and so elevates them that we wonder whether we can really be in the truth. What then can we do? We can remember that God understands everything. His word and his truth are greater than our feelings or our conscience. We may rest ourselves in his love for us and live in that love and by that love. We will not excuse ourselves of any sin, but neither will we needlessly accuse ourselves (cf. 1 Cor 4:3–5).

21 Christians are called to fellowship with God (1:3; 2:24). But if they are guilt-ridden and conscience-stricken, rather than seeking that fellowship or enjoying it, they will flee the presence of God. They will be unable to abide in him or claim their position as "his children." Nor will they dare seek answers to prayer that he alone can provide. On the other hand, those who have his peace in their hearts will have "confidence" not only at his appearing but in the ordinary here-and-now relationship to the Father, especially as it involves prayer. Believers will stand in his presence "naturally" as those who are supposed to be there, because he has so provided for them.

22 The fruit of this boldness is God's own openness to his children. He will never withhold any good thing from those who ask. The author does not give the basis for his assurance, but his words "because we obey his commands and do what pleases him" point directly to Jesus' own words in John 8:28–29: "I do nothing on my own but speak just what the Father has taught me . . . for I always do what pleases him." Jesus, who always did his Father's will, knew that his Father heard him: "I knew that you always hear me" (John 11:42), he says to the Father. Likewise Jesus assures his disciples, "In that day you will ask in my name. I am not saying that I will ask the Father on your behalf. No, the Father himself loves you" (John 16:26–27).

23 This verse specifies what command it is that the children must obey in order to receive whatever they ask of him (v. 22). It is "to believe in the name of his Son, Jesus Christ, and to love one another."

"Belief," which occurs here for the first time in 1 John, will be seen more and more as the issue between John and the "heretics." The "false teachers" do not "love"—that is clear—but the reason they do not love is that God's love is not in them, for they have not truly believed in Jesus Christ, the Son of God. To believe in Jesus Christ means in this context to believe the gospel about Jesus—that he is God's Son, that he came to save men and women from their sins, and that by believing in him they can have eternal life (John 3:16–18). The joining of belief and love in a single command shows how inextricably connected the two are in John's mind. Belief comes first because it is the basis for love (cf. 3:16), but love is the only expression of true faith.

The end of the command—"and to love one another as he commanded us"—recalls Jesus' own command given in the Gospel of John (13:34; 15:12, 17). The practice of the author to make no attempt to distinguish the subjects of verbs or the antecedents of pronouns as to whether Jesus or the Father is in view is characteristic of his writing. It is also characteristic of his theology. God is revealed in Christ Jesus. To see the Son is to see the Father; to know the Father is to know the Son. The deeds of the one are the deeds of the other. So completely are the wills of the Father and the Son joined that it is many times a matter of indifference as to which one is in view.

24 In this summary verse the author states for the first time in this epistle the mutual reciprocity involved in "living" in God. Obedience issues in the perfection of the "fellowship" between God and us. We "live" in him. He "lives" in us. We come to our "fellowship" with the Father through the "fellowship" the Son has with the Father (John 14:20; 17:21–23). The Son also enters into fellowship with us (15:4–5); and through him we have fellowship with the Father and with one another, just as the sign of our fellowship with the Father and with the Son is our love for them (cf. John 17:23–26). Clearly, Jesus' words in the Gospel of John are the basis for this expansion of the relation of love to "living" in God in 1 John.

The latter part of v. 24 characteristically furnishes the transition to the next section. The evidence that we abide in him is our obedience to his commands. The evidence that he abides in us is the presence of his Spirit, whom he gave to us (cf. Rom 5:5; 8:14–16). This is the first mention of the Spirit in 1 John. The author presupposes knowledge about the Spirit in his readers. He does not rehearse the teaching about the Spirit from his Gospel but only applies it to the particular problem at hand— distinguishing the true Spirit from false spirits (4:1–3) and receiving the Spirit's witness (5:6–7). The reference to the Spirit as the one "he gave us" is not an appeal to their existential experience of the Spirit but to their knowledge of the gospel as it had come to them from the eyewitnesses. The Father's giving or the Son's sending the Spirit to the disciples (John 14–16; 20:22) was a well-known event in the church (cf. Acts 1–2; Rom 8; Gal 4:6).

Notes

11 The phrase "to love one another" (cf. 3:23, 4:7, 11–12) is not essentially different in 1 John from the command "to love one's brother" (2:10; 3:10; 4:20–21) or "to love our brothers" (3:14). The reference is to the community of faith where Christian love must always begin and "abide."

14 The plural ἀδελφοί (adelphoi, "brothers") is used here "to show that the reference is to individual persons, whereas the singular is used when the reference is to the group viewed as a collectivity" (Haas, deJonge, and Swellengrebel, p. 90).

17 The Greek allows the genitival expression "love of God" to be descriptive, "the divine love," or possessive, "God's love," or objective, "love for God." But the subjective use, "love that comes from God," fits the context best.

21 "Confidence" translates παρρησία (parrēsia). "The word rendered **confidence** stood in ancient Greece for the most valued right of a citizen in a free state, the right to 'speak his mind' . . . unhampered by fear or shame. In our relationship to God such freedom of speech is not an inherent right, but is strictly dependent upon an equally frank and straightforward obedience to the divine will (verse 22)" (Dodd, *Johannine Epistles*, p. 93).

23 Πιστεύω (pisteuō, "believe") occurs in 4:1, 16; 5:1, 5, 10, 13. Πίστις (pistis, "faith") appears only in 5:4. In contrast to ἀγαπῶμεν (agapōmen, "we should love"), which is in the present tense, πιστεύσωμεν (pisteusōmen, "we should believe") is aorist, which stresses faith as an event, as when one "confesses" his faith in Christ (cf. 4:3) and acknowledges him as the Son of God (2:23).

3. *Warning Against the False Spirits*

4:1–6

¹Dear friends, do not believe every spirit, but test the spirits to see whether they are from God, because many false prophets have gone out into the world. ²This is how you can recognize the Spirit of God: Every spirit that acknowledges that Jesus Christ has come in the flesh is from God, ³but every spirit that does not acknowledge Jesus is not from God. This is the spirit of the antichrist, which you have heard is coming and even now is already in the world.

⁴You, dear children, are from God and have overcome them, because the one who is in you is greater than the one who is in the world. ⁵They are from the world and therefore speak from the viewpoint of the world, and the world listens to them. ⁶We are from God, and whoever knows God listens to us; but whoever is not from God does not listen to us. This is how we recognize the Spirit of truth and the spirit of falsehood.

This passage parallels 2:18–27, where the author warned against the presence of antichrists among those who had "gone out" from them. Now he directs a second warning to his followers, this time against the spirit of antichrist, who even now inspires false prophets among the dissenters (v.1). The false spirit can be detected because he will deny that Jesus Christ came in the flesh (v.3). The community of faith will overcome the false prophets because believers belong to God, and the Spirit in them is greater than the false spirit (v.4). The world listens to the false prophets (v.5), but the children of God listen to the apostolic declaration. Belief of the gospel is the true test of the Holy Spirit's presence and work (v.6).

1 The opponents not only lay claim to God but boast of their "inspiration" by the "spirit." Likely they gave evidence of their "inspiration" through "prophetic utterings" and perhaps even other signs such as ecstasies and glossolalia. Such "signs" were present in the religious milieu of the Greeks and Romans and most persons took them seriously. That they sometimes caused special problems in the early church is attested by Paul (cf. 1 Cor 12:3; ch. 14; 1 Thess 5:21). The warning is not against those who "feign" the Spirit's presence but against genuine evil spirits' inspiring the existence of false prophets—i.e., those who had left the community. By outward token these people were no less inspired than members of the faithful community. They were zealous in proclamation (cf. 2 John 7) and may have been even more successful than the faithful community in making converts from the world (4:5). Likely John saw in them the fulfillment of Jesus' warnings (cf. Mark 13:22) against false prophets in the "end times" (cf. 2:18).

The false prophets' success would itself be a problem and was probably used as an authenticating sign by them. Therefore, the need for some test to discern the presence of false prophets was all the more critical.

2 The test itself appears to hinge on the words "that Jesus Christ has come in the flesh." The false prophets may well have believed that Christ was the Savior of the world, but they probably denied the connection between the divine Christ with Jesus of Nazareth. At least they clearly denied that "the Christ" ever had come "in the flesh." This denial makes them not only precursors of Gnosticism but also of Docetism. The confession John urges speaks not only against those heresies but against any form of adoptionism as well. The clause "that Jesus Christ has come" reflects the author's clear view of the preexistence of the Son, who came from the Father and from the moment of his historical birth was Jesus Christ in the flesh.

How does this confession give evidence of the Spirit? For John, as for Paul, the truth of the Christian gospel is hid from the world (cf. 1 Cor 2:7–16). Only because there is a divine intervention and the darkness is removed can the light of the gospel be recognized (cf. 4:6).

3 Here a negative confession gives the counterpart of that in v.2, and the source of this denial is seen to be the spirit of antichrist. John reminds his followers that Jesus had warned that the Antichrist would come. It is now John's painful duty to announce that in the false teachers (2:18ff.) the spirit of antichrist is already present. By this the community was warned that the conflict between the false teachers and John was not a "leadership" or "personality" one. The Gospel itself was at stake. The struggle in the controversy was not against flesh and blood but against principalities and powers (Eph 6:12). Hence, whatever success the opponents had had within the community resulted from satanic inspiration.

4 The use of "dear children" shows the author's desire to address all the faithful in the community once more (cf. 2:1). They have indeed overcome the false prophets, because they resisted their teaching (v.5). So they establish the fact that they are "from

God"—that is "born of him" (2:29)—and that the one who is in them is "greater than the one who is in the world" (v.4). The false teachers do not have the Spirit of Christ living in them because "living" involves "fellowship," which is possible between God and his children only by the Holy Spirit. The false teachers are without this fellowship. Therefore they do not love because they do not know love. The antichrist can be "in the world" and evil spirits can be "in the false teachers," but "living in God" is possible only for the children of God.

5 In contrast to the "dear children" who "are from God" are the false teachers who "are from the world." The false teachers are successful "in the world" because their thinking, their theology, is accomodated to the world's beliefs. So their teaching is philosophically congenial to the prevailing currents of the day. Naturally the world hears such teachers gladly. The term "world" (*kosmos*) is probably to be understood in two ways: as a system of thought antithetical to Christian belief and as a description of those members of the community who were led astray by the false teachers. That some members of the community were easily persuaded to forsake the truth of the gospel should not bewilder the faithful. Although these members appeared to belong to the community, their willingness to hear and follow the false teachers showed their true colors.

6 The author repeats the description of the true followers as "we [who] are from God." The "we" probably is meant to include all the faithful but has particular reference to the true teachers. Whoever "knows" God, (i.e., has knowledge through fellowship with him by loving him and abiding in him and his Word) "listens to us"—not just to any words we may speak, but "listens to us" as we proclaim the word "heard from the beginning." The argument is parallel to that of Jesus in John 8:47: "He who belongs to God hears what God says. The reason you do not hear is that you do not belong to God" (cf. John 10:4–5; 18:37). So a second test for discerning the presence of the Spirit of God is added to the one developed in v.2. When people confess that Jesus came in the flesh, when they hear God speak to them in the gospel of his Son and are obedient to it, then the "Spirit of truth" has been present and active. When people deny the gospel, when they will not hear it as God's Word and will not confess that Jesus Christ has come in the flesh, then "the spirit of falsehood" has been at work.

Notes

3 An alternate reading to μὴ ὁμολογεῖ (*mē homologei*, "not acknowledge," "not confess") is λύει (*lyei*, "destroy," "annul"). Commentators are divided about which is the original and which is the explanatory gloss. It does not affect the meaning, because to "annul" that Jesus is from God, that he, the Son of God, has indeed come in human flesh into the world, would be an even more drastic way of referring to this denial (cf. Brooke, pp. 111–14; Bultmann, p. 62; Marshall, p. 207).

4 Here, as in vv.11, 18–27, protection against evil or victory over evil is ascribed both to an objective standard of doctrine and to the indwelling Spirit who illumines our minds to grasp and apply this victory; for "unless the Spirit of wisdom is present, there is little or no profit in having God's Word in our hearts" (Calvin, cited in Stott, p. 157).

6 The "Spirit of truth" occurs only here in 1 John, but see the Gospel of John 14:17; 15:26; 16:13. The phrase "the spirit of error" is unique in the NT but is comparable to "the spirit of the world" in 1 Cor 2:12. For reference to the two spirits in Jewish literature, see IQS 3.18 and Testament of Judah 20.1.

IV. Requirements for Fellowship With God Who Is Love (4:7–5:12)

The third main division of the epistle has as its major thesis an analysis of love. Love of one's brother was first introduced as a test of living in God who is light (2:9–11). The command to love received an even more significant treatment as a test of being born of God who is righteous (3:10–24). Here love of fellow believers finds its most complete representation in the Father's own being and activity.

1. Brotherly Love

4:7–12

> [7]Dear friends, let us love one another, for love comes from God. Everyone who loves has been born of God and knows God. [8]Whoever does not love does not know God, because God is love. [9]This is how God showed his love among us: He sent his one and only Son into the world that we might live through him. [10]This is love: not that we loved God, but that he loved us and sent his Son as an atoning sacrifice for our sins. [11]Dear friends, since God so loved us, we also ought to love one another. [12]No one has ever seen God; but if we love each other, God lives in us and his love is made complete in us.

7 The vocative "dear friends" (cf. 2:7; 4:1; lit., "beloved") and the imperative force of the verb make clear that the author is speaking primarily to the community itself. His intention is to provide final assurance that the community's commitment to mutual love is the explicit requirement of the gospel as revealed in God himself. Love for one's brother comes "from God." It is evidence of our being "born of God" that is as important as righteous behavior is (2:29). It is not a virtue innate in us nor is it learned behavior. It is "from God." He is the originator—the giver of love. Furthermore, whoever truly loves "his brother" not only is born of God (2:28; 3:24) but also "knows God."

8 Conversely, whoever does not love does not "know" God at all, for God in his very nature is love. To the statements, then, that God is light (1:5) and God is righteous (2:29), John adds the supreme statement "God is love" (4:8, 16). Love so conceived is not to be understood as one of God's many activities but rather that "all His activity is loving activity. If He creates, He creates in love; if He rules, He rules in love; if He judges, He judges in love. All that He does is the expression of His nature, is—to love" (Dodd, *Johannine Epistles*, p. 110). Since this is true of God, our failure to love can only mean that we have no true knowledge of God, we have not really been born of him, we do not have his nature.

9 The simple but profound statement "God is love" is explained by what God did. He "showed his love among us: He sent his one and only Son into the world that we might live through him" (cf. John 3:16–17). The author makes clear that the love he speaks of involves concrete and objective acts. God's love required him to send his Son. God's love in us requires deeds by which we show our love for one another.

The phrase "among us" (*en hēmin*) may be translated "in us," indicating the medium in which God revealed his Son and for whom the revelation was effective (cf. Brooke and Westcott), or "to us" (cf. Schnackenburg) or "for us" (cf. Bultmann).

"One and only" translates *monogenēs,* a word that both serves as "a predicate of value and designates the unique one as beloved at the same time" (Bultmann, p. 67).

The purpose of God's act is "that we might live through him. Death is man's present condition (cf. 3:14). God's act has as its intention not just our salvation (Gospel of John 3:17) but our 'living.' And it is to be a 'living' in love so that God's love is seen 'visibly working' in us and through us" (Westcott, p. 141).

10 "This" has as its point of reference God's act for us as stated in vv.9–10. In v.10 the author distinguishes *agapē* love from any love claimed by the false teachers. It is not that "we loved God" (3:17; 4:20) as his opponents claimed but that "he loved us." For the author, *agapē* love can be given to God only when it has first been received from God. It exists only as response to his initial love for us. Moreover, it is God's love for us that defines what true love requires, which is the commitment to sacrifice one's most beloved possession for another's gain. So for God, love required that he send "his Son as an atoning sacrifice for our sins."

The difference in understanding between John and the false teachers is never greater than in their understanding of love. The false teachers claimed to love God but understood love not in Christian terms but in those of Greek philosophy. As Dodd (*Johannine Epistles,* p. 111) points out, love in the Hellenistic world became a "cosmic principle, and the mystical craving for union with the eternal is given a metaphysical basis." In religious terms, love is perceived as "essentially the love of man for God—that is to say, the insatiable craving of limited, conditional, and temporal beings for the infinite, the Absolute, the Eternal" (ibid.). Two things derive from this understanding of love. First, love for God as it was expressed by the false teachers becomes primarily an exercise in self-gratification. As such, it expresses the vanity of those teachers. Second, one can never attribute love to God and say, for example, that God loves us. God as the Absolute is always passionless and unmoved. (On the meaning of *hilasmos,* see note on 2:2.)

11 The author continues to show that the true nature of love is unselfish and sacrificial. In 3:16 he appealed to Jesus, who laid down his life for his brothers, as the example for believers to follow. Now he directs attention to God's own example: "Since God so loved us, we also ought to love one another." The nature of the argument is not properly deductive but analogical, as Bruce (p. 109) has shown: "If the children of God must be holy because He is holy (Lev 11:44f; 1 Pet 1:15f) and merciful because He is merciful (Lk 6:36), so they must be loving because He is loving—not with the 'must' of external compulsion but with the 'must' of inward constraint: God's love is poured into their hearts by the Holy Spirit whom they have received (Rom 5:5)."

12 Here most commentators see a reference to the false teachers who may have claimed "visions" of God—visions from which their own knowledge was mediated to them (cf. Bultmann, p. 68; Schnackenburg, pp. 240–41). John's response is the blanket rejection: "No one has ever seen God." But the conclusion he moves toward is different from that expected from the Gospel of John. Instead of saying, "God the only Son, who is at the Father's side, has made him known" (John 1:18), he turns rather to love: "If we love each other," we know that God is present with us. As God was once present in his Son, so now he is present through the community of faith. And it is in this community that love has its ultimate fulfillment.

Stott (p. 164) warns against weakening this assertion: "We must not stagger at the majesty of this conclusion. God's love which originates in Himself (7, 8) and was manifested in His Son (9, 10) is perfected in His people (12). . . . God's love for us is perfected only when it is reproduced in us or (as it may mean) 'among us' in the Christian fellowship." Similarly, Westcott (p. 144) says, "It is through man that the 'love of God' finds its fulfillment on earth." With this conclusion, we can begin to understand a little better John's urgent concern for the "fellowship" of the community of believers. It was not an optional "blessing" or "fruit" of belief that so deeply concerned him but the basic question of God's presence and manifestation in the world.

The genitive in "love of God" is best taken as subjective—viz., the love that has its origin in God.

Notes

7 "The initial imperative, 'let us love one another,' leaves no doubt that πᾶς ὁ ἀγαπῶν *pas ho agapōn* ('he who loves') means the love of neighbor, even though no object is apprehended. . . . There is certainly no love without a *vis-a-vis*. The *vis-a-vis* of God is the world, as indicated in Jn 3:16. . . . If the love of God has as its object the world and thereby 'we', the object of those loved by God is accordingly the neighbors" (Bultmann, pp. 15, 66).

2. *Living in God and Living in Love*

4:13–16

> [13]We know that we live in him and he in us, because he has given us of his Spirit. [14]And we have seen and testify that the Father has sent his Son to be the Savior of the world. [15]If anyone acknowledges that Jesus is the Son of God, God lives in him and he in God. [16]And so we know and rely on the love God has for us. God is love. Whoever lives in love lives in God, and God in him.

In v. 12 the author linked living in God to loving one another. In 3:24 he linked living with God to obeying his commands. There, as here, the primary evidence for this relationship with God is the Holy Spirit. And it is the Spirit who enables us to testify that "the Father has sent his Son to be the Savior of the world" (4:14; cf. 4:2). Whoever confesses this also knows that God (by his Spirit) is present in them and that they live "in God" (v.15). And those who know they live in God know also that they live in his love (v.16).

13 Reciprocal abiding (2:24; 4:13, 15—God in us, we in God) is the final expression of fellowship with God. It is possible only through the gift of his Spirit, by whom the relationship with the Father and with the Son is sealed eternally. Reciprocal abiding makes possible God's love for us and our love for him. It is also the reason we can

love one another. No longer do we need to regard ourselves as "orphans" in the world (John 14:18).

14 To whom does the "we" refer in the statement "we have seen and testify"? The "we" certainly refers to all those, especially the apostles, who had direct knowledge of Jesus' earthly life; but it probably ought not to be limited to them. It is the Spirit working in them and in us who permits us to "see" in the historic event of Jesus' death God's act for our salvation. Although "no one has ever seen God" (v.12) at any time (the same Greek word *theaomai* is used), we do "see" by faith that the cross lifted up in Palestine was for our sins and for our salvation. We do "see" in Jesus our own Savior and Lord. We do "see" in the fellowship of faith the presence of his love. And because his Spirit in us gives us this "seeing" experience, we are commissioned to bear witness to the event. "When the counselor comes, whom I will send to you from the Father, the Spirit of truth who goes out from the Father, he will testify about me; but you also must testify, for you have been with me from the beginning" (John 15:26). Therefore, since there is such a close connection between seeing and testifying and the gift of the Holy Spirit, it is likely that the author meant his words to include his readers and to be applied to all Christians now as well as in the past.

15 The author goes on to state that "anyone" who "acknowledges" (*homologēsē*, lit., "confesses") God's act in his Son is included in the divine fellowship in which the Father is in the believers and the believers in the Father. Initially John connected the fellowship with obedience to the command to love one another (3:24). Then he showed its dependence on the gift of the Spirit (4:13). Here he shows that the fellowship is built on Jesus, who must be acknowledged as being one with the Father (2:23), as the one who came in the flesh (4:2), and as the Son of God who was sent to be the Savior of the world (4:14–15).

16 The same combination of knowing and believing is found in Peter's confession of Jesus in John 6:69, except that there the order is reversed: "We believe and know that you are the Holy One of God." The fact is that faith may lead to knowledge and knowledge may lead to faith. Here knowledge of God's love necessarily precedes the ability to "rely" on that love. The sequence of thought is this: First, we must know and rely on the fact that God loves us. Second, we come to realize through relying on his love (or having faith in his Son—the meaning is the same) that in his very nature God is love. Third, we discover that to live in God means to live in love. The fellowship we have with the Father and with the Son (1:3), the fellowship in which he lives in us and we live in him, is perceived as nothing other than a fellowship of love.

3. *Love Displaces Fear*

4:17–18

> [17]Love is made complete among us so that we will have confidence on the day of judgment, because in this world we are like him. [18]There is no fear in love. But perfect love drives out fear, because fear has to do with punishment. The man who fears is not made perfect in love.

The perfection or completeness of love is confidence. This confidence relates especially to the time of judgment (cf. 2:28), though John probably believed that "confidence" was the mark of a believer in every relationship to God (cf. 3:21; 5:14). He may have introduced the judgment theme in the context of the commandment to love because Jesus himself made this command so specific and established love as the basis for judgment. Not to love, therefore, is to disobey Jesus and to spurn the Father's own love in sending Jesus. To live in love, however, is to live in God; and this results in complete confidence for prayer and judgment.

17 The meaning of "because in this world, we are like him" is uncertain. The Greek literally says, "Because even as that one is, so also we are in the world." It is possible to understand this as an appeal to be like Jesus, the Holy One of God—viz., that "even as he is" refers to his eternal purity, love, righteousness, and perfect fellowship with the Father (Brooke, p. 124; Westcott, in loc.). Another possibility is to see it primarily in terms of the Incarnation (Marshall—"we live as Jesus lived"—p. 233). The appeal would then be to his example, as elsewhere in the epistle (e.g., 2:6). In view of the context, however, it is preferable to understand the words to mean that just as Jesus "abides" in the love of the Father (cf. John 15:10), an abiding that already marked his earthly existence and gave him "confidence" before God in the face of temptation, trial, and death, so "in this world" we also may abide in the Father's love and share in that same confidence (Bultmann, p. 73).

18 The other side of confidence is fear. If we truly abide in the Father's love, it follows that we will be without fear. "Perfect love drives out fear." The statement probably should be taken almost as a Christian truism as well as an allusion to the fear of God in judgment. Love and fear are incompatible. They cannot coexist. For the Christian love is first an experience of the Father's love for us. That "love" is so powerful and life changing that when we know it we are forever removed from the "fear" of God.

The fear spoken of here is not to be confused with reverence for God. Reverence will only deepen through the experience of God's love. The experience of the holiness of God's love makes us desire to be even more obedient to his commands. But it also removes us from the power of fear. Whatever may take place in this world cannot nullify the power of his love nor separate us from it. Similarly, if we experience fear in any portion of our life, to that extent we deny God's love and fail to trust him.

Notes

18 Ὁ φόβος κόλασιν ἔχει (*ho phobos kolasin echei*) may be rendered "fear brings its own punishment." Luther's translation—"fear has its own agony"—is based on this interpretation. Bultmann also prefers it.

4. Love Summarized

4:19-21

[19]We love because he first loved us. [20]If anyone says, "I love God," yet hates his brother, he is a liar. For anyone who does not love his brother, whom he has seen, cannot love God, whom he has not seen. [21]And he has given us this command: Whoever loves God must also love his brother.

19 In summarizing the command to love one's brother, the author begins with his most important truth. Love must never be conceived of as a "natural" experience of the natural man. There is such a "natural" love, but it must not be confused with the divine love (*agapē*). The love John speaks of originates with the Father. It became manifest in and through the Son and now characterizes the life of the children of God. Therefore he begins this summary by saying, "We love." Although the Greek verb form expresses either exhortation or description, here it is better to understand it descriptively: as the Father loves, and as the Son loves, so also will we love.

The love with which we love is not our own. We do not create it, nor do we even have the power to express it. It is always God's love or Jesus' love in us. But because we abide in the Father and in the Son, the love becomes also our own love. It is not that God reveals his love apart from us, or in spite of us, but that he invites us to love even as he loves. So we return to him his own love and love him with the gift of his love. So also we love our brother with the love God has loved us with.

20 The confidence we have in knowing that God loves us delivers us from fear but not from responsible action. In fact, God's love for us and in us sets us free to love our brother even as God loves him. To fail this test of love proves that one's claim to love God is a lie—just as the previous claims to have fellowship with God while walking in darkness (1:6), to know him while disobeying his commands (2:4), or to possess the Father while denying his Son were lies—and establishes the one making this claim as a liar. Bultmann (p. 76) shows that "liar" has a double sense: "The liar does not speak the truth" in that what he claims is false; and, second, his action shows that he has divorced "himself from the reality of God." The liar's life is a lie because it betrays the being and essence of God.

The second part of the verse is problematic. It can mean that if one is not able to love his brother, whom he can see, he certainly will not be able to love God, whom he cannot see. Or, if one does not practice the life of love by loving his brother, whom he can see, he will certainly be unable to express love for God, who is not even visible to him. Or, preferably, if one fails the test of loving his visible brother, he makes it certain that he does not love the invisible God and thus proves that there is no true love in him.

21 The final warrant of the life of love is obedience to the teaching of Christ. He gave the command that "whoever loves God must also love his brother." The quotation presents an unmistakable echo of Jesus' words in Mark 12:30-31, in answer to the question "Which is the most important commandment?" Jesus answered, "The most important one is this: 'Hear, O Israel, the Lord our God, the Lord is one. Love the Lord your God with all your heart and with all your soul and with all your mind and with all your strength.' The second is this: 'Love your neighbor as yourself' " (cf. John 13:34).

John makes clear that obedience expresses itself in a single command. Love for God and love of neighbor are inseparable. The one is not possible apart from the other. If one loves God, he cannot refuse love to the image of God that meets him in his brother. Dodd puts it thus: "Being the object of God's love, we are to love our neighbor in Him and Him in our neighbor; and that is what it is to remain in His love" (*Johannine Epistles*, p. 124).

Notes

21 The "he" mentioned may be taken as a reference to God who has given his command through his Son. Westcott (p. 155) argues, "The commandment was given in substance by Christ (John xiii. 34), but it came from God (ἀπό) as its final source." However, since the quotation represents so closely Jesus' own word, it seems likely that the NEB is right in concluding that it was Jesus' command the author had in mind.

5. *Love for the Father and Faith in the Son*

5:1–5

> ¹Everyone who believes that Jesus is the Christ is born of God, and everyone who loves the father loves his child as well. ²This is how we know that we love the children of God: by loving God and carrying out his commands. ³This is love for God: to obey his commands. And his commands are not burdensome, ⁴for everyone born of God overcomes the world. This is the victory that has overcome the world, even our faith. ⁵Who is it that overcomes the world? Only he who believes that Jesus is the Son of God.

The author now focuses on the relationship of the three fundamental elements so important to him in the knowledge of God: faith, love, and obedience. *Pisteuō* ("to believe," "to have faith"), first introduced at 3:23, becomes the primary term and pervades the section. In John *pisteuō* is "always connected with an object" (Bultmann, p. 59). Faith requires not only that something is held true, but that someone has entered into one's life. A commitment has been made and a relationship has been established that one can then only "confess" (cf. 3:23; 4:2, 4, 15).

1 The argument parallels 4:19. Even as we love only because God first loved us, so also our belief is possible only because we have first been "born of God." The author is not addressing the question of incorporation into the family of God but rather looks only at its result. "Believing" in Jesus (present tense in Gr.) is a direct consequence of our "having been born" (perfect tense in Gr.) of God and therefore becomes a "test" or proof of that birth. From this the author moves to a truism from nature: whoever loves his progenitor (*ton gennēsanta*, KJV, "him that begat"; NIV, "the father") will also love those similarly born, even his brothers and sisters.

2 This statement troubles commentators because it reverses what is expected. One anticipates a conclusion like this: "And this is how we know that we love God: by loving his children and obeying his commands." Instead the author concludes: "This is how we know that we love the children of God: by loving God and carrying out his commands." But as elliptical as this verse may be, it is probably best to assume that the author is saying exactly what he intends to say. Even as one cannot love God without loving his children, so also it is impossible to truly love the children of God without loving God also. If one claims he loves his brother and not God, he has not truly recognized his brother as one born of God and has not offered him the true love that comes from the Father. "If love to men proves the worth of our love to God, love to God proves the worth of our love to men" (G.G. Findley, cited in Bruce, p. 117).

The author cannot really talk of loving God, however, without also linking his words to obedience (i.e., "carrying out his commands").

3 The connection between love for God and obedience is meant as a protection against thinking of love for God as "emotional feelings" about God. True love (*agapē*) requires action. In respect to humankind, it means willingness to lay down one's life. In respect to God, it means a life of willing obedience, a relation of sonship with God, and service on behalf of God. It requires laying down one's life as being one's own possession and taking up a new life in response to a Lord and Master.

John now qualifies what he has just said by adding "And his commands are not burdensome." To the natural man the will of God is strange; the requirement for righteousness, foreign and hard. Even the law of love is a burden. But when God has entered into us and when we trust God's Son, then his yoke becomes gentle and the burden light (cf. Matt 11:30). We who have been born of God have within us a desire and a yearning for the Father. Seeking and hungering after righteousness becomes our joy. Living the life of love becomes our delight. The commands of God bring us the freedom and the liberty we so ardently long for.

4 "Everyone born of God overcomes the world." Here NIV personalizes the Greek word *pan*. Literally, however, *pan* has the sense of "whatever" or "everything"—viz., "everything born of God" (KJV, RSV). "It is not the man but his birth from God, which conquers" (Alfred Plummer, *Commentary on the Epistles of St. John,* CGT [Cambridge: Cambridge University Press, 1894], in loc.). Our being born of God is God's act on our behalf, the event through which he moves to overcome the world. The supernatural act by which human beings are being translated (the verb here is in the present tense) out of the kingdom of death into the kingdom of life through the Son—all this is in view.

The victory that overcomes the world is now identified with "our faith." The Greek literally says, "The victory that is victorious over the world." The participial form (*nikēsasa*, "that has overcome") is in the aorist tense. It may be taken as a simple statement of fact as NIV suggests or more likely as a reference to a past event. If the latter, the author would be emphasizing that the victory he refers to has already been won. By faith we now have access to what was once accomplished by and through the appearance of Jesus on earth.

5 Observe the progression of thought in what John says about how victory over the world is gained. It begins with the new birth, the begetting act of God (5:4a). It moves on to the believer's experience and act of faith (v.4b). It culminates in the confession that Jesus is the Son of God (v.5). The victory requires the whole process. The victory assures us that we too can love God and the children of God and that we too can obey his commands (v.3). Belief, love, and obedience are the marks of the new birth. And the life lived in the new birth is not a burden but a life of celebration. This was the experience of the apostles and also that of the early church. The Book of Acts is full of references to the victorious power of God against every principality and power. Paul's cry that "in all these things we are more than conquerors" (Rom 8:37) echoed throughout the Roman world. Whereas at first the victories were thought of in terms of alien powers on the outside, Christian consciousness soon perceived that the victory included the internal enemies that confront the conscience, assail Christian beliefs and standards, corrupt the soul, and negate the life of love and obedience to God.

The confession with which the victory is linked is again the confession that "Jesus is the Son of God" (cf. 2:22—4:15). This is where the author began. It is also where he will end. Every single tenet of belief in God, of knowledge about him, depends on the revelation and obedient confession and commitment that Jesus is the eternal life that was with the Father (1:2). He is the Son of God. The confession has in view the false teachers who acknowledge Christ the Redeemer but deny his historical identity, his true humanity. Verse 5 makes the transition to the final exposition regarding the Son and provides the base on which the final section develops: the witness of the Father to the Son.

6. *The Spirit, the Water, and the Blood*

5:6–12

[6]This is the one who came by water and blood—Jesus Christ. He did not come by water only, but by water and blood. And it is the Spirit who testifies, because the Spirit is the truth. [7]For there are three that testify: [8]The Spirit, the water and the blood; and the three are in agreement. [9]We accept man's testimony, but God's testimony is greater because it is the testimony of God, which he has given about his Son. [10]Anyone who believes in the Son of God has this testimony in his heart. Anyone who does not believe God has made him out to be a liar, because he has not believed the testimony God has given about his Son. [11]And this is the testimony: God has given us eternal life, and this life is in his Son. [12]He who has the Son has life; he who does not have the Son of God does not have life.

6a Jesus, who is the Son of God (5:5) and the Christ (5:1), came not just by water, but "by water and blood." This enigmatic statement has given rise in the church to many interpretations. Augustine linked the reference to John 19:34, where the piercing of Jesus' side produced water and blood. Calvin and Luther connected it to John 4 and 6 and saw in it a reference to the sacraments. Plummer and Candlish related it to OT sacrificial symbolism, the water of purification and the blood of the sacrifice. More commentators today, however, agree with Tertullian and see the water referring to Jesus' baptism and the blood to his death on the cross. Even though John's Gospel does not describe the water baptism of Jesus, the Johannine community could not have been ignorant of it.

The purpose of the statement seems clear. The author once more affirms that it is the historical Jesus who is the Christ, the Son of God. Although the false teachers may have acknowledged Christ as the Savior, the divine Son of God, they denied his true human existence. Like Cerinthus, they probably held that the Christ came on the man Jesus at his baptism and remained till the time of the Crucifixion. In this way they could deny that the Christ had ever been truly human and subject to suffering and death. The author rightly regards this as a denial of the redemptive activity of God. It was the Son of God who came into the world. It was this same divine Son who was baptized and received the Spirit. It was the Son who, with the Father's approval and in fulfillment of the Father's intention, shed his blood on the cross to redeem humanity. God would not be involved in man's redemption apart from the Christ's true humanity, suffering, and dying. Water and blood become, therefore, the key words of the true understanding of the Incarnation.

It is likely that once the author had arrived at his primary understanding, he saw in the incident of John 19:34 a divine confirmation of it. He may also have seen the reference to the water in John 4:10, 14 and the reference to drinking his blood in John

6:53 as confirmatory testimony. But these flow from the facts that are the historic base for them all. Jesus, the Son of God, came. He came through the water of baptism. He came also through the Cross. It is this coming by water and blood that is the basis of humankind's salvation.

6b "And it is the Spirit who testifies" (present tense; cf. John 14:26; 15:26; 16:8, 12), because the Spirit, as ultimate truth, is the only one capable of so bearing witness (cf. 1 John 3:24; 4:13). Man cannot receive the witness by himself. There are no human categories available to him through which he can understand it. God's redemptive act in Christ is not a bit of data humankind can deduce for itself by analogical reasoning. Like the Resurrection, it can only be announced. And this time it is not made known by angels (cf. Luke 24:6) but by the Spirit of God.

The Spirit bore witness historically in Jesus' baptism by coming down from heaven as a dove and remaining on him (John 1:32). At Jesus' death on the cross, the "blood and water" that flowed from his side bore witness and led to the following statement: "The man who saw it has given testimony, and his testimony is true. He knows that he tells the truth, and he testifies so that you also may believe" (John 19:35). But here in v.6 the present tense of the verb indicates that the author wants to show that the Spirit continues in his witness to the community of believers.

7–8 "For there are three that testify: the Spirit, the water and the blood." Does the author mean that the Spirit still witnesses through the biblical Word in which Jesus' baptism and death are recounted, or that the Spirit gives witness to the community of the efficacy of the historic baptism and death through the rites of water baptism and communion? Probably the author is pointing to the former as having priority but not so as to exclude the latter. Dodd says,

> The Spirit is, as we have seen, both a factor in the historical life of Jesus, and a continuing factor in the experience of the Church. Similarly, the baptism and the crucifixion are authenticated facts in history, and as such bear witness to the reality of the incarnate life of the Son of God; but further, the Church possesses a counterpart to the baptism of Christ, in the sacrament of Baptism, and a counterpart to His sacrificial death, in the sacrament of the Eucharist. Both sacraments attest and confirm to believers the abiding effect of the life and death of Christ. It seems likely that our author is thinking of these two sacraments as providing a continuing witness to the truth of Christ's incarnation and redemptive death. Their value as evidence lies precisely in their being concrete, overt, "objective" actions, directly recalling (or "representing") historical facts of the Gospel, while at the same time they are the vehicles of a suprahistorical life in the Church. As *verba visibilia*, they confirm the prophetic word, inspired by the Spirit. Thus the apostolic faith is authenticated against all false teaching by a threefold testimony: the living voice of prophecy, and the two evangelical sacraments; and **the three of them are in accord**" (emphasis his) (*Johannine Epistles*, pp. 130–31; cf. Bultmann and Westcott in Notes below).

But how does the Spirit give witness in the "living voice of prophecy"? Presumably he does it inwardly and supernaturally. The Spirit opens eyes and ears to perceive what God is declaring through his proclaimed word (cf. 1 Cor 12:3). He does not declare his own words but through inward conviction confirms the proclamation as being indeed the truth (cf. Acts 5:32). The Spirit provides what humanity is unable to acquire for itself. This witness of the Spirit accompanies every presentation of the word whether that presentation comes as a personal message or as the apostolic or inscripurated word.

9 The divine witness is not limited to the Spirit but includes the witness of the Father as well. His witness is greater than even the authenticated witness of man because of the nature of the one who gives it and of its greater trustworthiness (cf. John 5:36–37; 1 John 3:20). It was his voice that confirmed that Jesus' "passion" was an act in which God would glorify himself (John 12:28–30). So also it is God's own voice that is being heard again in the threefold witness.

10a Here the fact that the incarnate and crucified Jesus is God's own Son is clearly set forth. He who believes this testimony receives the Father's own witness in his heart—"that is, he is given a yet deeper assurance by the inward witness of the Spirit that he was right to trust in Christ" (Stott, p. 82). The inward witness is not a "small voice speaking within, but is the inbreaking of faith within the soul. It is the testimony becoming the possession of faith" (Schnackenburg, p. 265). Faith itself is God's own gift to the believer to lay hold of the Father. "Believing" becomes a "receiving," and the work of God in Christ results in cleansing from sin and forgiveness of sins and inward establishment of the love of God. Faith in the Son immediately becomes faith in the Father: "Whoever acknowledges the Son has the Father also" (1 John 2:23).

10b The gravity of receiving this witness is now demonstrated by the corollary: "Any one who does not believe [the witness borne by] God [about the Son] has made him out to be a liar." To receive the Son is to receive the Father. To deny the Son is to deny the Father. "The witness has been borne, once for all; it cannot be ignored or set aside. It has been borne by God Himself, in a case where His word alone can be final, as it concerns His own Son" (Brooke, p. 139).

The writer, then, cannot allow that one can profess belief in God, as did his opponents, and yet reject God's testimony to his own Son. Such rejection cannot be excused on the basis of ignorance. The evidence is too clear and too weighty. Rather, it is deliberate unbelief, the character of which in the end impugns the very being and character of God. If Jesus is not God's own Son in the flesh, then God is no longer the truth. He is the liar.

11–12 The witness is that through his Son God gave us eternal life. That Jesus is God's Son is established by God's own testimony from the time of Jesus' baptism up to and including his suffering and death. It is a testimony given through the Spirit and confirmed in the heart of the person who believes in the Son. The consequence of accepting this testimony from God is the fulfillment of the promise John made in 1:2 to bear witness and to testify to that eternal life that was with the Father and has now appeared to us in the Son. The witness has been given. Eternal life—which is nothing less than fellowship with the Father, with the Son, and with his people—is present in his Son. He who has the Son has this life. He who is without the Son is without life. It is not an idea nor a system of belief nor even a fact that is the ultimate object of faith; it is a Person. That Person is Jesus Christ. He is to live in us (3:24). His love is to abide and be made complete in us (4:12). We are to live in him (4:13). And this is life eternal.

Notes

7–8 KJV has in 5:7–8 the following: "For there are three that bear record in heaven, the Father, the Word, and the Holy Ghost: and these three are one. And there are three that bear witness in earth." NIV places these verses in a footnote. They are obviously a late gloss with no merit (see Marshall, p. 236). Some connect the "threefold witness" to Deut 19:15, which serves as a basis for the rabbinic law that no charge may be made against someone unless it is confirmed by two or three witnesses.

8 " 'Water' and 'Blood' therefore must have a different meaning than in v.6. What they now mean can scarcely be in doubt: they are the sacraments of baptism and the Lord's supper, which bear testimony for Jesus Christ as God's Son, since they mediate the salvation of the community imparted through him. This may also serve to explain why the 'spirit' as witness is combined into a unity with the two other witnesses. If this combination was initially prompted by the fact that the 'spirit' was called 'witness' in v.6, it nevertheless has a special meaning for the redactor: the two sacraments, baptism and the Lord's supper, 'are witnesses out of the power of the Spirit' " (Bultmann, p. 81). Similarly, Westcott (p. 176) says, "The witness here is considered mainly as the living witness of the Church and not as the historical witness of the Gospels. Through believers, these three, 'the Spirit and the Water and the Blood,' perform a work not for believers only but for the world" (cf. John 17:20–23).

V. Concluding Remarks

5:13–21

[13]I write these things to you who believe in the name of the Son of God so that you may know that you have eternal life. [14]This is the assurance we have in approaching God: that if we ask anything according to his will, he hears us. [15]And if we know that he hears us—whatever we ask—we know that we have what we asked of him.

[16]If anyone sees his brother commit a sin that does not lead to death, he should pray and God will give him life. I refer to those whose sin does not lead to death. There is a sin that leads to death. I am not saying that he should pray about that. [17]All wrongdoing is sin, and there is sin that does not lead to death.

[18]We know that anyone born of God does not continue to sin; the one who was born of God keeps him safe, and the evil one does not touch him. [19]We know that we are children of God, and that the whole world is under the control of the evil one. [20]We know also that the Son of God has come and has given us understanding, so that we may know him who is true. And we are in him who is true—even in his Son Jesus Christ. He is the true God and eternal life. [21]Dear children, keep yourselves from idols.

13 This verse makes the transition from the main argument to the Epilogue. It reminds us of John 20:31, where the author said he had written his Gospel so that his readers might believe in Jesus and receive eternal life in his name. John's first epistle is addressed to those who have accepted this belief but still need assurance that through this name they have indeed received eternal life. So the author refers six times (in addition to v.13) to what we believers know:

We know that he hears us—whatever we ask.
We know that we have what we asked.

We know that anyone born of God does not continue to sin.
We know that we are children of God.
We know also that the Son of God has come.
We . . . know him who is true.

(vv.15, 18–20)

The false teachers present a different "knowledge" as well as a different lifestyle. The author counters with a series of tests by which the believers can evaluate the false teachers' claims and practices. Walking in the light, obeying his commands, loving one's brother, being steadfast in the community of faith, doing what is right—these serve as tests of whether the life that is from God has been received. When it has been received, it is only because God's witness to his own Son as the source of that life has been accepted and believed. On this basis, we can expect God to hear us in prayer, free us from the presence and power of sin, and forgive our transgressions. Those who know these things know also that they have received eternal life.

14 The confidence we have in our life with Christ belongs not only in the future time of his coming (2:28) and of judgment (4:17) but also in the present and especially in the fellowship of prayer. We know that we have access to him (3:21) and that "he hears us." In John "hearing" does not mean simply to be listened to but to be heard favorably (cf. John 11:41–42). The expectation is, of course, linked to the qualifying clause "if we ask according to his will." This seems to reflect a natural dependence on Jesus' own teaching—"Thy will be done" (Matt 6:10)—and his example in Gethsemane—"Not what I will, but what you will" (Mark 14:36).

It is not "any" prayer that is answered but the prayer of the disciple who is in fellowship with the Father, who asks in Jesus' name (John 14:13; 15:16), who "remains" in him (15:7), and who obeys his commands (1 John 3:22). This is not meant to dampen the expectation we may have in prayer, but the condition for addressing God is to know he will hear and act. He who is in "fellowship" with God, who has received life from the Father, knows that he may address God in confidence. Prayer becomes not only a time for petitioning but of yielding one's life to the will and work of God. Prayer made in these circumstances is always heard because it is God's will that is being done and his intention for humankind that is being met. "When we learn to want what God wants, we have the joy of receiving his answer to our petitions" (Marshall, p. 245).

15 The author now goes on to state that the "assurance" for approaching God and asking him anything is absolute. A paraphrase of the text is as follows: "If we know that he hears us whenever we ask in his will, and we certainly do know this, then we may also know with equal certainty that we '*possess* the requests we have made' [Dodd, *Johannine Epistles*, p. 135] the moment we have prayed." Brooke (p. 144) sees the answer to prayer as fulfilled prophetically: "In the certainty of anticipation there is a kind of possession of that which has been granted, though our actual entering upon possession may be indefinitely delayed." This, however, seems to understate the author's position. That our petition is answered is not dependent on whether or not we have personally observed the answer.

Some answers to prayer are recognized immediately, others later, and some are not recognized in our lifetime. But this is not the author's point. When we pray as Jesus prayed, in full accord with the Father's will, we can know that we have our requests, because God has made them his own and his will must be done. What is required of us is simply the faith to believe that this is so, that his will will be done on earth as it is in heaven, and then decide to live accordingly. The author is exalting faith in the will of God and its relation to our privilege to pray. He is echoing Jesus' own words: "Therefore I tell you, whatever you ask in prayer, believe that you have received it, and it will be yours" (Mark 11:24).

16a The author now turns from assurance in prayer to the ministry of prayer. Although he does not give the basis for his statement, what he says about intercessory prayer follows logically from the tenor of his teaching. If love requires the willingness to lay down one's life for a member of the community (3:16), then it follows that if one sees a brother commit sin, he is obligated to intercede for him in prayer. For John it would be obvious that not to pray for a brother would be as much a betrayal of God's love as to withhold material aid from him if he hungered or thirsted (3:17). Moreover, when we pray for a brother or a sister who commits sin, we can know that the prayer we are praying is "according to his [God's] will" because Christ is the atoning sacrifice for sins; and "if we confess our sins," he is committed to "forgive us our sins and purify us from all unrighteousness" (1:9).

But why should a brother need such intercession? Why does he not pray for himself and make his own confession? We can only speculate as to John's answer. Perhaps here again it is a matter of assurance. The brother may need to be forgiven through intercessory prayer as an expression of the community's forgiveness. Because the sin was presumably committed after entrance into the community, the need to confess the sin to another and to have received assurance of forgiveness may have had special significance. Also, there might be an allusion here to Jesus' words in the Gospel of John: "If you forgive anyone his sins, they are forgiven; if you do not forgive them, they are not forgiven" (20:23).

16b The author comments that intercession is not required if it involves a "sin that leads to death." This is puzzling. We do not know exactly what the author has in mind. Judaism distinguished between deliberate or presumptuous sins—sins of open rebellion against God that are punishable by death—and sins of ignorance or inadvertence that can be atoned for (Lev 4; Num 15:22–29—cf. vv.30–31). First-century Judaism retained this pattern (see Notes). In the Johannine community some such distinction was presumably made, hence the limitation "sin that leads to death."

Conjecture as to whether there was one such sin—e.g., blasphemy against the Holy Spirit—or several—e.g., apostasy, murder, etc.—is fruitless. Nor is it the author's concern. He desires that intercessory prayer be made in all instances with the exception of sins that lead to death. Why does he make this exception? Presumably because he is speaking of spiritually efficacious prayer—prayer that will lead to eternal life. Such prayer can be made only for those who are rooted in God's life and love.

Who then is excluded from efficacious prayer? The text offers no clues. As has just been said, it might refer to the blasphemy against the Holy Spirit (Mark 3:29). But the content of the epistle may point to the surmise that the sin John has in mind may be that of false teaching. For life to be given to those who deny Jesus Christ, hate their brother, and refuse the witness of God would be a contradiction. Since such

149

persons deny the mercy of God, prayer for them would appear to be limited to asking for their repentance and conversion to God's truth.

17 Earlier John defined sin as "lawlessness" (3:4). Now he adds "unrighteousness" (NIV, "wrongdoing"). Possibly some in the community, knowing that the children of God were not to sin (3:9–10), attempted to deal with the problem of Christians' sinning by limiting sin to deliberate or lawless acts. If so, John will have none of it. All wrongdoing (*adikia*) is sin, even when done by the children of God. But not all sin results in death. The author aims first at honesty (cf. 1:8) and only then at resolution. Sin is not dealt with by denial but by confession and by community intercession for one another (5:16). Where this intercession occurs, the divine life of God is present and fellowship with God takes place. Within this life and fellowship, the blood of Jesus Christ purifies believers from all sin (1:7).

18 John concludes by stating three certainties that characterize his own position and that of his followers over against the false teachers: (1) We know that anyone born of God does not continue in sin (v.18). (2) We know that we are the children of God (v.19). (3) We know that the Son of God has come and has given us certain, definite knowledge about himself (v.20). Never has John wavered from the priority of the ethical requirement, nor does he do so now. Christians must not walk in darkness (1:7). They must not hate their fellow believers (2:10). They must not live of a sin (3:6).

However noble the sentiments expressed by the false teachers, the test of the truth of God is conduct. A sinful life is totally incompatible with the life received from God. John is not unaware of the difficulties involved in living the new life nor of the quality of the opposition from the evil one. John knows the wiles of the evil one and expects them. Nonetheless, the author has been adamant in his confidence that the evil one need not prevail. It is not the quality of strength in the life of the believer that gives him hope of prevailing but the presence of the power of God.

Already John has shown that if he who lives in him will not sin (3:6), no one born of God possessing the divine life of God will fall victim to the life of sin (3:9). To this he now adds that the Son of God himself will keep him safe from the evil one. NIV renders the article *ho* as an indefinite pronoun—"the one who"—but NEB supplies the subject and RSV capitalizes "he" to make clear that the reference is to Christ. John may first have used "born of God" for believers generally and then also for Christ to emphasize the relation between the two somewhat after the pattern of the Epistle to the Hebrews.

The phrase "keeps him safe" recalls Jesus' words in John's Gospel: "While I was with them, I protected them and kept them safe. . . . None has been lost. . . . My prayer is . . . that you protect them from the evil one" (John 17:12, 15). (For the evil one, see comment on 2:13b.) The phrase "touch him" obviously means "harm."

19 The second affirmation builds on the first one (v.18), but emphasizes the positive consequence: "We know that we are children of God" (lit., "we are of God"). The author now openly identifies himself with the community of faith and stresses the personal quality of the relationships involved in fellowship (*koinōnia*, 1:3) with the Father. We know we "belong to him," i.e., are "his children." And how is this known? It is not by boastful claims, like those made by the false teachers, but on the basis of the "tests of eternal life" that are substantiated by life and action. As Bruce (p. 127) says, "To claim to belong to the family of God is one thing; to exhibit the marks of His family, in the light of the criteria of obedience, love, and preseverance, is another thing. In the case of John and his 'little children,' these criteria have been met." In contrast to the true community that belongs to God (cf. John 8:47) is the rest of the world, which lies under the control of the evil one (cf. 2:15–17). Clearly there is no middle ground for the author. To be born of God is to be safe from the power of the evil one. Not to be born of God is to be wholly under the power of the evil one.

20 The third and final affirmation of John is in fact the summary of the epistle. It affirms the point of dispute with the false teachers. Christian faith has to do with Jesus Christ. He is the "Word of life" (1:1), "the eternal life" (v.2) that was with the Father and through the Incarnation came into human history. By his coming, humankind is enabled to know the true God and to have fellowship with him. But the false teachers said that this relationship was apart from the Son. Fellowship with God as they taught it came through divine knowledge of the subject. It was received through a process of speculative inquiry. From the beginning John denied this teaching. The reality of God can be known only through apprehending the reality that is in the Son. This comes through revelation, but it is a revelation grounded in the facts of history. It requires that one know Jesus Christ as God's Son and that one live his life entirely in him. One knows by this experiential life in the Son that he is also in the Father and that the Son is none other than the true God, the author of eternal life.

"He" in 20b is literally "this one" (*houtos*); RSV has "This is the true God." Grammatically the pronoun most naturally refers to Jesus Christ. Westcott, (p. 187) however, argues that in terms of subject emphasis it more naturally refers backwards to God, who earlier in the text was designated as the one who is true (20a): "This Being—this One who is true, who is revealed through and in His Son, with whom we are united by His Son—is the true God and life eternal." Stott supports Westcott, noting that all "three references to 'the true' are to the same Person, the Father, and the additional points made in the apparent final repetition are that it is *this* One, namely the God made known by Jesus Christ, who is *the true God*, and that, besides this, He is *eternal life*. As He is both light and love (i.5, iv.8), so He is also life" (italics his) (Stott, p. 196; cf. Brooke, pp. 152–53; Dodd, *Johannine Epistles*, p. 140). It is just as defensible, however, to argue that here at the climax of the epistle the author should ascribe full deity to Jesus. After all, this is the crux of his argument and the basis for his statement that he who is in Jesus is in the Father (cf. Bultmann, p. 90; Marshall, p. 254). (For Jesus Christ as the author of eternal life, see John 11:25; 14:6; 1 John 5:11.)

21 John closes on an affectionate note and with a final admonition. The phrase "dear children" (cf. 3:7; 4:4) serves to remind his readers of his genuine commitment to them. The exhortation "keep yourselves from idols" at first glance seems out of place. Idolatry has not so much as been mentioned in the epistle. Although the warning may be understood as a general admonition to "avoid any contact with paganism" (Dodd, *Johannine Epistles*, p. 141), it is more likely that the warning represents a final characterization of the "heresy" represented by the false teachers. False teaching is ultimately "apostasy from the true faith." To follow after it is to become nothing better than an idol worshiper, especially if it is a matter of the truth of one's conception of God. The author is blunt. The false teachers propose not the worship of the true God, made known in his Son Jesus, but a false god—an idol they have invented.

151

Notes

16a The Qumran community distinguished between sins requiring expulsion and those requiring penance. "Every man who enters the Council of Holiness and who deliberately or through negligence transgresses one word of the Law of Moses, on any point whatever, shall be expelled. . . . But if he has acted inadvertently, he shall be excluded from the pure mind and the Council. . . . For one sin of inadvertence (above) he shall do penance for two years. But as for him who has sinned deliberately, he shall never return; only the man who has sinned inadvertently shall be tried for two years that his way and counsel may be made perfect according to the judgment of the Congregation" (1 QS 8f., quoted from Houlden, p. 135).

16b In δώσει αὐτῷ ζωήν (dōsei autō zōēn, "he will give him life"), the subject of the verb dōsei may refer either to God (NIV, Marshall, Schnackenburg, Stott, Westcott) or to the one who prays (Bultmann, Brooke, Dodd).

19 Ἐν τῷ πονηρῷ (en tō ponērō, "in the evil one" (may be masculine (so NIV) or neuter ("under the domination of evil"). For Satan's power over the world, cf. John 12:31; 14:30; 16:11; Eph 2:2; 6:12.

20 Ἥκει (hēkei, "has come"; cf. John 8:42) clearly refers to Jesus' appearance in history (cf. 1:2; 3:5, 8).

Διάνοιαν (dianoian, "understanding") appears only here in the Johannine writings (cf. Eph 4:18; Col 1:21).

In γινώσκωμεν τὸν ἀληθινόν (ginōskōmen ton alēthinon, "we may know him who is true"), ginosōkōmen is in the present tense and emphasizes "a continuous and progressive apprehension" (Westcott, in loc.).

Ἀληθινόν (alēthinon, "true") has the force of "real" (NEB, "genuine") contrasted with the "idols" (v.21), which are false.

21 The command φυλάξατε ἑαυτὰ (phylaxate heauta, "keep yourselves") does not appear elsewhere in 1 John or in the NT, but comparable phrases are in 2 Cor 11:9; 1 Tim 5:22; James 1:27; Jude 21.

Εἰδώλων (eidōlōn, "idols") is used frequently in the literature of the period to refer to "false gods" (cf. 1 Cor 8:4, 7; 1 Thess 1:9).

2 JOHN

Glenn W. Barker

Outline

Text and Exposition

I. Introduction

1–3

¹The elder,

To the chosen lady and her children, whom I love in the truth—and not I only, but also all who know the truth— ²because of the truth, which lives in us and will be with us forever:

³Grace, mercy and peace from God the Father and from Jesus Christ, the Father's Son, will be with us in truth and love.

The introduction is a normal epistolary salutation. The author is identified as "the elder" (cf. 3 John 1); the recipients are identified as "the chosen lady and her children"; and an appropriate Christian greeting is extended: "Grace, mercy and peace from God the Father and from Jesus Christ, the Father's Son" (v.3).

1 The word that designates the author as "elder" is *presbyteros*, which can mean an old man, a senior person deserving respect, or a senior official of a local church (cf. Acts 11:30; 14:23; 1 Tim. 5:17). A special use of the word in the early church was to designate a church officer who had been a personal follower of one of the apostles (Eusebius *Ecclesiastical History* 3.39.3–4; Irenaeus *Contra Haereses* 5.33.3, 36.2). The author of this brief letter must have been so well known to those he was writing to that the title "elder" immediately identified him. That he assumes authority over them, though he is obviously not a member of their church, suggests that he was more than a local pastor. He probably held an influential position (like that of a bishop) in the region where his readers lived. Also he was probably so well established with his audience that he could simply call himself "the elder." That "the elder" was also the writer of the first epistle and that he was the apostle John is a valid inference (cf. Introduction to 1 John: Authorship and Date).

The designation of the letter's addressee raises questions. From ancient times opinion has been divided as to whether this letter was addressed to an anonymous noble lady, though she might have actually been called "Eclecta" (from the Gk. *eklekta*, "chosen"), as Clement of Alexandria supposed, or even "Kyria" (a direct transliteration from the Gk. *kyria*, "lady"), or whether it was addressed to a Christian community metaphorically identified as "the chosen lady and her children." Some commentators (Plummer, Ross, Ryrie) favor a person as the designee, while other commentators (Brooke, Bruce, Marshall, Stott, Westcott) favor a local church.

While a strict interpretation of the text supports an individual person as the addressee, the context supports an enigmatic reference to a community. Such a veiled allusion may have been, as Dodd suggests, a device for shielding the identity of the community from adverse action by public officials who opposed the Christian community. If the letter fell into unfriendly hands, it would seem to be nothing more than a private message to a friend. The reference to the elder's children would be a veiled way of referring to the members of the community; and the greetings extended to her from the children of her "chosen sister" (v.13) would be understood as being from the members of the community of the elder. The statement "whom I love in the truth—and not I only, but also all who know the truth" seems more appropriate as a reference to a church than to an individual. No dogmatic conclusion about the addressee is possible, however, because of the ambiguity of the text.

The linking of "truth" and "love" is of great importance. Because John's readers are in the truth—i.e., they know Jesus as the Christ, the Father's Son—they are also the recipients of God's love as it is known and manifested in the community of faith. And the love received by the community comes from all who know the truth. The community of love is as encompassing as the truth that is believed and lived.

The author is speaking in clear contrast to the heretics. They do not have the truth nor do they know what it means to be in the community of love.

2 John goes on to explain why the community of love can be so inclusive. Love relates to the truth, which lives in us and will be with us forever. Truth, for him, is more than what is objectively known. It is that which indwells the believer, permeating his whole existence. Because it is the truth of God, it also has no temporal limitation. It exists without end. Love and truth are themselves not passing sentiments; nor are they dependent on depths of emotional feeling or the strength of personal commitment that some believers might or might not possess. Love and truth originate in God. Like him, they endure without changing, and their splendor never fades.

3 At the time John's epistles were written, the salutation of a letter, according to secular practice, ended with a greeting. Most of the NT epistles follow this custom but give it a special Christian character, such as "grace and peace to you" (Rom 1:7; cf. 1 Peter 1:2) or "grace, mercy and peace from God the Father and Christ Jesus our Lord" (1 Tim 1:2). Here, however, John adds a significant variation to this custom. Rather than wishing or praying that God would grant them his peace, he turns it into a promise that God's mercy and grace will be ours if we truly remain in his truth and love. The words "truth and love" provide the transition to the next section, where they become the chief topic.

II. A Formal Word of Instruction (4–11)

1. An Exhortation

4–6

> ⁴It has given me great joy to find some of your children walking in the truth, just as the Father commanded us. ⁵And now, dear lady, I am not writing you a new command but one we have had from the beginning. I ask that we love one another. ⁶And this is love: that we walk in obedience to his commands. As you have heard from the beginning, his command is that you walk in love.

4 The author continues to follow the custom of his time by expressing his pleasure in writing to his readers. Like other Christian writers, John relates this note of joy to their spiritual state; for they are in this instance faithful to the truth.

The force of "some" in v.4 is disputed. Bruce and Stott do not understand its usage as pejorative. According to their reconstruction, the elder had met only some members of the community; and it is to them he refers. It seems more likely, however, that the news of the church had been brought to the elder and that part of this news was that the church had suffered division as a consequence of the work of the heretics. Brooke speculates that the majority had been led astray. Be that as it may, the author rejoices that some of the children remained true to the faith he had delivered to them.

Since the word for "truth" (*alētheia*) is not accompanied by the article, it is more normal for it to be rendered with almost adverbial force—"walking in truth" or "truthfully," meaning "authentically" (see Notes). However, NIV may be right in disregarding that possibility here in view of the usage of the word in v.2, where it occurs with the article and refers to the truth as the "divine reality." The following clause—"just as the Father commanded us"—seems more natural if it is "the truth" heard "from the beginning" (v.5) to which the author is referring (contra Bultmann). The commandment received from the Father is explained in v.5 as the commandment of love and in v.7 as belief in the Son (cf. 1 John 3:23: "And this is his command: to believe in the name of his Son, Jesus Christ, and to love one another as he commanded us").

5 It is clear that for the author the commandment of love has precedence here as it does in 1 John 4:21: "And he has given us this command: Whoever loves God must also love his brother." It is not that love precedes truth or belief but that love offers the clearest test of the truthfulness of the confession and the sincerity of the obedience given to God's commands. Belief may be feigned and confession only of the lips, but love is harder to counterfeit. The elder is not requiring something new but that which has been the supreme and final word "from the beginning." What the Father required (1 John 4:7), the Son manifested (1 John 3:16), and the Spirit makes available through life in him (1 John 4:13–15), the elder now asks for—viz., "that we love one another."

6 Four times in vv.4–6 the author uses the noun "command" (*entolē*). This is his way of making clear that what he is saying is a direct expression of God's will. And how does one know that he fulfills the will of God? The test of love is obedience to God's commands, and the test of obedience is whether one "walks in love." The argument is intentionally circular. Love of God that does not result in obedience to the Word of God cannot be the love that is God's gift in Jesus Christ. Jesus' own love was manifested by his obedience even to death. Love of God can finally be expressed only in action and truth (1 John 3:18). Do we love our brother? Are we prepared to die for him? Obedience that does not lead to the life of love in which we love one another even to death is not obedience offered to God. Not to love means to remain in darkness (1 John 2:11) and in death (1 John 3:14). Hatred of one's brother can never be defended as obedience to God. It is rather obedience and gratification of one's own sin—one's own evil nature (cf. 1 John 3:12).

2. *A Warning*

7–11

> [7]Many deceivers, who do not acknowledge Jesus Christ as coming in the flesh, have gone out into the world. Any such person is the deceiver and the antichrist. [8]Watch out that you do not lose what you have worked for, but that you may be rewarded fully. [9]Anyone who runs ahead and does not continue in the teaching of Christ does not have God; whoever continues in the teaching has both the Father and the Son. [10]If anyone comes to you and does not bring this teaching, do not take him into your house or welcome him. [11]Anyone who welcomes him shares in his wicked work.

7 This verse is reminiscent of 1 John 2:18, 27, and 4:1–3. The "deceivers" are those who have left the believing community for the world. It is unlikely that those who went out were members of the "lady's" community. More likely they were members of the original community of the elder. Nonetheless, they may have been known to the community here addressed and were therefore a risk to that community also. What distinguishes them is their unwillingness to acknowledge that Jesus Christ is come in the flesh. Curiously the tense is changed from the past tense "has come [*elēluthota*] in the flesh" (1 John 4:2) to the present participle "as coming [*erchomenon*] in the flesh." It would be possible, therefore, to interpret this as a reference to Jesus' return: he is coming (i.e., will come) in the flesh (cf. 1 John 2:28; 3:2). But since we know of no controversy in this area, this seems unlikely. Dodd obscures the sense by translating the participle *erchomenon* in the past tense, as if its meaning were simply identical with 1 John 4:2, and then offers the surprising explanation that "our author is not skilled in the niceties of the Greek idiom" (*Johannine Epistles*, p. 149).

It is far safer, however, to assume that the writer does know the difference between a present participle and a perfect (past tense) and that his intention is to say something beyond what he was saying in 1 John 4:2. What the present tense would emphasize normally in such a case is the timeless character of the event. As Bultmann suggests, this would be in line with the gospel's presentation in John 3:31; 6:14; 11:27. It is seen not simply as an event in history but as an "abiding truth" defining the union between humanity and deity that is present in Jesus' person. This union is not limited to Jesus' historical manifestation but remains true of him as the one at the right hand of the Father. As Brooke (p. 175) states it: "The incarnation was more than a mere incident, and more than a temporary and partial connection between the Logos and human nature. It was the permanent guarantee of the possibility of fellowship, and the chief means by which it is brought about."

8 There is a difficult textual problem here that allows for two quite different meanings. NIV reads "Watch out that you do not lose what you have worked for," as does RSV. But RV, NEB, and JB accept the alternative reading: "Watch out that you do not lose what we have worked for." Bultmann and Schnackenburg support the reading, whereas NIV, Brooke, Marshall, and Westcott support that of the NEB. The textual evidence is so divided that it is difficult to make a choice. On balance the more difficult reading "we" is preferable and, in fact, coincides with similar feelings expressed by Paul in writing to the Galatians: "I fear for you, that somehow I have wasted my efforts on you" (4:11; cf. v.19: "My dear children, for whom I am again in the pains of childbirth until Christ is formed in you").

As messengers of Christ, the apostles could not help but feel completely involved in the lives of their charges (cf. Phil 2:16). Whether or not they actually planted all the churches or whether missionaries were responsible for some of them is beside the point. Paul did not establish the Christian communities in Rome and Colosse. Yet he accepted full responsibility for them in terms of the apostolic message. As one in charge of the message that was "from the beginning," all the apostle John's labors were directed to the maintenance of the truth of Jesus Christ as one come in the flesh. If anyone failed to continue in this message, then in a real sense John's apostolic mission had failed. That the reader would lose was self-evident. But so would the community of faith and "the elder" himself.

A "full reward" (*misthon plērē*, NIV, "rewarded fully") suggests that John envisions two possibilities. Verse 8 appears to address the situation when a reader is partially deceived and so loses some of his reward for faithfulness and perseverance. One receives according to his labor. (For the concept of "rewards," see Matt 5:12; John 4:36; 1 Cor 3:8; Rev 11:18; 22:12.)

9 This verse, which is John's second possibility, suggests a more radical departure from the faith: "Anyone who goes too far." NIV's translation—"Anyone who runs ahead"—may be too weak for the verb *proagōn* in this context. The NEB rendering— "Anyone who runs ahead too far"—is supported by Westcott's paraphrase: "Everyone that advances in bold confidence beyond the limits set to the Christian Faith" (p. 219). The situation here in v.9 implies not a loss of reward but of God himself, the loss or nonattainment of eternal life as promised in 1 John 2:25.

The "teaching of Christ" can be construed as an objective genitive—i.e., the teaching about Christ—as Bultmann and Marshall read it. The reference would then be to the teaching that Jesus Christ has indeed come in the flesh. But it is equally possible that the genitive is subjective and refers to Jesus' teaching in v.5 that "we love one another" (cf. Brooke, Schnackenburg, Stott, Westcott). It is of little importance, however, which alternative is accepted, because the author holds equally to both positions. For Jesus Christ to be acknowledged as the one come in the flesh is fundamental to the faith, and for us to love one another is equally fundamental. To confess the former requires that we do the latter. To have the Father and the Son is to have precisely what the false teachers have lost. To give up the Son is to lose the Father (cf. John 5:23; 14:6–7).

10–11 The last warning extended to the reader is both the most objective and the most final. "If anyone comes to you and does not bring this teaching, do not take him into your house or welcome him." The author is not certain what will happen in the lady's community. Probably he expects that the false teachers will soon arrive with their pernicious propaganda. If so, the situation is dangerous. The false teachers must not be shown hospitality, as if they were brothers in the faith. Because they are deceivers, it would be a mockery of the Father and a sin against Christ to give those who deny the Son and hate the brethren a place of respect within the community of faith. To do so would be to become a partaker in their unbelief and hatred of the truth.

The statement is all the more remarkable since it comes from the "apostle of love." Moreover, the command to extend hospitality is deeply rooted in the tradition (Rom 12:13; 1 Tim 3:2; 5:3–10; Titus 1:8; Heb 13:2; 1 Peter 4:8–10). It was an absolute demand that brothers in Christ be supported, fed, and housed by the local congregations they visited. Nevertheless, the elder invokes a higher principle here. False prophets, antichrists, and deceivers are not to share in the provision of hospitality. Even the Christian greetings that might be given ever so casually are forbidden in the case of the false teachers. One cannot serve God and mammon simultaneously (Matt 6:24). One cannot be a partner of God and a partner of the devil (1 Cor 10:20).

Clearly the elder's words are an offense to some today and are not considered "a sufficient guide to Christian conduct" (Dodd, *Johannine Epistles*, p. 152) or worthy of the church. Admittedly great care should be exercised before applying such a radical withholding of hospitality from anyone. For the elder it was applied only to antichristians who were committed to destroying the faith of the community. The issue involved more than disagreements in interpretation or personal misunderstandings among members of the body of Christ. It was radical and clearly defined unbelief, and it involved active and aggressive promotion of perversions of truth and practice that struck at the heart of Christianity.

But ought not persons who had gone so far astray be dealt with all the more in love? Do they not require even more by way of grace, mercy, and forgiveness of Christ? At the personal level, Christians should always be prepared to turn the other cheek and seek tirelessly to be reconciled with others. But only those whose own faith is secure and whose understanding beyond corruption can do this. Unfortunately, the community of the elect lady was not yet in this position. It was not mature enough to deal with such deadly deviations; in fact, it was more likely that it might be destroyed by them. The responsibility of parents may furnish an analogy. Parents must discriminate as to whom even among their relatives they entertain in their home. Some relatives might be of such questionable character as to menace the moral, spiritual, and physical welfare of the children. Such relatives must be excluded. Parents must balance their concern for their relatives with their responsibility for their children. Notice that John does not suggest that the elect lady and her children deal with the false teachers in hatred or retaliate against them. Instead, he counsels that the false teachers be kept at a distance lest their heresy destroy the young church.

We today can only be grateful that the infant church took heresy regarding the person of Christ seriously. Christianity stands or falls with its Christology. From the human point of view, if John and other apostolic leaders had tolerated the "antichrists" who denied the basic truth of the Incarnation, the church might never have survived. We today are the beneficiaries of the spiritual discernment and moral courage of John and others like him.

III. Conclusion

12–13

> ¹²I have much to write to you, but I do not want to use paper and ink. Instead, I hope to visit you and talk with you face to face, so that our joy may be complete.
>
> ¹³The children of your chosen sister send their greetings.

12–13 The epistle closes with a quite normal wish. The elder acknowledges that there is much more he might say, but he recognizes that it will be more effective if he were to say it in person. The phrase "face to face" (lit., "mouth [*stoma*] to mouth") suggests an intimacy that requires personal presence. When the community of believers enjoys fellowship in Christ, one of the results of their fellowship is the joy of the Lord.

The children who sent greetings were doubtless members of the elder's community who understood the plight of the community of the chosen lady; and they wished to share the elder's concern to strengthen the bonds of love that unite all saints.

Notes

1 Ἐν ἀληθείᾳ (*en alētheia*, NIV, "in the truth") is anarthrous (without an article) here and therefore should be understood as having an adverbial force—viz., "truly," as in John 1:47;

7:26; 8:31; 17:8. Marshall (p. 61), however, argues that "in view of the significant role which 'truth' plays in these letters, a deeper sense may already be present here." But if this were the author's intent, how natural it would have been to include the article as he did in v.1b! A more judicious decision would be to follow the example of NEB and not supply the article where none is present. The practice of supplying the article (so RSV, JB, NIV) almost inevitably obscures any difference in the text and encourages what might well be over-interpretation, particularly in the case of 2 John 1 and 3 John 1.

4 Compare Paul's words in Rom 1:8: "First, I thank my God through Jesus Christ for all of you, because your faith is being reported all over the world" (cf. 1 Cor 1:4; Phil 1:3; Col 1:3; 1 Thess 1:2; 3 John 3–4).

7 The question has been raised as to whether John's view contradicts Paul's statement that "flesh and blood cannot inherit the kingdom of God" (1 Cor 15:50). Paul thinks of the flesh as that which must die and be transformed. The "fleshly" body must become a "spiritual body." John, however, as well as Luke, thinks of flesh as defining the human reality of a person. When Jesus' disciples were startled when he appeared to them after the Resurrection, he said to them, "Look at my hands and my feet. It is I myself! Touch me and see; a ghost does not have flesh and bones, as you see I have" (Luke 24:39). John understands that Jesus arose from the dead in his physical body (John 20:27) and that his glorification was in that same body (John 20:17). Both John and Paul recognize the need of the transformation of the flesh but used different terms to define it.

(For "deceiver and the antichrist," see comment at 1 John 2:18ff.)

3 JOHN

Glenn W. Barker

Outline

Text and Exposition

I. Salutation

1

¹The elder,

To my dear friend Gaius, whom I love in the truth.

Third John is a genuine letter written by "the elder" to a man named Gaius in another community. Although the letter is highly personal, it is also clearly official. The elder expresses thoughts that are meant to be shared with other members of the community. Concern for the situation in the church is the occasion for writing. The letter implies that Gaius was in a specially influential position and commends and supports him.

1 The elder (cf. comment on 2 John 1 and Introduction to 1 John: Authorship and Date) addresses Gaius as "my dear friend," and his warm affection for Gaius permeates the entire letter. Although the name Gaius occurs elsewhere in the NT (cf. Acts 19:29; 20:4; Rom 16:23; 1 Cor 1:14) and is common enough in the literature of the time, his identity, aside from what is said of him in this letter, is unknown to us. He may have been a member of the church Diotrephes appears to have headed. But whether he held any official position in it is uncertain. The pronoun in the phrase "whom I love in the truth" is emphatic but probably not, as Westcott suggests, in contrast to the attitude of some other detractors of Gaius.

On NIV's rendering of *en alētheia* as "in the truth," see note on 2 John 1.

II. Personal Words to Gaius

2–4

²Dear friend, I pray that you may enjoy good health and that all may go well with you, even as your soul is getting along well. ³It gave me great joy to have some brothers come and tell about your faithfulness to the truth and how you continue to walk in the truth. ⁴I have no greater joy than to hear that my children are walking in the truth.

2 The elder, wishing good health to Gaius does not mean that Gaius was ill. The wish was a conventional one and though it does not rule out the possibility of particular concern for Gaius's health, it does not necessitate it. Here the elder commends him by praying that things will be well for his physical health as they have proved to be for his spiritual health. Implied in this verse is a tribute to the wholesome state of Gaius's spiritual life. Of how many Christians could their physical health be equated with their spiritual health? But the elder knew his man!

3 Behind this verse we see the flow of Christians between the early churches as well as between the Johannine ones. And it went on in the second century also. It may have been occasioned in some instances by a change in personal circumstances and in others because of opposition and persecution. However, it may have been more intentional than this and may have represented, particularly among the Johannine churches, a commitment to live as a fellowship of Christians deeply concerned for one another.

Traveling missionaries and evangelists may have indeed swelled the ranks of those who moved back and forth. Yet it would probably be too much to read into the term "brothers" an exclusive reference to them. In any event there was a lively flow of persons between the church where Gaius was a member and the elder's community. Moreover, these men appear to be reporting to the elder as a normal and expected activity. They tell him about Gaius's faithfulness to Christian truth as well as about his sincerity and faithfulness in his daily living. In vv.5–8 the elder specifies the conduct he has in mind. Nowhere in this letter, however, does he refer to the theological issue before the church. Westcott's (p. 226) comment may well be correct. "The words evidently point to some difficulties from false teaching which Gaius had boldly met, though as yet the issue of his work was uncertain."

4 The importance for the church of Gaius's stand for the truth is seen in the elder's next comment. There is no more important news he can receive, no greater joy he can experience, than that his own "children" (i.e., his own converts to the faith) are living in fidelity "to the truth." The word "children" could of course designate less specifically all for whom John feels pastoral responsibility. Westcott sees the possessive pronoun *ema* ("my") used here as indicating a stronger relationship (cf. Bultmann also).

III. Commendation for Gaius's Hospitality

5–8

> ⁵Dear friend, you are faithful in what you are doing for the brothers, even though they are strangers to you. ⁶They have told the church about your love. You will do well to send them on their way in a manner worthy of God. ⁷It was for the sake of the Name that they went out, receiving no help from the pagans. ⁸We ought therefore to show hospitality to such men so that we may work together for the truth.

5 Again the writer's warm feeling shines through as for the third time he addresses Gaius as his "dear friend" (cf. vv.1–2). Now he commends him for his hospitality to Christian brothers who came from the elder to visit the church, even though they were at the time unknown to Gaius. It is likely that Gaius's actions were quite in contrast to what others in the church did. As Westcott (p. 227) surmises, Gaius may have incurred the displeasure of some in his church. Although hospitality was required of all Christians (Matt 10:10; Rom 12:13; 1 Tim 3:2; 5:10; Heb 13:2), it was sometimes necessary to refuse it (2 John 10).

6 Part of what the traveling brothers had reported to the elder was the wholehearted way—involving, perhaps, risk to his standing in the community—in which Gaius had entertained them. On returning, they had testified to this before the whole church, and this increased the elder's pride in "his son in the faith." He had not only entertained the traveling brothers but had shown them *agapē* love.

It seems that these brothers had returned, perhaps carrying letters from the elder;

and they again needed Christian hospitality. The admonition to send them on their way "in a manner worthy of God" shows the supreme importance assigned to hospitality. The phrase probably means that the traveling brothers were to be recognized as servants of God and supported as such. In such instances, Christians were to provide hospitality as if the Lord himself were being welcomed (cf. John 13:20; Gal 4:14–15; Heb 13:2).

7 That they went out "for the sake of the Name" shows that they were missionaries. Assuredly "the Name" is Jesus Christ (cf. Acts 5:41), and the sending body is either the elder's community or a company of believers known to the elder and Gaius. That they could make no preparation and accept nothing from pagans shows how strongly the Johannine community depended on the word of Jesus: "Take nothing for the journey except a staff—no bread, no bag, no money in your belts. . . . Whenever you enter a house, stay there until you leave that town" (Mark 6:8, 10). Whether it was Jesus' words "Freely you have received, freely give" (Matt 10:8), as Marshall conjectures, or simply common sense that forbade them to take support from pagans, we do not know. What we do know is that wandering preachers and missionaries of pagan deities were common in the Roman world. Deissmann also recounts how profitable it became for some of them and what distrust it occasioned (*Light from the Ancient East* quoted in Dodd, *Johannine Epistles*, p. 160).

It was difficult enough accepting gifts from the church, as Paul showed, let alone taking help from unbelievers (cf. 1 Cor 9:14–18; 2 Cor 12:16–18; 1 Thess 2:6–9). Although Paul acknowledged the right of the traveling missionaries to be supported by the church (1 Cor 9:14), he was well aware of the risks this entailed. Nonetheless, for the mature Christian community such support was encouraged and gladly received (cf. Phil 4:10–18). Both for the giver and receiver there was a blessing to be received. In the Johannine community such support was certainly a part of the sacrifice one Christian owed another. Even a Christian's life was not beyond the limit love required (1 John 3:16–17).

8 Whether this call to practice hospitality is based on the principle that by their support church members may be fellow laborers with missionaries in proclaiming the gospel (cf. 2 Cor 8:23; Col 4:11) or whether such support guarantees participation in the truth is not clear. In the Johannine community, *koinōnia* ("fellowship") required the former, while obedience to the commands of Christ demanded the latter. The author could be ambiguous if he desired because both alternatives were involved. However, the preferable understanding would support the NIV rendering.

IV. Complaints Against Diotrephes

9–10

> [9]I wrote to the church, but Diotrephes, who loves to be first, will have nothing to do with us. [10]So if I come, I will call attention to what he is doing, gossiping maliciously about us. Not satisfied with that, he refuses to welcome the brothers. He also stops those who want to do so and puts them out of the church.

9 This paragraph brings us to the nub of the problem the elder is writing about. He had already addressed a letter to the church through its leader Diotrephes. That letter is lost, perhaps destroyed by Diotrephes himself. Its contents are not, however, difficult to imagine. On the basis of what the elder wrote Gaius, we can surmise that he had written the church asking them to extend hospitality to the traveling missionaries he had sent out. It may also have included a request for support that would speed them on their way. Diotrephes chose to thwart the elder's intention either by suppressing the letter or opposing the request before the congregation. He also had threatened the expulsion of any in the church who were considering offering hospitality to the elder's emmissaries. In fact, some may already have been forced out of the church.

Why Diotrephes was opposing the elder is not clear. The elder's statement that Diotrephes "loves to be first" could simply reflect personal rivalry. Or it could reflect an inflated and dictatorial ego. The elder's prominence in the community was obviously longstanding. Diotrephes may have been troubled by the elder's continued influence over the church Diotrephes was leading. If Diotrephes was a younger man, the elder's age may have been a problem. That there was a deeper split, perhaps involving theological differences, is not supported by the text.

The elder commends Gaius for his faithfulness to the truth and for living according to the truth. Does this indicate that the elder suspected Diotrephes of wavering in opposition to the false teachers in the area? Does the statement that he "will have nothing to do with us" and that he is "gossiping maliciously about us" and "refuses to welcome the brothers" indicate that he is not really committed to the commandment of love the elder contends so unremittingly for? If so, Diotrephes had as yet shown no theological deviation regarding the person of Christ. If he had, we can, in view of his other actions, be quite certain that the elder would have exposed him and pronounced judgment on him. But quite apart from doctrinal deviation, the opposition of Diotrephes would have the effect of weakening the elder's position in the community and making the work of the false teachers that much easier.

Another cause for the problem may have been that the elder may have expanded the activity of the missionary emissaries in order to stem the tide of false teaching flooding the area. The presence of these missionaries would have been an effective deterrent to schism and would have strengthened the hand of the elder in dealing with this threat to the gospel. But his actions may have been resented by Diotrephes as eroding the local autonomy of the churches. The "malicious gossip" referred to may have been that the elder was using the presence of false teachers as a pretext for establishing his own authority more completely over the churches.

Exactly how Gaius fits into all this is unclear. Dodd surmises that he was the leader of another local church in the area and on that basis the elder writes to him. Dodd senses the difficulty of placing Gaius in the same church as Diotrephes. Why should he be telling Gaius about what Diotrephes is doing when presumably Gaius would already know about it firsthand? Marshall conjectures that Gaius may have lived in a nearby village—perhaps a day's journey away—and therefore did not know all that was taking place in the church. If so, that would explain how Gaius could be a member of the same church, as the letter implies, and yet not know all its workings.

A commonly accepted reconstruction of the situation is that the letter reflects the circumstances of the transition from the apostolic period to a time of more rigid, episcopal church government (Adolph Harnack, *Über die dritten Johanesbrief*, T.U. 15:3b [Leipzig: Hinrichs, 1897], in loc.). The tension between Diotrephes and the elder is then seen as a conflict between one of the first monarchical bishops and one of the last of those possessing immediate apostolic authority (cf. Dodd, Houlden, Marshall). (The idea is given a perverse twist by Käsemann, who sees the elder himself as a heresiarch and Diotrephes the episcopal representative of the orthodox party [E. Käsemann, "Ketzer und Zeuge," ZTK 48 (1951), 292–311]!)

Although Harnack's theory is not implausible, it goes beyond the evidence. The elder does not object that Diotrephes should have authority, but he does object to its misuse to the detriment of the truth. The real conflict is not between two types of belief. It is between two levels of commitment to the work of God: Diotrephes is more interested in furthering his own position than in furthering the work of God (cf. Stott, pp. 226–27).

10 Exactly how the elder intended to deal with Diotrephes is unclear. John's statement that he "will call attention to what he [Diotrephes] is doing" suggests that John planned to confront Diotrephes, perhaps personally, and expose his conduct before the whole church, unless he completely repented. There seems to be an implication that Diotrephes' misdeeds were not yet fully known to the congregation; and perhaps it was the elder's hope that once they were revealed, the church would either censure or expel Diotrephes from his position.

How are we to explain the sharp words and drastic response on the part of the apostle of love? Do they not represent a contradiction to his teaching? More probably they represent the response of one who sensed that the very nature of the gospel was threatened by such hypocritical conduct on the part of one of its ministers. Diotrephes' actions against the elder were reprehensible by any standard; but they were even more so on the part of one who probably had been of the fellowship of the elders, who knew the message of love that had been received, and who had pledged to live a life according to the commandment given by the Son of God. For such a leader of the church to give way to personal pique and selfish ambition was unthinkable.

Moreover, the wickedness involved spread beyond the vicious innuendos and lies directed against the elder. It extended to those wholly innocent of possible wrongdoing. The hospitality due the missionary "brothers" in order to speed them on their way in their service of the gospel had also been singled out for abuse; and they were denied the welcome due them as members of the household of faith. Because they came from the elder, they suffered the consequences of guilt by association. The harshest treatment of all had been directed against those whose conscience required them to extend hospitality to the brethren. Because they dared to disobey Diotrephes on this matter, they had been cast out of the congregation.

Such contradiction to the gospel by word and deed as done by Diotrephes could not be condoned, and indeed it was not. It was no longer Diotrephes who was on trial for his action but the elder and all those who believed like him. Silence on their part in the face of such total rejection of the truth and the life of the gospel would have been as hypocritical as Diotrephes' earlier action.

It was no pleasant experience that awaited the elder, but "truth" without love is no truth at all. Diotrephes was condemned not because he violated sound teaching regarding the person and nature of Jesus Christ but because his "life" was a contradiction to the truth of the gospel. This condition required action by John and by the congregation.

V. Exhortation and Endorsement of Demetrius

11–12

> ¹¹Dear friend, do not imitate what is evil but what is good. Anyone who does what is good is from God. Anyone who does what is evil has not seen God. ¹²Demetrius is well spoken of by everyone—and even by the truth itself. We also speak well of him, and you know that our testimony is true.

11 That the elder admonishes Gaius not to "imitate what is evil but what is good" need not imply that he fears for Gaius's character. It is rather for his encouragement in continuing to do good. He may have expected Diotrephes and his supporters to exert intense pressure on Gaius to give up his support of the elder and his missionaries. In that event, Gaius would have no option but to take his stand on principle. To give in to pressure against one's convictions is to submit to evil. Whatever its source or whoever its advocates, evil can never be reconciled to God. Even to contemplate giving in to evil means that loyalty to God's revealed will is jeopardized.

Why does the elder appeal to imitators? Because it is the nature of God's revelation that truth (vv.1, 3), love (v.6), and righteousness (v.11) have been modeled first in Jesus Christ and then by those who are faithful to his commandments. Humankind does not have in its nature a dependable standard by which to judge itself. It must always measure its understandings and actions by God himself, for whom love, truth, and righteousness are absolute attributes. In Christ these same attributes have become available to all who love God and desire to obey his commands. To show them forth in our lives proves that we are "from God." All goodness proceeds from him; our perseverance in goodness demonstrates that in Jesus Christ we have seen God.

12 The elder now commends Demetrius, of whom we know no more than what is said of him here. For some reason John felt it important for Gaius to know and trust him. Apparently he was also a supporter of the elder. Some have conjectured that Demetrius was the bearer of the letter or that he was a traveling missionary. The elder honors him with a threefold tribute: (1) He "is well spoken of by everyone." (2) He is well spoken of "by the truth iself." (3) The elder also "speaks well of him." This strong backing of Demetrius leads us to think he had been given a special mission that required unusual trust, but one that the elder did not choose to describe here.

How the truth could speak well of Demetrius is somewhat puzzling. Bultmann sees "the truth" as a personification. If so, it could stand for God, Christ, the gospel, the revelation. It seems more likely, however, that it is the truth of the gospel in Demetrius's life the elder is referring to. Like Gaius, Demetrius is "walking in the truth." His life matches his confession. In Pauline terms, he manifests the fruit of the Spirit. In Johannine terms, he lives the life of love. The clause "and you know that our testimony is true" reminds us of John 21:24.

VI. Personal Remarks and Farewell Greetings

13–15

> ¹³I have much to write you, but I do not want to do so with pen and ink. ¹⁴I hope to see you soon, and we will talk face to face.

> ¹⁵Peace to you. The friends here send their greetings. Greet the friends there by name.

13-14 John's statement that he wished to write more parallels not only 2 John 12 but also John 20:30. It is characteristic of his style as is also his expressed desire to see Gaius soon and talk with him "face to face" (cf. comment on 2 John 12).

15 The closing word again bears the mark of the warm relationship existing between John and Gaius. John extends "peace" to him, knowing that his situation may become very difficult in the days ahead. He also reminds him that all who are with John are also Gaius's friends. Then he concludes by asking Gaius to greet his friends in the church. This last remark supports the assumption that the elder's real desire is that Gaius will in fact share this letter with the members of the church.

Notes

1 On this form of epistolary address, see Funk, p. 425.
2 Marshall's statement (p. 83) that "there is some probability that Gaius was not in the best of health" based on v.9 is only conjectural. If Gaius's health were really a problem, it seems unlikely that he would be able to exercise the hospitality he is commended for; and it might be even less likely that in such a warm personal note his health would have been referred to in such a perfunctory way.
3 Καθώς (kathōs, "and how") may be understood as introducing the author's own personal knowledge. "The brothers came and told about your faithfulness just as indeed you are faithful" (Bultmann, p. 98, n.6).
11 Ὁ ἀγαθοποιῶν (ho agathopoiōn, "one who does what is good") occurs only here in the Johannine writings. "To be from God" reminds us of 1 John 2:3–5; 33:4–10; 4:7.

JUDE

Edwin A. Blum

JUDE

Introduction

1. Authorship

The first verse identifies the author of this letter as "Jude, a servant of Jesus Christ and a brother of James." "James," an English form of the Hebrew name "Jacob," was a popular name among the Jews in NT times because of its patriarchal connection. Likewise popular was "Judah," the name of Jacob's fourth son, founder of the tribe of Judah. "Jude" is an English form of "Judas" (*Ioudas*), the Greek form of "Judah." The name gained added luster from Judas Maccabaeus, a national hero of the Jews, who led the revolt against Antiochus Epiphanes in the second century B.C. But the perfidy of Judas Iscariot may perhaps have led practically all major English versions (except the RV) to use the form "Jude" rather than "Judas" in translating this letter.

Can Jude be identified with any certainty among the number of men in the NT named Judas? BAG lists eight possibilities (pp. 380–81). The link of Jude with James provides the best clue for identifying the author of the letter. After the martyrdom of James the son of Zebedee under Herod Agrippa I (c. A.D. 44; cf. Acts 12:2), the only James who is well enough known in the early church that the unspecified use of his name would be generally recognizable was James of Jerusalem. Paul called him "James, the Lord's brother" (Gal 1:19). Later, according to Hegesippus, he became known as "James the Just."[1]

If the James of Jude 1:1 can be so identified, Jude was the brother of the leader of the Jerusalem church (Acts 12:17; 15:13; 21:18; 1 Cor 15:7; Gal 1:19; 2:9, 12) and the half-brother of Jesus of Nazareth (Matt 13:55; Mark 6:3). If the Jude of this letter was the half-brother of Jesus, he did not believe in the messiahship of Jesus until after the Resurrection (John 7:5; cf. Acts 1:14 ["his brothers"]). This probably explains the humility with which Jude introduces himself in 1:1 as a servant (slave) of the brother (now recognized as the Messiah) he had denied.

In a story that comes from Hegesippus and is related by Eusebius, this trait of

---

[1]Eusebius, *Ecclesiastical History* 2.23.

175

humility was shown by the grandsons of Jude, "said to have been the Lord's brother according to the flesh."[2] (This is "the only mention of Jude [the man] in ecclesiastical history" [HDB, s.v.].) The story tells how the grandsons were brought before Domitian, the Roman emperor (A.D. 81–96), and accused of belonging to the royal house of David. The emperor questioned them about the Christ and his kingdom, and they explained that it was a heavenly kingdom that would come at the end of the age. So the emperor dismissed them as simple peasants with no royal pretensions.

Modern objections to the authorship of the letter by a half-brother of Jesus include the fact that its language seems very Hellenistic for an author who grew up in Galilee. In addition, the vocabulary abounds in ornate and rare words (there are thirteen words not found elsewhere in the NT). Yet it is unreasonable to dogmatize about what facility in the Greek language and literature or what knowledge of Jewish apocalytic writings (cf. the possible use of the Assumption of Moses in v.9 and the Apocalypse of Enoch in v. 14) the half-brother of Jesus might have had. Greek was the lingua franca of the Mediterranean world, and the presence of the Decapolis to the east and to the south of the Sea of Galilee provided ample opportunity for Greek influence on nearby Nazareth.

Hughes has surveyed the evidence regarding the languages Jesus used in his ministry and concludes that, while more work needs to be done in this field, it is certainly probable that Jesus spoke Greek fluently.[3] His half-brother Jude grew up in a multilingual environment. Turner describes the language of Jude as revealing a Jewish Christian author who had a distinctly Hellenistic style. In addition, Turner finds evidence of biblical Greek in Jude's vocabulary.[4]

Schrage opposes the authorship of the letter by the Lord's half-brother on the ground that it bears the marks of the beginning of early Catholicism (*Frühkatholizismus*). "Early Catholicism" is a step in the development of the Catholicism of the later Roman church. Schrage finds support for his view in the "Catholic" salutation of the letter as well as in the letter's artistic style and its appeal to tradition (v.3). From this slender evidential base, he alleges a late date of composition that would rule out the possibility that Jude the half-brother of Jesus wrote the letter (Balz and Schrage, pp. 219–20).

None of these objections are weighty, since the appeal to tradition is common in Paul's letters (cf. 1 Cor 11:23ff.; 15:3ff.).[5] The salutation and artistic style of the letter do not prove a late date. Christianity spread rapidly in the ancient world; so a "polished" work may well have been sent to the church at large in Jude's time.

2. Date

The letter is so short that it contains little to help fix its date of composition other than the points mentioned above and inferences that can be drawn from the heresy

---

[2] Ibid., 3.20.

[3] Philip Edgcumbe Hughes, "The Languages Spoken by Jesus," *New Dimensions in New Testament Study*, edd. R.N. Longenecker and M.C. Tenney (Grand Rapids: Zondervan, 1974), pp. 127–43.

[4] Nigel Turner, James H. Moulton's *A Grammar of New Testament Greek*, vol. 4, *Style* (Edinburgh: T. & T. Clark, 1976), p. 139.

[5] See also F.F. Bruce, "Scripture and Tradition in the New Testament," *Holy Book and Holy Tradition*, edd. F.F. Bruce and E.G. Rupp (Grand Rapids: Eerdmans, 1968), pp.68–93.

the author opposes. If the author was the younger half-brother of Jesus (the older half-brother being the influential James of Jerusalem), the most probable time of writing would be between A.D. 40 and 80. If the letter was used by Peter in 2 Peter, the writing would have to be sometime prior to Peter's death or before A.D. 65. However, Peter's use of Jude is not certain (cf. Introduction to 2 Peter: Special Problem). Guthrie thinks Jude could have been written in the period between 65 and 80. The heresy of the false teachers could have developed quite early. So all things considered, the letter may most probably be dated about 60 to 65.

3. Canonicity

If 2 Peter utilized Jude and if Peter wrote 2 Peter (both positions are disputed), then 2 Peter is the oldest witness to Jude, and its "apostolic" character or canonicity is, in principle, settled at a very early date. In the early church fathers, a number of allusions to Jude have been identified (cf. Bigg, pp. 305–9). The Muratorian Canon (c. 200) states that an epistle of Jude was accepted in the Catholic church.[6] Tertullian, Clement of Alexandria, and Origen all knew the book.

Eusebius, in speaking of the Epistle of James, says, "It is to be observed that its authenticity is denied since few of the ancients quote it, as is also the case with the epistle called Jude's which is itself one of the seven called Catholic; nevertheless we know that these letters have been used publicly with the rest in most churches."[7] Eusebius later ranks Jude as a book of the church that has been spoken against (*Antilegomenōn*) and distinguishes it from the spurious books (*Notha*).[8] Schelkle (p. 144) says that Jude was considered canonical by the end of the second century in Rome, Africa, and Egypt.

On the other hand, there were doubts about the letter. Those who spoke against it objected to its use of noncanonical writings and noted also the limited number of citations of the letter in the literature of the early church. These doubts were overcome, and the worth of the book was recognized by the church. Didymus of Alexandria (c. 395) defended the book, and since then little objection to its canonicity has been voiced.

4. Place of Origin

The lack of internal clues makes determining the letter's place of origin a problem. Egypt and Palestine are common guesses.

5. Destination

Since the address is so general—"To those who have been called, who are loved by God the Father and kept by Jesus Christ" (v. 1)—it is quite possible that the author

---

[6]Cf. English text in E. Hennecke and W. Schneemelcher, edd., *New Testament Apocrypha*, 2 vols. [London: Lutterworth, 1963–65], 1:44–45).

[7]*Ecclesiastical History* 2.23.25.

[8]Ibid., 3.25.3.

intended the letter to be circulated to a number of churches. Against this are the internal indications that the author knows the conditions within the church or churches to whom he writes (v.4). It is possible, however, that Jude itinerated and thus knew the dangers affecting the churches of a region or a circuit of churches within a region. The fixing of the destination remains speculative. Asia Minor, Syrian Antioch, or even Palestine are common suggestions.

6. Purpose

Jude had desired to write on the subject of the church's teaching ("the salvation we share," v.3). But he found it necessary to warn his readers concerning innovators who were smuggling false teaching into the churches. Quite likely, these teachers had an itinerant ministry in imitation of the apostles. Both Paul (cf. Gal, Col) and John (cf. 1 and 2 John) faced the problem of false teachers who promoted a different gospel and erroneous instruction.

Jude's purpose is to give a strong denunciation of the errorists. He evidently hopes that by his concise but vigorous exposure of them, the church will see the danger of their error and be alert to the coming judgment on it. Jude also wants to reassure the church by showing that the fact that such scoffers would come was part of the content of apostolic prophecy. In his last paragraphs, he calls the Christians to exercise their faith within the received common instruction. He also praises God as the one who is able to keep both the church and individuals from falling. Christians may have confidence that the God who began a good work of salvation within them (Phil 1:6) will keep them (v.1) and finally bring them safely into his glorious presence (v.24).

The Book of Jude has been called "the most neglected book in the New Testament."[9] There may be various reasons for its neglect, e.g., its brevity, its citation of noncanonical Jewish writings, and its burning denunciation of error. Yet Christians and the church today need to listen to Jude's contribution to biblical revelation. The emphasis on a "fixed" core of truth known as "the faith" needs to be pondered. Jesus is God's Word to man (cf. Rom 6:17; Heb 1:1–4). "God is light; in Him there is no darkness" (1 John 1:5ff.) is the apostle John's summary of the revelation of God in Jesus. God is righteous and true and he hates sin and error.

Contemporary culture is becoming indifferent to the question of truth. Christians have found truth in Jesus (Eph 4:21). Jude warns of the dangers in the mixture of error with this truth. So his eloquent tract for maintaining the purity and truth of the Christian faith is needed in view of the relativity and syncretism so common today. While it must be granted that some Christians have been and are still intolerantly dogmatic about relatively minor theological issues, there is also the great danger of accepting uncritically all teaching or positions as valid and thus compromising God's once-and-for-all self-disclosure in Jesus.

---

[9]Douglas J. Rowston, "The Most Neglected Book in the New Testament," NTS, 21 (July 1975), pp. 554–63.

7. Special Problems

At least two special problems confront the student of Jude: the identity of the heretics and the relation of Jude to 2 Peter. For a discussion of the second problem, see the Introduction to 2 Peter.

Regarding the first problem, the identity of the heretics, Rowston[10] states "that Hermann Werdermann[11] is the only modern scholar to investigate the matter fully." Werdermann called the error "libertine gnosis" and did not identify it with any known system. But since 1913, the time of Werdermann's work, the amount of knowledge concerning Gnosticism has greatly increased.[12] While the exact historical background of Jude is still uncertain, much more information is available (e.g., from Nag Hamadi in Egypt [ancient Chenoboskion]) to supplement previous sources (e.g., Plotinus, Irenaeus, Tertullian, Hippolytus, Origen, Epiphanius, and Clement of Alexandria.[13]

The emerging picture of the world of Gnosticism is very complicated. Generally speaking, the Gnostic world-view was hostile toward the world and all worldly ties. From this perspective, Gnosticism branched into ascetic and libertine divisions. For the libertine Gnostic the idea of "thou shalt" or "thou shalt not" does not come from God (who is absolutely transmundane) but from the Archons (or the demiurges) who are related to this world. Salvation (pneumatic freedom) involves the intentional violation of the rules of the Archons. Gnosticism also could cause a nihilism. In some systems, the Gnostic despaired of this world to such an extent that body and soul were meaningless. Only the acosmic pneuma would transcend this universe to reach the unknown God.

Against this kind of thinking, Jude's strong polemic becomes understandable. The heretics were antinomian; they did not observe Christian moral instruction. Though the false teachers spoke about the pneuma (spirit) and claimed to be spiritual, they were really *psychikoi* ("soulish,' "psychic," "unspiritual") and did not have the "Spirit" (v. 19). Their lives gave evidence of bondage to the world, not liberation from it (v. 8). Their rejection of Jesus (v. 4), their blaspheming of angels (v. 8, 10), their complaining and cynicism (v. 16) all fit libertine Gnosticism.

The ultimate threat of this Gnostic faith to Christianity lay in its denial of God's revelation in Christ. To follow the Gnostic path led to a radical rejection of all God's Word to man and to a substitution of a different salvation. The means of salvation became an esoteric teaching, and salvation did not free the whole person (body, soul, spirit) from the bondage of sin. This world was negated and the knowledge of the one, true God hidden. Jude's vehement opposition to this kind of error was justified in the light of the significant issues that were involved.

8. Bibliography

(See Bibliography for 1 Peter, pp. 216–17.)

---

[10]Ibid., p. 554.
[11]*"Die Irrlehrer der Judas und 2 Petrusbriefs* (Gutersloh: C. Bertelsmann, 1913).
[12]Cf. Hans Jonas, *The Gnostic Religion* (Boston: Beacon, 1970).
[13]Ibid., pp. 37–42.

9. Outline

I. The Salutation (1–2)

II. The Reason for the Letter (3–4)

III. The Warning Against the False Teachers (5–16)
   1. Examples of God's Judgment in History (5–7)
   2. The Description and Doom of the False Teachers (8–13)
   3. Enoch's Prophecy of the Coming Judgment (14–16)

IV. The Exhortations to the Believers (17–23)

V. The Doxology (24–25)

Text and Exposition

I. The Salutation

1–2

¹Jude, a servant of Jesus Christ and a brother of James,

To those who have been called, who are loved by God the Father and kept by Jesus Christ:

²Mercy, peace and love be yours in abundance.

1 This brief letter begins with the customary self-identification of the author. He is "Jude" (cf. Introduction: Authorship). There were eight different individuals in the NT with that name; but a process of elimination makes it probable that the Jude of this letter is the brother of Jesus and James (cf. Matt 13:55; Mark 6:3). Modestly he calls himself a "servant" (*doulos;* lit., "slave") of Jesus Christ, and as such he belongs to him. While Jude's being Christ's servant is not without distinction (e.g., "Moses my servant," Josh 1:2), it is probably mentioned here to imply that what he is about to write is what his Master wants him to say. He also calls himself "a brother of James." The self-identification of linking himself to his brother makes sense only if the brother is well known to the recipients of the letter. The James (*Iakōbos*) spoken of here is one of six persons of that name mentioned in the NT and, on the basis of NT evidence, is "the Lord's brother" (cf. Jos. Antiq. XX, 200 [ix. 1]). He was the author of the Epistle of James and became the head of the church in Jerusalem (cf. Introduction: Authorship).

The readers are "the called" (*klētois;* cf. DNTT, 1:271–76), which in Pauline theology stresses the sovereign activity of God's grace in summoning to salvation. The term "the called" is almost synonymous with "a Christian" (Kelly, p. 243). Second, they are "loved by God the Father" (*tois en theō patri ēgapēmenois;* lit., "beloved in God the Father"). Many MSS read "sanctified" (*hēgiasmenois*), which is close in appearance to *ēgapēmenois* and occurs in 1 Corinthians 1:2. These factors may have caused an accidental substitution of the latter for "beloved in God the Father." This reading makes good sense; for the Father, who is love (1 John 4:16), has set his love on his people (cf. Deut 7:6–8). Third, those to whom Jude is writing are "kept [*tetērēmenois*] by Jesus Christ." There is no "by" in the Greek text. Some have argued that the "in" (*en:* NIV, "by") with "God the Father" was displaced (Mayor, EGT, 5:253) and should be taken with Jesus Christ. As the text stands, it could be translated "kept for Jesus Christ," with the thought that God the Father preserves the Christian for his Son (cf. vv. 24–25; John 17:15).

2 "Mercy, peace and love be yours in abundance" is typical of the greeting, or prayer, that was customary in ancient letters. Jude omits the word "grace," which is used in the salutations of practically all the other NT letters. Perhaps his reference to "mercy," "peace," and "love" is a way of showing facets of God's grace to men. It seems correct to understand all three as indicative of what God does for us. Mercy is his compassion, peace is his gift of quiet confidence in the work of Jesus, and love is his generosity in granting us his favors and meeting our needs.

II. The Reason for the Letter

3-4

> ³Dear friends, although I was very eager to write to you about the salvation we
> share, I felt I had to write and urge you to contend for the faith that was once for
> all entrusted to the saints. ⁴For certain men whose condemnation was written about
> long ago have secretly slipped in among you. They are godless men, who change
> the grace of our God into a license for immorality and deny Jesus Christ our only
> Sovereign and Lord.

3 Jude tells his "dear friends" (*agapētoi;* lit., "loved," "beloved"; cf. vv. 17, 20) how
he came to write this letter. He had to write a positive statement of the Christian faith.
Whether he was actively engaged in writing or only in the process of thinking about
it is not clear from the Greek *pasan spoudēn poioumenos graphein* (present participle
and infinitive—i.e., "making every effort to write").

"The salvation we share" (*tēs koinēs hēmōn sōtērias;* lit., "our common salvation")
is that which all Christians now participate in. First Peter 1:5 speaks of a "salvation
that is ready to be revealed in the last time." Both are true. Christians have been saved
(Titus 3:5), they now possess salvation (Jude 3; cf. Heb 6:9), and they long for Christ
who "will appear a second time, . . . to bring salvation to those who are waiting for
him" (Heb 9:28).

By saying "I felt I had to write," Jude explains that a compelling obligation to the
people of God prompted him to write for their spiritual good. His letter is intended
to exhort the readers to struggle for "the faith that was once for all entrusted to the
saints." "To contend" or "struggle" translates *epagōnizesthai,* a word that occurs only
here in the NT. However, related words do occur in the NT (cf. TDNT, 1:135–40).
The basic meaning of this word is that of the intense effort in a wrestling match (cf.
agōnizomenos in 1 Cor 9:25). The verb form is a present infinitive, showing that the
Christian struggle is to be continuous.

"The faith" is the body of truth that very early in the church's history took on a
definite form (cf. Acts 2:42; Rom 6:17; Gal 1:23). Without doubt, the form of the faith
as a body of recognized truth became clearer as time passed. Jude stresses that this
faith has been entrusted "once for all" (*hapax*) to the "saints" (*tois hagiois*—the ones
set apart by God for himself). Basically the Christian faith cannot be changed; its
foundation truths are not negotiable. (This conviction is not, of course, peculiar to
Jude; see the similar emphasis in Gal 1:6–9 and in 2 John 9.)

4 Jude goes on to explain the reasons why he was compelled to write. Ungodly men
had "secretly slipped in" (*pareisedysan,* "crept in unawares") among the believers.
Paul uses the related word *pareisaktos* of Judaizers who had "infiltrated" Christian
congregations to spy on their freedom in Christ Jesus (Gal 2:4). Concerning these
men, the Greek says *hoi palai progegrammenoi eis touto to krima,* which KJV
translates as "who were before of old ordained to this condemnation," while NIV has
"men whose condemnation was written about long ago." The word *prographō* means
to "write before," either in the same document or in a previous one. The reference
could be to God's writing down from eternity the destiny (i.e., the reprobation or
punishment) of the wicked. But it is more likely that it refers to previously written

predictions about the doom of the apostates (so Mayor, p. 24; BAG, p. 711; contra Schrenk, TDNT, 1:772).

After stating the destiny of these men, Jude describes them as "impious" or "ungodly" (*asebeis*), a term often used of notorious sinners. This general word is made more specific by the two specific charges that follow. First, they "change the grace of our God into a license for immorality." Evidently their understanding of grace and perhaps of the forgiveness of sins led them to feel free to indulge in all forms of sexual depravity (*aselgeian*, cf. comments at 2 Peter 2:2). Second, they "deny Jesus Christ our only Sovereign and Lord." Exactly how they deny Jesus Christ, Jude does not say. Certainly they denied him by their immoral living that ran counter to his commands. Perhaps also they denied him in their teaching of a Christology that denied either his full humanity or his full deity. NIV's translation of *ton monon despotēn kai kyrion hēmōn Iēsoun Christon* ("Jesus Christ our only Sovereign and Lord") is defensible because of the one article (*ton*) with two nouns and the use of *despotēs* in 2 Peter 2:1 in reference to Christ. However, *despotēs* is commonly used of the Father (Luke 2:29; Acts 4:24; and LXX), and the word "only" (*monon*) makes it more difficult to apply *despotēs* to Jesus. Thus the translation would be "the only Sovereign [the Father] and our Lord Jesus Christ." If this is adopted, then the error of the godless men was more likely a moral rather than a theological one (cf. Titus 1:16; "They claim to know God, but by their actions they deny him").

III. The Warning Against the False Teachers (5–16)

1. *Examples of God's Judgment in History*

5–7

> [5]Though you already know all this, I want to remind you that the Lord delivered his people out of Egypt, but later destroyed those who did not believe. [6]And the angels who did not keep their positions of authority but abandoned their own home—these he has kept in darkness, bound with everlasting chains for judgment on the great Day. [7]In a similar way, Sodom and Gomorrah and the surrounding towns gave themselves up to sexual immorality and perversion. They serve as an example of those who suffer the punishment of eternal fire.

5 As did Peter in 2 Peter 1:12, Jude states that his readers already know what he is about to say but that he will remind them of it. So he gives them three examples of the Lord's judgments: on the unbelievers at the time of the Exodus, on the fallen angels, and on Sodom and Gomorrah. In each instance the objects of judgment are notable rebels against the Lord. In v.5 there is a difficult textual problem (cf. Notes). However, NIV gives the sense.

The first example is that of Israel, who experienced the great display of God's grace in the Exodus, saw and heard his revelation at Sinai, and received his care in the wilderness; yet a number of them disbelieved and rebelled. Obviously this is not an instance of people being saved and then losing their salvation. Jude describes the rebels as "those who did not believe" (*tous mē pisteusantas*). The Israelites were physically delivered from bondage, not by their faith as a nation, but by God's covenant love and mercy. The warning in this judgment is against unbelief and rebellion.

6 The second example is of the fallen angels. The most likely reference here is to the angels ("sons of God," cf. Gen 6:4; Job 1:6; 2:1) who came to earth and mingled with women. This interpretation is expounded in the pseudepigraphical Book of Enoch (7; 9.8; 10.11; 12.4), from which Jude quotes in v.14, and is common in the intertestamental literature and the early church fathers (e.g., Justin *Apology* 2.5). These angels "did not keep their positions of authority" (*tēn heautōn archēn*). The use of the word *archē* for "rule," "dominion," or "sphere" is uncommon but appears to be so intended here (cf. BAG, p. 112). The implication is that God assigned angels stipulated responsibilities (*archē*, "dominion") and a set place (*oikētērion*). But because of their rebellion, God has kept or reserved (*tetērēken*—perfect tense) these fallen angels in darkness and in eternal chains awaiting final judgment. Apparently some fallen angels are in bondage while others are unbound and active among mankind as demons.

7 The third example of judgment is that of the cities of the plain, Sodom and Gomorrah. In v.7 NIV is so concise that it slides over the significance of the pronoun "these" (*toutois*). Kelly (p. 253) translates this verse thus: "Just as Sodom and Gomorrah and the surrounding cities, which practiced immorality in the same way as these and lusted after different flesh, stand out as an example, undergoing as they do a punishment of everlasting fire." The key factors are "these" (*toutois*—masculine, referring to "angels" [v. 6], not cities [feminine], and the words "different flesh" (*sarkos heteras*). Thus the sin of Sodom and Gomorrah was seeking union with "different flesh" in a way similar to what the "sons of God" (angels?) did (Gen 6:2) when they mingled with "the daughters of men" (humans).

Normally angels do not marry, nor do they have substantial bodies, though at times they have assumed bodies or appeared in a bodily form as divine messengers (Gen 19:1ff.; Zech 1:9ff.; 2:1ff.; Matt 28:2ff.; Mark 16:5; Luke 24:4ff.; John 20:12ff.; Acts 1:10f.). In Genesis 19 angelic messengers in the form of men visited Sodom; and the men of the city, motivated by their homosexuality and supposing the messengers to be men, desired them. So they "went after different flesh." God destroyed the cities of the plain by raining fire and brimstone from heaven on the cities (Gen 19:24)— possibly the divine use of a natural catastrophe associated with the volcanic activity of the area.

Notes

5 This verse has suffered confusion in the history of the transmission. UBS (3d ed.) lists nine different readings and gives its choice as πάντα, ὅτι ὁ κύριος ἅπαξ (*panta, hoti ho kyrios hapax*, "all things, that the Lord once"). Nestle (26th ed.) follows UBS. Other readings replace κύριος (*kyrios*, "Lord") with θεός (*theos*, "God"), Ἰησους (*Iēsous*, "Jesus"), or even θεὸς Χριστός (*theos Christos*, "God Christ"). The Byzantine tradition has ἅπαξ τοῦτο ὅτι ὁ κύριος (*hapax touto, hoti ho kyrios*, "once this, that the Lord"). It appears that *kyrios* is correct, that *panta* ("all things") is to be accepted above *touto* ("this"), and that *hapax* ("once") is being used in a series with τὸ δεύτερον (*to deuteron*, "second," "second time").

2. The Description and Doom of the False Teachers

8–13

> [8]In the very same way, these dreamers pollute their own bodies, reject authority and slander celestial beings. [9]But even the archangel Michael, when he was disputing with the devil about the body of Moses, did not dare to bring a slanderous accusation against him, but said, "The Lord rebuke you!" [10]Yet these men speak abusively against whatever they do not understand; and what things they do understand by instinct, like unreasoning animals—these are the very things that destroy them.
>
> [11]Woe to them! They have taken the way of Cain; they have rushed for profit into Balaam's error; they have been destroyed in Korah's rebellion.
>
> [12]These men are blemishes at your love feasts, eating with you without the slightest qualm—shepherds who feed only themselves. They are clouds without rain, blown along by the wind; autumn trees, without fruit and uprooted—twice dead. [13]They are wild waves of the sea, foaming up their shame; wandering stars, for whom blackest darkness has been reserved forever.

8 Jude now links the examples of God's judgment (vv.5–7) to the false teachers whom he calls "dreamers" (*enypniazomenoi*). Though this word might refer to pretensions of prophecy, it more likely refers to their carnal sin that leads them to live in a dream world. "In the very same way" (*homoiōs mentoi kai houtoi*) points back to the sins of Sodom and Gomorrah (v.7). The false teachers pollute "their own bodies" (lit., "flesh") in various forms of sexual excess, doubtless including homosexuality. Their rejection of authority (*kyriotēta*, "lordship") implies that they repudiated Jesus as Lord (*kyrios*) over their lives.

The third sin of these false teachers is that they "slander celestial beings." How and why, Jude does not say. Perhaps their materialistic and fleshy bent led them to deny all spiritual forces—good or evil.

9 The false teachers should have learned from the example of the archangel Michael. Oral tradition and apocryphal literature tell of a struggle over Moses' body. According to Clement of Alexandria (*Adumbr. in Ep. Judae*), Origen (*De princ.* 3.2.1), and Didymus of Alexandria (*In Ep. canon brevis enarr.*), Jude is quoting from the apocyphal Assumption of Moses, only small portions of which have survived. Accordingly, the devil, it seems, claimed the right to the body because of Moses' sin of murder (Exod 2:12) or because he (the devil) considered himself the Lord of the earth. Michael is mentioned in Revelation 12:7, and 1 Thessalonians 4:16 refers to "the voice of the archangel." In Daniel 10:13, 21 and 12:1, Michael is a great prince or mighty angel for Israel. Yet in spite of Michael's power and dignity, he dared not bring a "slanderous accusation" against the devil but referred the dispute to the sovereignty of God. So if he, a mighty archangel, had respect for celestial powers, Jude is saying, how much more should the mere human false teachers do so? (On the struggle over Moses' body, cf. TDNT, 4:866, n. 211.)

10 "Yet these men" (*houtoi de*) connotes contempt. They, unlike Michael, presume to speak evil against what they know nothing about. (Later, in v.19, Jude explains that they do not have the Spirit.) These "dreamers," however, do have knowledge, but only on the instinctual level of animal passion. So like the "unreasoning animals" (*aloga zōa*), they are destroyed (by God) through the things they practice.

185

11 Again Jude turns to the OT—this time for another triad of examples. Because of their coming judgment, he pronounces "woe" (*ouai*) on the false teachers as Jesus did on the scribes and Pharisees (Matt 23:13, 15–16, 23, 25, 27, 29).

1. The false teachers have "taken [*eporeuthēsan*] the way of Cain." The verb *poreuomai* connotes a moral or religious "walk" (cf. TDNT, 6:575). Cain's way was the religion of his own works without faith (Heb 11:4) and led to the hatred and murder of his brother (1 John 3:12–13). Like Cain, these men belong to the evil one, manufacture religion, and kill the souls of men by error.

2. They have abandoned themselves to Balaam's error (cf. comments on 2 Peter 2:15–16). Balaam was the prototype of all greedy religionists who lead God's people into false religion and immorality (cf. the events at Baal-Peor, Num 31:16–19). The combination of *exechythēsan* (passive from *ekcheō*, "pour on," here, "abandoned themselves"; NIV, "they have rushed") and *planē* ("error") indicates that the false teachers were wholly consumed by their love of money.

3. "They have been destroyed in Korah's rebellion." Numbers 16:1–35 tells of the drastic punishment inflicted on Korah, Dathan, Abiram, and 250 other rebels against Moses' authority. So, with a bold disregard of anachronism, Jude says of the false teachers, "They have been destroyed [*apōlonto*, the aorist tense, i.e., completed action] in Korah's rebellion." It is a striking way of saying that their doom is certain and settled.

12–13 Now, with burning eloquence, Jude piles figure upon figure (six of them in all) to describe the errorists:

1. The false teachers are "blemishes at your love feasts." Translators are divided on which of the two usages of *spilas* (cf. BAG, MM) is preferable here. Some (e.g., Alford, Weymouth, NASB, Kelly [p. 269]) render it "rocks" or "hidden rocks"; others (e.g., KJV, RSV, NEB, NIV, TEV) render it "spots" or "blemishes." In either case, the metaphor is a striking one. The rendering "hidden rocks" connotes the danger of shipwreck of the faith; "spots" or "blemishes" parallels 2 Peter 2:13 and connotes defilement. The "love feasts" were communal meals in which the early church ate together and observed the Lord's Supper. "Eating with you" is too tame a translation of *syneuōchoumenoi*; with its connotation of sumptuous eating, it might better be translated "feasting with you." "Without the slightest qualm" (*aphobōs*, lit., "without fear") means that the false teachers do not recognize the terror of the Lord against those who mock his Son's death shown in the Supper (cf. 1 Cor 11:27–32; Heb 10:26–31).

2. Jude goes on to depict the false teachers as "shepherds who feed only themselves"—a figure that points to all the biblical warnings against the false shepherds who care nothing for the flock (e.g., Ezek 34:8; John 10:12–13).

3. They are like clouds that promise rain but are "blown along by the wind" and "without rain" (*anydroi*, lit., "waterless"). Thus the false teachers are wind, devoid of refreshment, promise, and performance.

4. They are, Jude says, like fruit trees in late autumn, long past the harvest, bearing no fruit. Furthermore, they are trees not only fruitless but also uprooted—thus "twice dead."

5. Next is the metaphor of the restless sea (v.13). For modern man, the sea is often a thing of beauty; to ancient man, less able to cope with the sea's fury, it was a terror. (Rev 21:1, with its promise of no more sea, reflects this attitude.) Isaiah (57:20) compares the wicked to the sea: "The wicked are like the tossing sea, which cannot

rest, whose waters cast up mire and mud." The errorists are busy, restless, untamed. Their product is like the foam or scum at the seashore. "Foaming" (*epaphrizō*) is another of Jude's words that occur in the NT only in his book.

6. The final metaphor (*asteres planētai*, "wandering star") is astronomical. The ancients called the planets "wandering stars" because of their movements. The reference here could be to meteors, shooting stars, comets, or planets; but planets is the most likely meaning. An unpredictable star would provide no guidance for navigation; so false teachers are useless and untrustworthy. Their doom is the eternal darkness that is reserved for them (cf. 2 Peter 2:4).

3. Enoch's Prophecy of the Coming Judgment

14–16

> [14]Enoch, the seventh from Adam, prophesied about these men: "See, the Lord is coming with thousands upon thousands of his holy ones [15]to judge everyone, and to convict all the ungodly of all the ungodly acts they have done in the ungodly way, and of all the harsh words ungodly sinners have spoken against him." [16]These men are grumblers and faultfinders; they follow their own evil desires; they boast about themselves and flatter others for their own advantage.

14 Enoch, who "walked with God; then he was no more, because God took him away" (Gen 5:24), is not specifically called "the seventh from Adam" in the OT. But in Genesis 5 and also in 1 Chronicles 1:1–3, he is the seventh in order (counting Adam as the first). Here, however, Jude quotes not Genesis but the Book of Enoch (also called "The Ethiopic Book of Enoch")—the longest of the surviving Jewish pseudepigraphical writings and a work that was highly respected by Jews and many Christians. Those who wonder about the propriety of Jude's quotation of this noncanonical book should note that he does not call it Scripture. Paul also quoted from noncanonical writers statements he considered true. See Acts 17:28, where he quoted Cleanthes and Aratus (*Phaenomena* 5); 1 Corinthians 15:33, where he quoted Menander (*Thais* 218); and Titus 1:12, where he quoted Epimenides (*De oraculis*). Lawlor (p. 102) argues that Jude is not quoting the Book of Enoch but a prophecy of his given to Jude by inspiration. This is possible, of course, but unnecessary. The prophecy does not give any startling new information but is simply a general description of the return of the Lord in judgment (cf. Deut 33:2; Dan 7:10–14; Zech 14:5; Matt 25:31).

15–16 The stress is on two words, each used four times: "all" (*pantōn*) and "ungodly" (*asebeia, asebeō, asebēs;* cf. v.4). Jude finds Enoch's prophecy a good summary of the universal divine judgment on the impious and all their deeds.

Verse 16 completes Jude's denunciation of the false teachers as "grumblers" (*gongystai*). In 1 Corinthians 10:10 the related verb *gongyzō* is used by Paul of the rebels in the wilderness (cf. LXX Exod 16–17; Num 14–17; cf. also TNDT, 1:728–37). Jude also calls the false teachers "faultfinders" (*mempsimoiroi*), a term that underlines their critical attitude and habitual complaining. (Both *gongystai* and *mempsimoiroi* occur only here in the NT.) "They follow their own evil desires" might be translated "they live by their passions." "They boast about themselves" is literally "and their mouth speaks haughty [or bombastic] words," which reminds one of Antiochus Epiphanes (cf. Dan 7:8–11; 11:36). "Flatter others for their own advantage" reinforces Jude's stress on the venality of the false teachers. Here the literal sense of the Greek text ("honoring faces for the sake of advantage") is highly picturesque.

187

IV. The Exhortations to the Believers

17–23

> [17]But, dear friends, remember what the apostles of our Lord Jesus Christ foretold. [18]They said to you, "In the last times there will be scoffers who will follow their own ungodly desires." [19]These are the men who divide you, who follow mere natural instincts and do not have the Spirit.
> [20]But you, dear friends, build yourselves up in your most holy faith and pray in the Holy Spirit. [21]Keep yourselves in God's love as you wait for the mercy of our Lord Jesus Christ to bring you to eternal life. [22]Be merciful to those who doubt; [23]snatch others from the fire and save them; to others show mercy, mixed with fear—hating even the clothing stained by corrupted flesh.

17–18 "But, dear friends" (*hymeis de, agapētoi;* lit., "but you, beloved") makes the transition from the burning denunciation in vv. 8–16 to the preparation of the believers for their necessary struggles. They must remember (cf. v.5; 2 Peter 1:12–15) the previously spoken words of the apostles. The apostles (the Twelve plus Paul) must have had a wide ministry of which we have little knowledge, and their preaching was part of the oral deposit of faith for the early churches. One of their prophecies was a prediction of mockers in the last time who would live ungodly lives. So the church was to be vigilant, for the last time was seen to be at hand and the ungodly mockers on the scene. The "last time" (Gr., singular) is the age of messianic salvation and judgment that culminates in the judgments of the Second Advent. Since the apostles have predicted this time, the church should not be surprised or discouraged but prepare itself for action.

19 Again Jude returns to his triadic pattern of describing the false teachers.

1. He calls them "men who divide you" (*apodiorizontes*). This extremely rare word (only here in the NT) may mean that "they made distinctions," perhaps as the later Gnostics divided Christians by classifying them into groups of initiates ("spiritual") and lesser ones, which translates the word *psychikoi*.

2. Next he calls them men "who follow mere natural instincts," *psychikoi* (lit., "soulish," "psychic," "unspiritual"; cf. BAG, p. 902; TDNT, 9:656–63). *Psychikoi* was very likely used by the Gnostics as a slander of the orthodox when the fact was that they themselves were living on the natural level. Here Jude turns the word against the false teachers. The church today is plagued by false teachers claiming superior knowledge and experience; yet their lives are often worse than those of the average pagan.

3. Finally he says that they "do not have the Spirit" (*pneuma*). *Pneuma* is without the definite article (*ho*) in Greek—a fact that has led some to translate this as "they do not have a spirit" and teach that man is dichotomous until conversion, when he becomes trichotomous. But this view is without biblical support. The use of *pneuma* without the article for the Holy Spirit is common in the NT (cf. John 3:5; 7:39; Gal 5:16). In spite of all their vaunted claims and teaching, the false teachers are devoid of the Holy Spirit.

20–21 The repetition of "beloved" (*agapētoi;* NIV, "dear friends") personalizes the message and redirects attention back to the believers. (In v.17 Jude had started his exhortations to the faithful but returned to one final salvo against his opponents.) Now he gives them a fourfold exhortation for their spiritual profit.

1. Christians are to be "building themselves up" (*epoikodomountes,* present participle) in their "most holy faith." In the NT "the faith" is the orthodox body of truth and practice from the apostles (cf. Acts 2:42; 20:32; Rom 6:17). It is "most holy" because the Spirit gave it concerning God's "holy servant Jesus" (Acts 4:27, 30). Christians build themselves by having fellowship with the Lord and his people, by continuing in the gospel and in the Word of God, and by worship—especially by remembering the Lord at his table.

2. Christians are to be praying (present participle) in the Holy Spirit (cf. Rom 8:26–27; Gal 4:6; Eph 6:18). Because all believers have the Spirit, they are to pray according to the Spirit's will (set forth in the written Word and made known by inner promptings) to accomplish God's work by God's power.

3. Christians are to keep themselves in God's love (v.21; cf. vv.1–2). The realm of God's love is in Jesus Christ; those who depart from Christ depart from the love of God. Those who reject the commands of Jesus reject his love (cf. John 15:10: "If you obey my commands, you will remain in my love").

4. Christians are to keep their attention fixed on the "mercy of our Lord Jesus Christ [that brings them] to eternal life." True eschatology keeps present reality in focus. The mention of mercy reminds Christians that salvation is never a matter of good works and that only in Christ is their hope of salvation (cf. comments on v.3). "Eternal life" in this verse refers to the future aspects of the presently enjoyed salvation.

22–23 These verses contain certain minor textual problems. The most important is whether three groups are in view (NIV, UBS 3d ed., Nestle 26th ed.) or only two (Nestle 25th ed., B, Clement of Alexandria). The shorter reading of B is split against other good members of its family (e.g., 1739). The stronger MS support for the longer reading is also reinforced by the triadic pattern of Jude's thought. Accepting the longer text, the three groups are (1) those who are hesitating (according to most texts), (2) those who need to be saved from the fire, and (3) those who need pity because of contamination.

The first command is to show mercy to those who are doubting (or hesitating). This group of people are "at odds with themselves" (reading *diakrinomenous* and understanding this verb as "doubt" or "waver" rather than "dispute"). The teaching and example of the false teachers have caused them to be uncertain about the truth of Christianity. They must be dealt with patiently and mercifully by showing them Christian love. The second group needs to be dealt with directly and vigorously. Salvation is God's work, and here Christians are portrayed as God's instruments for snatching brands out of the fire (cf. Zech 3:3). The picture is of a person slipping into the eternal fire but rescued from error by the grace and truth of God.

The final group of people appears to be deep in the immorality of the false teachers. Their very clothing is "stained by corrupted flesh." Perhaps the figure is that their depravity has made them infectious. Christians are to show mercy as in the first case, but now they are to be fearful lest the infection spread to them. Yet even here God's wondrous grace can exchange the excrement-covered garments (cf. Zech 3:3, Heb. text) for festive garments of righteousness. For no one, not even the most defiled sinner, is beyond salvation through faith in Christ's redeeming work.

V. The Doxology

24–25

24To him who is able to keep you from falling and to present you before his glorious presence without fault and with great joy— 25to the only God our Savior be glory, majesty, power and authority, through Jesus Christ our Lord, before all ages, now and forevermore! Amen.

24 Jude's message of warning and doom might have depressed and discouraged his readers. Beset by so much false teaching and immorality, how can Christians ever reach heaven? The answer lies only in the power of God. So this doxology, surely one of the greatest in the NT, reminds us of God's ability to bring every one of his own safely to himself. God "is able to keep [us] from falling" (or "stumbling"). Furthermore, he is able "to present [us] before his glorious presence [lit., 'his glory'] without fault" (*amomos*, used of Christ as a faultless lamb in 1 Peter 1:19; cf. comments there). "With great joy" (*agalliasei*) is the response of Christians for their completed salvation (cf. DNTT, 2:354).

25 "To the only God our Savior" points to the monotheistic nature of the faith by showing that the Father is the Savior as well as the Son. Whatever the false teachers may say, there is only one God and Savior. To "God our Savior . . . through Jesus Christ our Lord" (notice the intimate pronouns "our . . . our") belong four attributes: (1) "glory" (*doxa*), a word with many associations and connotations difficult to capture in a few words—perhaps "radiance" or "moral splendor" comes close to its meaning (cf. DNTT, 2:44–48; TDNT, 2:232–55); (2) "majesty" (*megalōsynē*), which refers to God's greatness (Kelly [p. 293] suggests "awful transcendence"); (3) "power" (*kratos*); and (4) "authority" (*exousia*)—the last two stressing his might and "the sovereign freedom of actions He enjoys as Creator" (Kelly, p. 293). The solemn time notation "before all ages, now and forevermore" indicates that these attributes of God suffer no change and that therefore his divine plan will surely be carried out. Salvation is completely secure because God's own purpose stands and because he is able to do all that he wills (Isa 46:9–10).